D1005866

The Storm
Gathering

A Keystone Book is so designated to distinguish it from the typical scholarly monograph that a university press publishes. It is a book intended to serve the citizens of Pennsylvania by educating them and others, in an entertaining way, about aspects of the history, culture, society, and environment of the state as part of the Middle Atlantic region.

The Storm Gathering

The Penn Family
and the American Revolution

Lorett Treese

A Keystone Book

The Pennsylvania State University Press
University Park, Pennsylvania

Library of Congress Cataloging-in-Publication Data

Treese, Lorett, 1952–
    The storm gathering : the Penn family and the American Revolution
    / Lorett Treese.

        p.   cm.
    "A Keystone book."
    Includes bibliographical references and index.
    ISBN 0-271-00858-X
    1. Pennsylvania—History—Colonial period, ca. 1600–1775—
    Biography.   2. Penn family.   I. Title.
    F152.T84   1992
    974.8′02′0922—dc20
    [B]   92–5573
                                                                         CIP

Copyright © 1992 The Pennsylvania State University
All rights reserved
Published by The Pennsylvania State University Press,
Suite C, Barbara Building,
University Park, PA 16802-1003
Printed in the United States of America

It is the policy of The Pennsylvania State University Press to use acid-free paper for the
first printing of all clothbound books. Publications on uncoated stock satisfy the minimum
requirements of American National Standard for Information Sciences—Permanence of
Paper for Printed Library Materials, ANSI Z39.48–1984.

Contents

List of Illustrations

Maps

Figures (between pages 118 and 119)

For MAT

Preface

On a hot summer day in Philadelphia, the old sash windows at Christ Church are open wide. Visitors wander in steadily, most wearing shorts and T-shirts, some holding cameras or fanning themselves with transit maps. From time to time a tour bus stops and a group of people alight and troop in to occupy the wooden pews and listen to background information presented by one of the hostesses. Those who walk to the front of the church find a grave-marker set into the brick floor: "Here lieth The Body of The Honorable JOHN PENN Esq. One of the late Proprietaries of PENNSYLVANIA. who died February 9th A.D. 1795 Aged 67 Years."

A young girl reads the inscription on John Penn's grave-marker and hesitates, then avoids stepping on it by taking a giant step. A few moments later a woman stops at the marker and wonders out loud, "Was he any relation to *William* Penn?" The hostesses do not mention John Penn, although they point out the personal pews of some of Christ Church's other famous worshipers from the Revolutionary War era.

This book was written for all the men, women, and children who seek to understand the American Revolution, and particularly events in Pennsylvania around that time. It covers the period in Pennsylvania between the end of the French and Indian War (1763) and the demise of the Penn proprietorship (1779). It is also the story of how the Revolution affected and transformed the family of William Penn.

The voluminous correspondence of Penn family members and their officers and appointees, housed at the Historical Society of Pennsylvania in Philadelphia, is the basis of this book, and I would like to thank the staff of the library and manuscript department at the Historical Society for their patient and helpful assistance. I also want to thank the staff at the Library Company of Philadelphia for their help with early newspaper sources, which added much color to the story. In addition, I am grateful for the assistance of the staffs at the Falvey Memorial Library at Villanova University and at the Winterthur Library, especially those persons who handle interlibrary loans. I would like also to thank my editor at Penn State Press, Peter J. Potter, and my manuscript editor, Peggy Hoover. And particular thanks go to Donald B. Kelley of Villanova University for his generous advice about the text.

I reserve my warmest thanks for my husband, Matthew Treese. Without his encouragement and unfailing support, this book would never have been completed.

A Note on Double-Dating

Prior to 1752, when England adopted the Gregorian Calendar and changed New Year's Day from March 25 to January 1, events occurring between these dates literally fell into two different years and were often officially recorded with "double dates," for example, 1701/2.

Introduction

During the night of August 4, 1777, three cavalrymen from the Philadelphia Troop of Light Horse arrived at an elegant country house named Lansdowne outside Philadelphia and demanded to see Former Governor of Pennsylvania John Penn, who was living there in quiet retirement. They threatened to arrest him if he did not sign a "parole," a written promise that he would do nothing unfriendly to the new entity people were calling "the United States," give no intelligence to the British forces that were shortly expected to invade Pennsylvania, and consider himself a prisoner of war.[1]

Like the cautious man he was, John Penn listened carefully and examined the document. Then he became angry: These soldiers had no right to come at such an hour, disrupt his household, and frighten his wife. He was no criminal, and he would not be bullied into signing anything. He kept the messengers waiting until early the next morning, then sent a note suggesting that they return on Friday at a decent hour and call on him like the gentleman he was. At that time, he would tell them whether he would sign the parole.[2]

John Penn and his wife, Anne, must have spent the night considering their predicament and reflecting on how quickly their position in Pennsylvania had changed. As recently as 1773 John and Anne had returned from Europe to the thriving city of Philadelphia. John was the grandson of William Penn, revered founder of Pennsylvania, and in 1773 he had been Pennsylvania's governor and a joint proprietor of the province, entitled to one-quarter of the income from the sale of the vast Penn family lands. Money from land sales was beginning to make the family quite rich, and both the colonial assembly and the people of Pennsylvania had warmly welcomed him home. His prospects had seemed so bright.

But Pennsylvania was a "commonwealth" now, and no longer a proprietary province. The previous summer, in 1776, Pennsylvania had joined the other colonies in declaring independence from Great Britain. Representatives of the people of Pennsylvania had drawn up a new constitution that had taken away John Penn's governing powers and given them to a "Supreme Executive Council." The Penn family still owned a great deal of land, but procedures for selling it had been confused and disrupted by politics. John Penn's personal income had been drastically affected. Suddenly threatened with bankruptcy, he had been forced to let servants go and retire to his country estate.[3] There he hoped to take no part in the uprising—but rather to quietly preserve what he could of his personal fortune and wait for the trouble to end.

Since the summer of 1776 there had been plenty of trouble. That fall and winter, Pennsylvania had been essentially governed by a body called the Council of Safety—led by moderate, not radical, Patriots, but men who could not control the mobs intent on seeking out Loyalists. Such mobs had taken it on themselves to identify the "enemies of the people," beat them up, and loot their homes. People had been thrown into jail for singing "God Save the King" or even for no reason at all.[4] In February 1777 Pennsylvania's legislature, by then controlled by radicals as well as moderate revolutionaries, had made treason punishable by death, and during the summer the assembly had passed a "test act" making it possible to imprison any male over eighteen who refused to swear allegiance to the state. There had also been talk of confiscating the property of those who joined or aided the British.[5]

Yet that summer the tide appeared to be turning. The fleet of British General William Howe had been sighted off Delaware Bay, and the British were expected to occupy Philadelphia any day. The Patriot cause no longer looked so hopeful. Anne Penn suspected that Pennsylvania's revolutionary leaders wanted to secure and confine the former governor as a hostage to be exchanged for any Patriot leaders who might be captured. This, she believed, was the reason behind the demand that he sign a parole.[6]

John Penn now faced a difficult decision. If he refused to sign the parole, would he be cast into some crowded, filthy prison where people had been known to die of fever during the hot Philadelphia summers? Would his estates be confiscated by the revolutionary government? If he did sign the parole and the rebellion was quelled, would he be considered a traitor to England? What would happen to his family then? John decided not to sign the parole.[7]

He waited at home all day Friday, but the cavalrymen never returned. Saturday, Sunday, and most of Monday passed before he was again confronted with the American Revolution. At four o'clock on Monday afternoon the three cavalrymen came back, this time accompanied by three others. When John Penn again refused to sign the parole, they told him he must appear before the president of Pennsylvania's Supreme Executive Council. "It was an indignity I never could submit to," John Penn later wrote. When he said they had no authority to summon him in such a manner, they threatened to take him by force.[8]

Many years as governor of Pennsylvania had made John Penn an expert negotiator. After what he termed "much conversation"[9] a compromise was worked out. He would go to Philadelphia and stay at the house of his father-in-law, former Chief Justice William Allen. The president of the Supreme Executive Council could communicate with him there.

The next day, the cavalrymen called at William Allen's house on Water Street, where John and Anne Penn waited. For a third time, John Penn refused to sign the parole. The cavalrymen, he wrote, "informed me that I must consider myself as their Prisoner."[10] The cavalrymen and some Continental soldiers kept the Penns under house arrest for three days.

Although the Penns could not leave, rumors flowed freely into the Allen house. John Penn heard he might be suddenly and forcibly taken to Hartford, Connecticut, or to Fredericksburg, Virginia. There were plans to "carry [him] off immediately without giving [him] time to make the smallest preparations for [his] Journey."[11]

Anne Penn was determined to share her husband's exile, but neither she nor John wanted to go to Virginia, where they knew Patriot spirit ran high. Although they were neutrals, not Loyalists, John Penn had been an officer of the crown. If the Penns were sent to Virginia they could expect nothing but the basest threats and insults. A trip to Virginia, John wrote, "would be evidently at the risk of our lives."[12]

John Penn finally weakened and decided to sign the parole, but when he sent word to Congress, that body haughtily declared it "inconsistent with the dignity of the Congress to rescind a solemn resolution upon a verbal application only."[13] They wanted a written application from the former governor. A humbled John Penn wrote John Hancock: "I am ready to sign the Parole whenever it shall be offered to me, & shall be much obliged to you if you will be pleased to make known this request to the Congress."[14]

That night John Penn signed the parole and was freed. A few days of quiet followed before General Howe landed at the head of the Elk River on August 25 to make his way north to Philadelphia, at which time the secretary of war sent John Penn a message that he would have to leave Pennsylvania after all. Apparently Patriot leaders had panicked and now feared he might help the British despite his pledge to the contrary. The government would, however, allow John Penn to name the place he found "most agreeable." He chose the Union Iron Works in the Jerseys, where his wife's family had a farm they called "the Union" about fifty-five miles from Philadelphia. The Board of War protested that the Jerseys harbored too much Tory sentiment, but John Penn insisted. It was finally agreed that the Union Iron Works would be his place of indefinite exile.[15]

John Penn was concerned about his wife, but the idea of a separation was not too disheartening because he was not going far and Anne could join him later. As a woman, she was an obvious noncombatant who would probably be allowed to cross both British and American lines. While still in Philadelphia, she might also be able to petition General Howe to make a deal with the Patriot forces and get her husband exchanged and released.[16] After the British occupied the city, Anne did manage to get a few letters to John's aunt, Lady Juliana Penn, in England. She wrote Lady Juliana about her husband's plight and the general situation in Pennsylvania in 1777, concluding sadly, "There appears to be no prospect of relief but from the termination of the War."[17]

But could even the end of the war restore the lives of Penn family members to what they had so recently considered normal? Their standing in Pennsylvania and their relations with its citizens had been very different only a few years before!

1

"Receive What Moneys Thou Canst Get In"
The Penn Proprietorship

In 1732, long before it occurred to anyone in England that the American colonies might fight for their independence, Thomas Penn made his way from England to America. Just thirty years old at the time, Thomas was the first member of the Penn family to set foot in the province since his father, William Penn, left Pennsylvania in 1701. His arrival had been anxiously anticipated for some two years.

On August 11, 1732, Governor Patrick Gordon received a message that the Honorable Mr. Penn had finally reached America and gone ashore at Chester. The governor quickly made plans for an appropriate reception, dispatching his secretary to convey his compliments and congratulations on a safe journey. Then he rallied his advisory council and other important gentlemen of the city and set off to greet Thomas Penn personally. As word of Mr. Penn's arrival spread quickly throughout the city, many other Philadelphians, driven by their curiosity to see a son of the founder, tagged along.[1]

The governor reached Chester in time to share a midday dinner with

Thomas Penn before accompanying him back to Philadelphia. When they arrived at the Schuylkill ferry, they met the city's mayor, aldermen, and city recorder Andrew Hamilton, who had prepared a speech. Because neither Hamilton nor anyone else knew much about Thomas Penn, the speech naturally focused on the merits of his father: Thomas Penn was welcomed into Pennsylvania's capital, where he had been "long and impatiently expected" and where all citizens were grateful for William Penn's "wise and just laws." Thanks to William Penn, Pennsylvanians had "Liberty of Conscience" and "Freedom from Spiritual Tyranny." "We are indeed strongly prejudiced in favour of a Son of the great Mr. Penn," Hamilton concluded.[2]

Thomas Penn thanked everyone briefly, and as he stepped within the city limits, ships in the Delaware fired their guns in salute. A battery of cannon on Society Hill fired off a second salvo as people lining the streets cheered while he made his way to the governor's residence.[3]

Such a warm and handsome welcome was appropriate for the special place the Penn family had in Pennsylvania society. Pennsylvania had been established as a proprietary colony in 1681 by a charter from Charles II that made William Penn a type of feudal lord who technically answered only to the king. William Penn had been given absolute ownership of all the land in Pennsylvania, plus mining rights and use of the province's waterways. The charter allowed him to sell, lease, or grant land as he saw fit; establish courts like those in England and outline court procedures; make laws with the advice and approval of the colony's free men or their elected representatives, so long as those laws were reasonable and in accordance with the laws of England; and appoint people to execute the laws, including sheriffs and justices of the peace. In short, the proprietor represented the British crown in Pennsylvania, but in return for that honor the proprietor was duty bound to uphold the crown's privileges and prerogatives.[4]

Like the feudal lords of the Middle Ages, William Penn had to present a symbolic tribute of two beaver skins each year at Windsor Castle, but the Pennsylvania proprietor was also required to uphold British trade regulations and send all laws passed in Pennsylvania to England for review by the king's Privy Council.[5]

Except for these restrictions, the proprietor had the right to establish any type of government he wanted. An idealistic William Penn wanted to found an English colony where all religious dissenters, including members of the Quaker sect like himself, would be tolerated. Pennsylvania would not be the first refuge for Quakers—many had already found relative religious freedom in the Jerseys and the Carolinas[6]—but Pennsylvania *would* be the first colony in which Quakers were expected to play a significant role in government. Penn was traditional about who would wield power. The proprietary family and the province's large landowners would be members of his government's upper house, while the elected representatives of smaller landowners would sit in a lower house. The upper house would make the province's laws, and the lower house would affirm them.[7] William Penn was not establishing a democracy. He and his landed aristocracy would command and the people would obey.

Before the end of the seventeenth century, William Penn's experiment in government was under attack. The elected representatives of the people wanted to wrest the lawmaking power away from the upper house. Penn's government was further disrupted in the early 1690s when the crown accused the proprietor of tolerating too much piracy and illegal trade with the French. British monarchs William and Mary briefly relieved William Penn of his government and appointed their own governor. This royal appointee, however, found it difficult to deal with the province's contentious Quakers, and the crown restored governing powers to William Penn, who then made his second and last trip to Pennsylvania. Before returning to England, he restructured the government and provided Pennsylvania with a new constitution.

Adopted in 1701, the new constitution became known as Pennsylvania's Charter of Privileges. In drafting it, William Penn bowed considerably to popular will. The people's elected representatives in the Pennsylvania assembly would be allowed to initiate legislation, while an appointed governor would approve or veto their laws. This governor would be advised by an appointed council that would act as a cabinet. Therefore, rather than making laws, the proprietors would be acting through appointees to suggest or prohibit certain measures. They would depend on those same appointees to protect their interests and those of the crown.

The land and the government of Pennsylvania were two separate entities. In his will, William Penn tried to keep the valuable land for his descendants and relieve his family of the increasingly troublesome government. He left the government to trustees with instructions to sell it back to the crown, and he left his American lands to his second wife, Hannah Callowhill Penn, who was to distribute certain designated parcels to his children by his first wife and divide the bulk among her own sons.[8]

But could the proprietorship legally be divided this way? If part of Penn's will was invalid, would the entire proprietorship pass to the elder branch of the Penn family—William Penn's descendants by his first wife? William Penn died in 1718. Springett Penn, a grandson of William Penn by his first wife, tried to assert what he felt were his rights to the Penn government soon after his own father died in 1720. Hannah Penn brought suit to establish the validity of her husband's will. The British Court of Chancery debated the case until July 1727, when it was decided that the sons of Hannah would inherit the entire proprietorship.[9] Hannah's sons were further assured of their inheritance in 1731 when William Penn's surviving descendants by his first wife agreed to release all claims to the land and government of Pennsylvania in exchange for a sum of money.[10]

Thomas Penn had been born while his father's fortunes were dwindling. Though William Penn had expected Pennsylvania to be a lucrative investment, it had brought his family relatively little money during his own lifetime. During Thomas's youth, the Penns had often been strapped for cash. In case it proved to be Thomas's fate to make his own way in the world, he had been apprenticed to a London mercer (a cloth merchant) named Michael Russell.[11] William Penn's death saddled the family with a contested estate and considerable debt. Once their inheritance of the proprietorship was assured, it was still uncertain whether this would prove to be an asset or a liability to William Penn's sons.

If the Penns were to make money in Pennsylvania, their income would come from the sale of land. William Penn had made provision for all the land in Pennsylvania to be divided into three categories. In the first category was common land, for sale to settlers at uniform prices. The second category included various tracts occasionally granted to members of the Penn family as personal estates. The third category consisted of the often controversial "proprietary tenths" or "proprietary manors"—when a new tract of land was made available for sale, one-tenth of the best land was theoretically reserved as a proprietary manor. Such manors did not operate as real feudal manors; they were simply estates held jointly by the proprietors where land was generally rented rather than sold.[12]

A settler desiring to buy land in Pennsylvania went to the secretary of the land office to get a warrant for a survey and pay a portion of the purchase price. Settlers were supposed to name only the number of acres they wanted. They were not to request specific tracts, although they frequently did request land adjoining an existing claim or near a certain body of water. Upon receiving the warrant, the surveyor general appointed a deputy surveyor to make a survey. When the survey was returned to the land office, that office would issue a patent after full payment was received.[13]

After William Penn's death, a number of factors discouraged settlers from following these procedures and kept their money from flowing into Penn coffers. Land office procedures made it very easy for surveyors to become land speculators. Surveyors could manipulate the system so that large areas were not settled until they had laid out choice claims for themselves or their friends.[14] Land sales were further complicated in the early 1700s when the proprietors of Maryland questioned whether their border with Pennsylvania—defined very specifically as 40° north latitude in William Penn's charter—might actually be north of Philadelphia.[15] In 1732 Lord Baltimore signed an agreement acknowledging that Maryland's border with Pennsylvania was roughly fifteen miles south of the city, but he soon backed out, and the issue remained uncertain until the 1760s. In the meantime, settlers hesitated to pay the land office for land that might end up in another province. A third problem was the uncertainty created while Chancery debated which branch of the Penn family would inherit the proprietorship. It was many years before the Pennsylvania land office could guarantee clear titles.

These uncertainties did not discourage settlers from flocking to Pennsylvania and establishing homesteads there. William Penn had made occasional but unsuccessful attempts to discourage squatters, and after his death the problem intensified. By 1726 the Pennsylvania land office estimated that about 100,000 people were either illegally settled or simply had not paid their purchase money or taken all the steps required to complete a land purchase. It was hoped that a Penn family member would come to Pennsylvania and help sort the matter out.[16]

To make the proprietorship profitable, the Penns would also have to demand their quitrents—fees that were due annually from all landowners. In a proprietorship, payment of a quitrent made one "quit and free" from standard feudal service to one's lord. The annual payment also confirmed a land title and symbolized the landowner's acknowledgment of the proprietor's overlordship. A quitrent was usually a standard sum of money, but it might also be something symbolic, such as a peppercorn or a red rose.[17]

From the start, quitrents had been difficult to collect. After the death of William Penn, many settlers saw no sense in paying until the proprietorship was confirmed to one branch of the Penn family or the other and until the boundary dispute with Maryland was settled. If the land office could not grant clear title, settlers reasoned, how could purchasers be expected to pay quitrents?[18] Squatters had little intention of ever paying unless the system caught up with them. As the eighteenth century progressed and quitrent arrears mounted, the essentially feudal nature of quitrents also came to seem increasingly outdated and foreign to the people of Pennsylvania.

By the time Thomas Penn arrived in Philadelphia in 1732, he and his brothers, John and Richard, had been confirmed as Pennsylvania's proprietors and their major boundary dispute had been settled. The eldest brother, John, possessed a half share in the proprietorship, while the two younger brothers were junior proprietors, each holding a one-quarter share. The Penn brothers agreed that one of them should reside in Pennsylvania to work with the land office and the Penn receivers to see that procedures were followed and funds were collected. They decided the meticulous Thomas Penn was the best candidate for ensuring that they got the money they were entitled to.

The young proprietors laid some groundwork in a letter to their receiver general, James Steel, in 1730. They instructed Steel to copy his rent rolls, listing arrears owed, and estimate the total amount of money the people of Pennsylvania collectively owed the Penn family. Steel was also to list surveys that had not been "perfected" or correctly completed.[19] In preparation for his arrival, Thomas Penn personally ordered Steel to enclose some land for his horses and to lay in a large cask of Madeira wine for his use. He also sent Steel some cash with instructions to "treat" (entertain) important gentlemen who remembered the proprietary family kindly and could be counted on to help in the future.[20]

The sudden death of his business partner in London prevented Thomas Penn from leaving as early as he had planned, so Thomas instructed Steel to "receive what moneys thou canst get in and let them be remitted to my Brother John."[21] Throughout 1731 Thomas Penn was expected at any moment. That spring James Steel penned an amusing account of how the governor, the mayor, the magistrates, and the "principal Inhabitants" of Philadelphia had trooped to the docks to attend the landing of a ship only to find that the exciting rumor they had heard was false—there was no Penn family member on board.[22]

When Thomas Penn finally did arrive, he established himself in a house on Second Street and built a modest country retreat about two miles out of town near modern-day Twentieth and Hamilton streets.[23] He immediately began devoting himself to business, and his preoccupation with good organization and his attention to detail prompted him to order a cabinetmaker to build him a case with forty-eight pigeonholes so he could file his documents neatly.[24]

Under Thomas Penn's direction, proprietary manors were duly laid out and the land office began issuing patents and warrants in a regular manner. Thomas's exacting nature was evident in a letter to Lancaster leader Samuel Blunston in which he offered the opinion that surveys should not be made unless the persons applying made some agreement to take warrants immediately. "Several Tracts were surveyed soon after my Arrival," he wrote, "and the Persons have never thought more of applying and think they have nothing more to do till they can conveniently pay their money and get a Patent."[25] With Thomas Penn in charge, settlers came to understand that if they ignored procedures someone else could claim their land.

Thomas Penn was also serious about collecting the quitrents due his family. In 1732 Pennsylvania adopted a paper currency, but Thomas hoped to keep quitrents payable in sterling or at least to make them payable at the current, not the original, exchange rate, because paper money tended to depreciate in value over time.[26] In 1734 he wrote his brothers about people whispering that the Penns would make use of the English courts of chancery to recover their quitrent arrears and that he hoped the rumor would squeeze more cash out of the family's debtors.[27] In 1739 the Pennsylvania assembly compromised with the Penn family, acknowledging that quitrent arrears had been detrimental to the proprietors. These arrears were to be payable in paper money, but at the current exchange rate, and the family would also be awarded a lump sum plus an annual stipend.[28]

Concerned that the executive branch of the Penn government had grown too weak, Thomas considered the idea of a Penn family governor. In 1735 he wrote his brother John that he himself had been governor in all but name and suggested that the more popular John, who had been born in Pennsylvania, might become governor. At the same time, he seemed to be soliciting some sort of recognition for the three years he had spent doing business in the family's behalf. "I have applyed my time closely to Business and that not of the most easy or pleasing sort," he wrote.[29] In the end neither Thomas nor John became the province's governor. The Penns feared that the Board of Trade might oppose their holding the governorship personally or that they might shock important London Quakers by accepting an office that required one to take an oath. Although Thomas and his brothers were drifting away from their father's faith, they did not want to appear to be giving up William Penn's principles for temporal advantage.[30] Instead, the Penns would more actively exert their influence through their appointed governors.

Thomas Penn left Pennsylvania in 1741. In his mind he had justly asserted his family's rights as landlords and proprietors over their tenants and dependents. Throughout the rest of his life he would continue to insist on what was due the Penn family and strive to maintain a balanced government in Pennsylvania by exerting the privileges his father's charter of 1701 guaranteed the proprietors. His goal appeared to be money. Perhaps he remembered his own straitened youth and resented those who had become rich in Pennsylvania, seemingly at Penn family expense. During his stay in Pennsylvania, Thomas managed to make a little extra cash by dealing as a merchant. In 1735 he wrote Samuel Blunston: "If thou shouldst see any good Flax that can be had for 6 a pound here I should be well pleased to have a Tun if it could be had in three Weeks at this place."[31]

By the time Thomas Penn left Pennsylvania, the citizens who had welcomed him so warmly had decided he was cold, aloof, and greedy. While he resided in Pennsylvania, Pennsylvanians had appeared to cooperate with the proprietary family because it was in the common interest to fight the continuing border disputes with Maryland.[32] But Thomas's tough new land policies and grasping nature had actually compromised the popularity of the Penns.

Before returning to England, Thomas Penn appointed several agents to manage the land office and collect quitrents to his satisfaction—the first of many appointees he would rely on to carry out the proprietary objectives as he defined them. Thomas was determined to prevent any further lapses to the detriment of his family. In 1741 he wrote James Steel that he had landed safely back in England after an extremely rough journey. He added, "I must press on you—dispatch in the Rent Rolls and [I] have sent a Ream of large paper for the copying them upon."[33]

2

"Proprietary Affairs Suffer Much"

The Penn Family in the Mid-Eighteenth Century

Not long after Thomas Penn returned to England, he was forced to deal with a family crisis concerning his nephew John. In 1747, when he was just eighteen, John was talked, or perhaps tricked, into an imprudent marriage. The Penns did not like to talk about it, but John's uncle Thomas briefly sketched the sad story on a scrap of paper inserted in a letter addressed to James Hamilton, then governor of Pennsylvania. To ensure that a clerk wouldn't be able to spread rumors about this family embarrassment, Thomas wrote the note himself.

John had been staying with a schoolmaster named Dr. Cox, and the next thing the Penns knew, Cox's daughter[1] "claim[ed] him for her husband, having with the rest of her Family basely plotted to rob his Family of him."[2] The girl said they had been married in London's Fleet Street, where the buildings had notice boards advertising quick, cheap marriages with no questions asked. Because John was underage, it was illegal for him to marry without his parents' consent, but once such marriages had been contracted they were considered binding.

It was not unusual for adventurers to lure young members of the gentry into hasty or secret marriages. Lord Hardwicke's Marriage Act of 1753 was intended to protect British heirs and heiresses from just such pitfalls by clearly defining legal marriage and making marriage itself a public and well-documented affair, but it came just a little too late for John Penn.[3]

And John may have been more than a blameless young dupe. "I am so conscious of the Crime I have committed,"[4] he wrote his uncle, without explaining whether he was referring to the marriage itself or to something more. From the Cox family perspective, John had "gained an ascendance over [his wife's] affections" and it had been his "deliberate choice" to marry her. His bride had "sacrificed her Duty to show her confidence in [him]."[5]

Contemporaries sometimes used the word "indolent" to describe John Penn. Friends and family members remarked that he was "fat" and advised more exercise. Did he also have a sensuous nature? Thomas Penn was convinced that his nephew had been the victim and not the seducer. The erring young man was quickly reclaimed by his uncle, separated from his wife, and disabused of any lingering romantic notions. Thomas wrote that John had "seen the villany of these people in the proper light and as much detests them as I do."[6]

If the Coxes were scheming adventurers, why had they singled out John Penn? By 1747 William and Hannah Penn's oldest son, also named John, was dead. Thomas Penn had inherited his older brother's interest in the Pennsylvania proprietorship, while his nephew John's father—Thomas's younger brother, Richard—had retained his one-quarter interest. John's uncle Thomas, however, was not yet married, and until Thomas Penn produced his own heir, young John stood to eventually inherit the entire proprietorship.

Richard Penn, the younger John's father and brother of Thomas, lived modestly and had little to do with the proprietorship. He had married a physician's daughter, Hannah Lardner. When young John Penn married, his father commanded a comfortable but not luxurious annual income of about £1,000 to £1,200.[7] Richard's humbler family never moved in Thomas Penn's social circles. When Thomas finally did produce a son, Richard politely declined an invitation to the christening, claiming he did not want to cultivate relationships among Thomas's more exalted connections. He also pleaded a general ignorance of proprietary matters, professing a "known deficiency in the knowledge of those affairs which alone can make such Acquaintance Useful."[8] Richard was content to support his brother and to follow his administrative lead.

Thomas Penn continued directing his agents and placemen in Pennsylvania by letter. He meticulously reviewed their replies and accounts and seemed to enjoy the work. Toward the end of his life he wrote one contact: "The greatest pleasure I now enjoy is that of receiving letters from and about business in General."[9] Thomas intended that young John would eventually have an important position in the Penn organization, for despite John's unfortunate marriage he liked him. In one letter to John, he came as close as he could to genuine warmth when he wrote, "I will always be ready to do every act of Friendship for you: and you may depend on an Home wherever I have an House."[10]

After wresting John from the clutches of the Cox family, Thomas made arrangements that would prevent John from seeing his wife for an undetermined but decidedly lengthy period. He engaged a Frenchman, Robert Dunant, to travel to Geneva as John's governor. Upper-class underage men traveling or studying in foreign cities generally lived and worked with such older, trusted, responsible guardians. Thomas Penn gave Dunant a salary of £200 a year, plus travel expenses, and specified that John was "put entirely under [his] direction." Perhaps anticipating pursuit by the Coxes, Thomas also gave Dunant authority to remove John to another location at his own discretion.[11]

Far from resenting arrangements that would separate him from a woman he had once, perhaps, loved, John was happy to escape. He may have feared becoming victimized again and felt that the separation was anything but cruel. Several years later he implied that the trip to Geneva had been his own idea when he wrote Thomas Penn: "A long while before I left England I proposed it to you as the only method I could think of of being safe."[12] Throughout his exile on the continent, his letters repeatedly thanked Thomas for his "kindness."[13] He promised, "I shall always observe the advice that you give me on ev'ry point,"[14] and he protested that his loyalty to his uncle derived not from "fear" or "interest" but from "gratitude" and "friendship."[15]

At one point John admitted to his uncle, "Had it not been for Your Kindness toward me what would have become of me, perhaps [I] might have been starving with hunger & want."[16] Why was John Penn so grateful? John's own father, Richard, on hearing of his marriage to Miss Cox, refused to see him or have anything more to do with him. He refused even to receive letters from his son, which forced John to send regards to his immediate family in letters to his uncle. John asked his uncle Thomas to "recommend [him] to [his] Papa as a true Penitent" ardently hoping to be "restored to [his] former situation."[17] Several letters express a real fear that he might not ever be welcome home again.

Things were actually not that bad. Thomas Penn was passing John's letters on to Richard, who was generally pleased to hear news of the son both he and his brother still affectionately called "Jack." Perhaps John's father felt he should suffer the traditional penalty for such a lapse, or perhaps the Penns were making it clear that the Coxes could not hope to profit from an unwanted connection with the family.

Life in Geneva was not unpleasant for John Penn. At his uncle's direction he studied geometry, trigonometry, natural law, civil law, history, and French. John preferred his music lessons, however, and proudly told his uncle he could play "second fiddle"[18] at concerts. He also attended balls and assemblies, took afternoon walks on the city's fortifications, traveled around the lake with other gentlemen students, and joined a club the students called "The Circle."[19] Thomas Penn was suspicious about this club, but John reassured him it was just a group of young men who gathered in a rented room each afternoon to take tea, play cards, and perhaps have supper. No females were involved.[20]

John attempted to keep his marriage secret from the gentlemen with whom he studied and socialized in Geneva, so there were several tense moments when he heard from his wife. John did not welcome this communication and never called his wife by her Christian name when he mentioned her in letters to his uncle. Instead he wrote that he had heard from "a certain quarter" or "those quarters" again.

The first letter came about nine months after he left England. John told his uncle, "She is sure my letters must have been stop't in the post, as she does not doubt but I have wrote to her." John had not written and had no intention of doing so. He burned his wife's letter.[21] A few months later a Geneva merchant with connections in London sought John out and delivered a letter addressed to a young man "who has done very ill in not writing to his friends & those who wish him well." The merchant was instructed to obtain an answer, so John informed his bride that he hoped "she would never trouble me any more with her letters."[22] About a month later a letter from England questioned a Geneva merchant about Master Penn's living arrangements. Did he have a governor? How long was he going to stay abroad?[23] Then three years of silence followed, as the Cox family apparently concluded they could not hope to influence John by mail.

Both Thomas and Richard Penn feared and discouraged communication between John and the Coxes. They were afraid the Coxes would extort money from John or, worse yet, lure him back to his bride and force the Penns to acknowledge the connection. When John proved negligent in answering his uncle's letters, Thomas feared that just such a thing had occurred. If John had absconded, his uncle sternly warned, he would "surely repent it." A clear threat appeared in Thomas Penn's words: "If it should be as I fear, years of misery must be your portion."[24] The Penns need not have worried. John might disappoint the family by not writing often, but his complete dependence on them prevented him from even contemplating such rebellion. John acknowledged this to his uncle: "I know what the consequences of deceiving you would be."[25]

In 1751 John received a letter from a male member of the Cox family expressing the family's opinion that John had not written because he had been under "slavish restrictions" and urging him to throw off his dependence on his uncle and return to a woman who still felt affection for him.[26] The letter hints that John's wife and her family might not have been as evil and mercenary as John's uncle and father chose to think. Yet John was unmoved. He duly reported the letter to his uncle, saying, "You will easily guess why it was wrote just at this time & not before."[27] John Penn had come of age, and in the intervening years Thomas Penn had married and produced an infant son. John was no longer in line to inherit the entire Pennsylvania proprietorship.

Thomas Penn's marriage was quite different from the hasty, covered-up union his nephew had entered. On August 22, 1751, in St. George's Church in Hanover, forty-nine-year-old Thomas Penn married twenty-seven-year-old Lady Juliana Fermor, daughter of the first Earl of Pomfret.[28] His marriage marked the end of Thomas's association with the Quaker faith. The Quaker convention of addressing all acquaintances as "thee" and "thou" regardless of rank had long since disappeared from Thomas Penn's correspondence. After the wedding he also attended Church of England services with his wife.

Lady Juliana came from a well-connected family, and a friend described her as "just what a lady of quality should be"[29]: She was engaging, she was beautiful, but she was also a woman of sense and educated and intelligent. Apparently she liked to read. In one letter, her brother recommended the latest book on French history.[30] In another letter written years later, Lady Juliana wrote a friend that the distractions of London interrupted but did not halt her "studies."[31]

Thomas Penn was proud of her, and their marriage was a happy one. He always referred to her by title as "Lady Juliana." Both he and his wife were extremely fond of their children, whom Thomas generally called "the Little People" or "Lady Juliana's very Little Family." Thomas grieved for those of his children who did not survive childhood and was always genuinely solicitous of his wife's health. In later years she returned the favor, managing the Penn business correspondence during her husband's illnesses and writing the letters he dictated or suggested to her. She was more than just a secretary, for she understood the political situation affecting her husband's organization and became a real asset to the Penns.

Shortly after Thomas Penn's marriage, John was permitted an abbreviated version of a grand tour, leaving Geneva in October 1751 to visit Turin, Milan, Parma, Modena, Florence, and Rome. His trip included at least one exciting moment, when his chaise overturned on an icy, dangerous road in the Alps. John lost both his "pocket book" and his writing box in the snow, so he could not provide the full story of his journey that his uncle was anxious to read nor account for the £375 the trip had cost.[32] Thomas Penn considered £375 far too much, and John discovered that excessive spending was one sure way to make Uncle Thomas angry. John had to justify the expenditure, saying, "I saw no gentleman in Italy who made less figure than myself," and swore he simply could not have lived on any less.[33]

Thomas forgave John, and John's father was also ready to see and forgive him. On his return from Italy, John was directed to go to a French port and come to England secretly, lest the Cox family discover his presence and prove importunate to the Penns. Thomas told his nephew to "take passage for England alone, leaving your servant behind, as without you come un-attended there will be no possibility of keeping your coming over private."[34] Richard Penn often visited Bath for his health, so he found a nearby town where John could stay and they could visit. John was told to make his way to the White Hart at Holt. His father suggested that he conceal his identity and "take a name, which may be Pyke as I suppose his Linnen is marked with a P."[35] Despite these cloak-and-dagger efforts, it is possible that the Coxes did discover the whereabouts of their erstwhile inlaw. While contemplating a second trip, John wrote Thomas Penn: "We have already had an example of the unwary, the last time I was in England."[36] All in all, John was happy to see and be received by his family before embarking on a much longer journey.

Thomas Penn wanted his nephew to serve a kind of apprenticeship in Pennsylvania. In 1752 he wrote several Pennsylvania officials that his nephew would soon be arriving and outlined what he expected of them and of John during this visit. To Richard Peters at the land office he wrote: "We do not send with him any Powers, he goes to spend two years and make himself Master of all our Concerns," adding, "I wish he may turn out a Man of Business."[37]

Peters was an important man in Thomas Penn's organization and was likely to sympathize with John's peculiar marital situation. In his own youth he had married a servant girl and compounded the error by remarrying before he knew for certain that she had died. A charge of bigamy had driven him to exile in America. Over the course of a long career in Pennsylvania, Peters also served as provincial secretary, clerk of the governor's council, secretary of the board of property, and chief negotiator in Indian affairs, as well as president of the College of Philadelphia. Peters had already expressed the hope that Thomas himself would return to look after the squatter problem, which had grown worse after his departure.[38]

Thomas Penn told Peters that John would live with James Hamilton, who had been governor of Pennsylvania since 1748. Hamilton was instructed to treat him as "a young man just come into the World,"[39] offering advice and correction as necessary. John was ordered to behave himself while in Hamilton's house, but the arrangement turned out less well than expected. The governor liked to spend time alone with his books, which often left John companionless except for his violin.

John Penn arrived on November 22, 1752, and found Philadelphia much more agreeable then he had expected. While he resided there, Philadelphia was emerging as an important city in the British Empire. Its skyline was already dominated by a new State House and the impressive spire of Christ Church, and it was such a busy port, one visitor remarked, that nearly everyone was somehow engaged in trade. Through the port of Philadelphia, merchants shipped the produce of Pennsylvania's rich hinterland and imported fine manufactured goods.[40] John's initial letters mentioned attractive women and well-regulated assemblies. His one criticism of Philadelphia was that it lacked paved streets.

John quickly perceived a certain tension in the politics of Pennsylvania. In February 1753 he urged his Uncle Thomas to come to Pennsylvania and defend the rights of the proprietary family against those who wanted to "engross all the power of government,"[41] but Thomas warned him not to join in political disputes.[42] John protested that he was carefully avoiding such arguments, but he observed that there were many disaffected people in Pennsylvania who did not wish the family well.[43]

At the time of John's visit, Quakers essentially controlled the assembly, having maintained their influence in the province despite repeated attempts by Thomas Penn to oust them from politics. Penn's quarrels with the Quaker assembly had arisen over Pennsylvania's defense. When war with Spain had threatened in 1739, the Penn governor had suggested that the Quaker-controlled assembly raise a compulsory militia. The pacifistic Quakers had balked, preferring to soothe their consciences by meeting demands for military support as they had in the past—by donating money "for the King's use." An angry Thomas had tried and failed to get the British Board of Trade to unseat Quaker legislators, citing the contradiction between their religious principles and their duty to defend the colony.[44] In Pennsylvania, Thomas's fellow advocates for defense had too little popular support to vote the Quakers out of office in the early 1740s. Thomas Penn's unpopular land policies may have contributed to this defeat, leaving the proprietary family with little support throughout the 1740s.[45] Before he had been in Pennsylvania long, John Penn complained that no prominent Quakers had come to call on him, though other gentlemen had.[46] Apparently, by 1752, Pennsylvania's Quaker leaders felt confident enough to snub Thomas Penn's own nephew.

Thomas fought back by trying to strengthen the executive branch of the Penn government. The assembly had long been raising more money than it needed for specific purposes, creating surpluses that the assembly spent as it pleased, so Thomas Penn instructed his governor to pass no bills that would raise money unless the governor was given a say in expenditures. He ensured that these orders would be followed by having the governor pledge £5,000, which would not be returned if the governor violated Thomas's instructions. The assembly regarded such absentee direction as a form of foreign dictatorship, and Thomas Penn's proprietary instructions caused bitter resentment among the assembly members for the proprietary family from the 1750s on.[47]

While John Penn remained in Pennsylvania, events were taking place that would lead to the French and Indian War. In the spring of 1754 the French began asserting themselves in the Ohio Valley. By May, Philadelphia received the ominous news from a young George Washington that French soldiers had appeared at a fort he and other Virginians were building on the Ohio near the Monongahela. According to their reports, shots had already been fired.[48]

The assembly members earned much popular criticism for their apparent inability to meet this threat. By the summer of 1755, Pennsylvania settlers were chiding them for inaction and blaming them for Indian attacks on the frontier. Thomas Penn further frustrated the assembly by instructing his governor to veto any bills taxing the proprietary estates. The legal nature of the proprietorship meant that he was well within his rights despite the frontier crisis. By the time John Penn left the province, popular opinion would drive the assembly to raise money on Thomas Penn's terms and exempt the Penn family estates from taxes from 1755 to 1758. This only

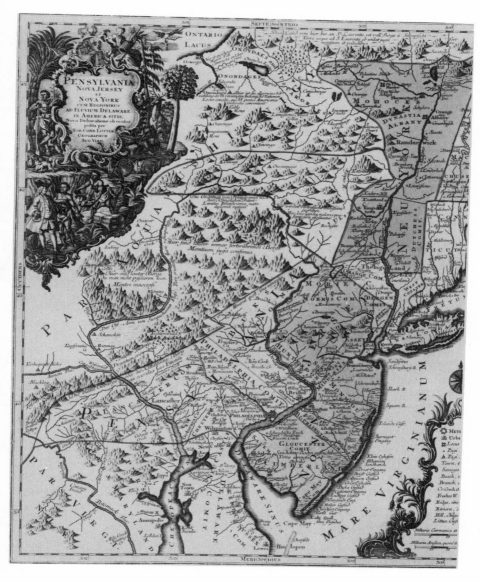

Map 1. Pennsylvania, New Jersey, and New York, circa 1750. (Courtesy, The Historical Society of Pennsylvania)

intensified the assembly's resentment of Thomas because it appeared to be deliberate tax-dodging on the part of the province's largest landowners.[49]

Thomas Penn was also busy extending the influence of the Penn family by placing potential allies and supporters in appointive positions. The proprietors' most important officer was their governor, who was empowered to appoint other proprietary and provincial officers. The governor was advised by a council whose members were also appointed and scrutinized by Thomas Penn. The sale of land was managed by the land office, whose officials were, again, Penn family appointees. Upon becoming chief proprietor in 1746, Thomas Penn had begun filling these positions with non-Quaker gentlemen from a small political faction dominated by the wealthy Presbyterian merchant William Allen.[50] Known today as the proprietary gentry, their members also included Richard Peters and James Hamilton, whom Thomas Penn had entrusted with the care of his nephew.

John Penn would have moved among this proprietary gentry during his stay in America. This exclusive group generally enjoyed inherited wealth and derived additional earnings from the fees and salaries of their offices. Occasionally, in return for their loyalty, they received grants of land that did not require cash downpayments, and this enabled them to increase their incomes through the rents and profits of considerable landholdings. Though they were not rich by the standards of eighteenth-century Europe, they lived the life of lesser British gentry, complete with townhouses, carriages, and country estates. When John visited Philadelphia they dominated several important organizations, including the College of Philadelphia and the Philadelphia Corporation (nominally the city's governing body), and interacted socially at Philadelphia's prestigious Dancing Assembly.[51]

As a member of the proprietary family, John Penn would have had limited contact with other social groups. He would not have been welcome in exclusively Quaker organizations, nor would he have associated with the city's lesser merchants, whose incomes were more equal to the successful self-employed artisans that contemporaries called "mechanics." And he would have had little reason to interact with the city's sailors or unskilled workers. Although all Philadelphians lived in relatively close quarters, the elite managed to separate themselves from the lower orders by surrounding their houses with thick party walls to ensure privacy. They went visiting in chairs, chariots, and carriages, which further cut off communication with their inferiors.[52] Thomas Penn wrote John that the lack of paved streets did not matter much because "no one" went about the town on foot.[53]

John had arrived bearing orders that he be placed on the governor's council.

The council members welcomed him and showed their respect for the Penn family by resolving to "place him at their Head; and that when he shall have taken the legal Qualifications, he should be considered as the First named or Eldest Counsellor, on the Death or Absence of the Governor, or Lieutenant Governor."[54] John proudly wrote that at council meetings he held "the next place to the governor."[55] Thomas Penn advised him to study the minutes of past council meetings that he might be "more fit to act whenever . . . called to it."[56]

John also tried to make himself useful by looking after his long-absent uncle's property—including his estates, his livestock, and his slaves. At that time Thomas Penn was contemplating a return visit, so John supervised a renovation project at Springettsbury, the old country house Thomas had built outside Philadelphia. John reported sadly that his uncle's pheasants were dead and that the Penn deer, an important mark of a gentleman's estate, had escaped from their paddock. He also discovered that a slave named Cato had a drinking problem.[57] Thomas Penn was glad for his nephew's services but not always happy for the bad news. He lamented the loss of his deer and his pheasants and advised John to send Cato to the country if he did not reform.[58]

Together with Richard Peters, Benjamin Franklin, and Isaac Norris (another assembly member), John Penn traveled to the Albany Conference in 1754. Although this was an important attempt at intercolonial cooperation intended to improve relations with the Indians, to John it was primarily a chance to travel and see more of America. He returned by way of Long Island,[59] and his correspondence with his uncle did not even comment on what had taken place at the conference.

John Penn's letters to his uncle mention little about politics or the Penn land business in Pennsylvania. His brief and infrequent messages touched on nothing of importance to the Penn family. Thomas Penn began to wonder whether his nephew's stay in America was doing John or the family any good and whether John was ready for the kind of responsibility Thomas wanted him to assume. When Governor Hamilton resigned, Thomas could have reshuffled his organization and perhaps made John governor, but instead he relegated his nephew to the status of boarder in the new governor's home.

At about the same time, Thomas Penn became aware of just how much money his nephew had spent and sensed that something was wrong. In a short period John had received £800 from Richard Hockley, the Penns' receiver general, plus a £200 prize from the lottery.[60] By the end of 1755 Hockley informed Thomas that John had received a total of £1,600 and was £200 or £300 in debt. The problem was that John had taken up with an Italian musician, an "Insinuating Fellow of debauch'd principles."[61] Thomas chided John for the expenses, wondered whether he was unhappy, and suggested that John travel in Europe for a while, perhaps visiting Germany or Holland, until he was ready to engage in family business. Only if he had already volunteered for the army would John be provided with more money and permitted to stay. If John was serving under General Braddock he would be allowed another £500 to outfit himself properly.[62] Despite John's protests that he had been slandered and his rationalizations that no gentlemen from Pennsylvania had joined Braddock's army,[63] Thomas ordered John to return to Europe. Though angry, Thomas expressed his best wishes for his nephew's real happiness.[64]

John's marital problems meant that he could not expect to come home. Earlier in 1755, John's father had told Richard Peters, "That worst of men Dr. Cox and his Daughter are suing him for a support,"[65] apparently hoping for a legal settlement that would force the Penns to pay John's wife an allowance out of his estate. Thomas's lawyer was fighting the case, but John was still ashamed of the whole situation and was slow to provide the necessary details. On the advice of Peters, John decided to return to his father's house in England rather than wander aimlessly through Europe.[66] Richard Penn believed his friend must be mad to suggest such a thing. In the summer of 1755 Richard anxiously wrote his brother asking how they might prevent John from returning directly home.[67]

Where John went and what happened to him and his wife remains a mystery. Surviving correspondence fails to mention John until a year later, when his father wrote Thomas Penn to say he had no objection to John's being presented to the king.[68] The letter indicates that the blot on John's character had by then somehow been erased, perhaps by the early death of Dr. Cox's daughter. The Cox family is not mentioned in any later Penn correspondence. Whatever the truth about his marriage, and whatever had occurred to dissolve it, his youthful error shaped John Penn's later life. His subsequent behavior was extremely conservative, and all his later decisions were carefully made.

John continued to travel and write letters to his uncle about the places where he was staying. In 1760 he stayed at Gordon Castle outside Edinburgh, and he described the city and the sights he and his companion, Colonel Morris, had seen.[69] Later letters indicate he was taking a new interest in Thomas Penn's lands in America and in Penn family dealings with the Pennsylvania assembly. Sometime between 1755 and 1763 John apparently became the man his uncle wanted. Pennsylvanians soon heard he would be returning—this time as their governor.

In the dark days of 1754 Thomas Penn had warned John that his father might "prefer your Brother to you and give him your estate,"[70] but John's younger brother turned out to be a poor alternative. When John had first sailed to America, young Richard Penn Jr. was enrolled at Cambridge to study law. Proud and deeply resentful about being the younger son of a younger son, Richard often complained about life's unfairness. He told his Uncle Thomas that at Cambridge "some of [his fellow students] look but shy upon me, as being only a Pensioner, and expect some difference be paid to them."[71] Richard never graduated, and he later admitted he had done poorly at the "Laborious study of the Law."[72] During the summer of 1761, when he was twenty-six years old, Richard blamed his family for his bad luck, implying it was their fault for choosing a career they should have perceived he had no talent for. He mentioned his disappointment that Uncle Thomas had failed to get him a position that paid a salary—"some small thing that might have been suitable for me." His family's neglect had forced him to pay an irksome attendance on Sir James Lowther, who had also failed to secure him a good position in the army.[73]

Thomas Penn sent back a stinging reply. He would have been glad to discuss young Richard's career during Richard's recent visit, but, as Thomas put it, Richard's "inclinations had [him] to other places." Richard, his uncle continued, had no right to expect the life of a gentleman "without applying as all other young men do to a profession for a support and advancement in the world." The younger sons of peers and gentry always worked for a living. Failure at his studies had made him unfit for any office, and Thomas was not about to bear the blame for Sir James Lowther's inability to help. The Penns were not responsible for plans they knew nothing of. Richard could now choose the army or the church, or beg some money from his father, to which Thomas Penn would add. Young Richard might then go to the East Indies and try to set himself up as a merchant. Thomas Penn softened the blow by closing his letter with an offer of £100 if Richard really needed it.[74]

Richard apparently accepted none of these alternatives and continued to drift. When John Penn became governor of Pennsylvania, Richard was permitted to visit the province—his uncle and father hoped he would eventually find himself and prove useful to his family. Other than that, there were no firm plans for Richard's future in the Penn organization, and Richard would always resent it.

James Hamilton was again serving as governor early in 1763 when he received a very private letter from Pennsylvania's proprietors containing news that would reach no one else by that ship: John Penn had finally claimed his birthright by expressing serious interest in becoming governor and taking on the Penn family business in Pennsylvania.[75] In later letters Thomas Penn assured his other officers it had always been John's right to claim this position and that John had not been appointed because the Penns were dissatisfied with Hamilton, whom Thomas respected and liked. In fact, Thomas assured Hamilton he could have the income from tavern licenses (a major perquisite for Pennsylvania's governor) for the full following year.[76]

Despite all the advance notice, some Pennsylvanians expressed a certain surprise at John Penn's arrival. A rumor surfaced that the ailing Richard Peters had been asked to put off a sabbatical in England to advise a young and inexperienced governor,[77] but that was not true. Thomas Penn had suggested that Peters postpone his trip because the provost of the College of Philadelphia was also in England and it would have been detrimental to the institution to have two senior officers absent at the same time.[78] Both John and Thomas had merely expressed satisfaction that Peters would be there to greet the new governor and give him advice based on lengthy experience in managing Penn family affairs.[79]

Thomas Penn wrote Richard Peters's brother William that John would be able to devote more attention to the land office than James Hamilton had, "as it is my Nephew's business as much as that of being Governor."[80] John looked forward to the increased responsibility. He observed to Thomas, "I often hear it said that the Proprietary affairs suffer much for a want of a proper regulation among their officers."[81]

John Penn arrived in Philadelphia on October 30, 1763, and the next day his commission was read and he took his oath of office. Then Governor John Penn, his council, the mayor, the city recorder, the aldermen, and the sheriff all marched to the courthouse, where the commission was read again—this time to the assembled public. Guns were fired from the battery, and citizens rang the bells at Christ Church.[82] A short time later Philadelphia's more prominent merchants met at the courthouse and proceeded to John Penn's residence, where Mayor Thomas Willing delivered a welcoming address signed by 169 of them. "An elegant Entertainment for his Honor was held at the State House," Philadelphia newspapers said. Key government officials attended together with "such military Gentlemen and Strangers as were in town."[83]

Even the usually hostile assembly participated in this outpouring of welcome and goodwill. They congratulated Penn on his appointment and offered their "sincere thanks for the warm Professions you are pleased to make of doing every thing in your power that may tend to the advantage and prosperity of the Province & to cultivate and improve Harmony and a good Understanding with Us."[84]

John Penn was so feasted and feted that he complained to Thomas Penn that the surfeit of visits and addresses it was impossible to avoid left little time to arrange his personal household affairs. The house intended for his residence had been left in poor repair by its former occupant, Governor William Denny, who had destroyed or sold about half the furniture and "hardly left a sauce pan" in the kitchen.[85] But John got no peace. One by one, representatives of the city's various religious groups and public institutions called to address him, and the new governor gave polite answers to Philadelphia's Baptists, Quakers, and Roman Catholics and to the ministers and wardens of Christ Church, the treasurers of Pennsylvania Hospital, and the city's Library Company.

Many of the welcoming speeches contained ominous allusions to the dreadful situation on the frontier. Despite the warm welcome, everyone knew that John Penn had arrived at a very bad time. Perhaps in appointing his nephew governor, Thomas Penn had been vicariously fulfilling an old desire to become governor himself. Certainly he hoped to exert more control over the province's executive branch of government through a Penn family member. Yet even Thomas would have delayed the appointment of his inexperienced and untried nephew if it had not been for all the red tape and if arrangements had not been too far advanced when all the trouble started.

Thomas Penn could only hope that John was ready for the crisis that would immediately face him.

3

"To Kill Us All, and Burn the Town"

The Paxton Boys

Soldiers manning Fort Bedford in western Pennsylvania were alarmed one day in June 1763 when James Clark's dog arrived at the fort wounded and alone. They went looking for Clark and found him dead with an Indian spear in his belly. He had been scalped and his corpse "inhumanly mangled."[1]

In July, about thirty or forty miles from Carlisle, Indians rushed William White's house. White was shot down at his door, but the four other men and one boy with him managed to pull him inside. They held their assailants off until the Indians set the house on fire. Then the Indians picked them off as they tried to escape through the windows. Only one man got away, through a hole in the roof.[2]

In September a letter from Sinking Spring reported that a party of patrolling soldiers had come across a young boy with another horror story to tell. They followed the boy to the house of John Fincher, where they found Fincher, his wife, and two sons dead. Fincher had been a Quaker, and before he died he had offered his Indian assailants food and begged them to spare his family. Neighbors later reported they had heard a girl screaming—presumably Fincher's daughter, as the Indians were carrying her away.[3]

The soldiers were able to track these particular Indians to Nicholas Miller's house, where they found the bodies of four murdered children. Pressing on, they overtook their prey. After exchanging fire, the Indians rode off leaving two captured Miller children behind. The soldiers concluded these were the same vicious marauders who had attacked Franz Huber's family, carrying off Huber's wife and three children. Three other Huber children survived scalping, but two later died.[4]

News from the frontier during the summer of 1763 shocked the residents of the more settled parts of Pennsylvania. How could such things be happening in William Penn's peaceful colony, where the founder had promised to treat the Indians fairly? Such appalling stories seemed to be coming from a foreign land. Indeed, Pennsylvania's frontier would have seemed very foreign to some Philadelphians. As one traveled west from the Delaware, the nature of Pennsylvania society changed.

Surrounding the strongly Quaker communities of Philadelphia, Bucks, and Chester counties, a broad belt of German communities stretched from Bethlehem to Lancaster. William Penn had invited these Germans by promoting Pennsylvania in northern Europe. In the years following 1709 a huge wave of Swiss and Germans fled their war-torn principalities and came seeking the religious freedom William Penn had promised. Some Germans were Lutheran, others were Catholic, others belonged to the German Reformed churches. Still others belonged to the "pietistic" sects which sought to purify the practice of Christianity. The German immigrants shared a different language and tended to isolate themselves, rarely interfering in colonial politics.

In 1763 Pennsylvania's Germans were enduring Indian attacks together with their neighbors settled farther north and west, the people that have come to be known as Pennsylvania's Scots-Irish. These people of Scottish descent had lived for a time in Ulster. William Penn's secretary, James Logan, believed they would make good frontier settlers, so he encouraged them to come to Pennsylvania and head west. Between 1717 and 1740 many flocked to the province and settled in the Susquehanna Valley and upper Berks County.

From the start, Pennsylvania's Quakers had been suspicious of the Scots-Irish, most of whom were Presbyterian. The Quakers considered them lawless, bigoted, superstitious, and overzealous, and they were afraid the Scots-Irish would eventually outnumber them and begin to persecute them for their faith. They tried to prevent this by denying growing Scots-Irish communities equal representation in the assembly that drew up Pennsylvania's laws.

Additional evidence of the lack of understanding between the city and the frontier was the alarming news of Indian attacks that arrived just as Philadelphia was celebrating peace at the end of the French and Indian War. In January 1763 Governor James Hamilton had received orders to proclaim peace. He and his council members had marched to the courthouse attended by the mayor and various army officers. The assembly had joined them while Hamilton's secretary read the peace proclamation "in the presence of a great Concourse of People."[5] By the end of July, Hamilton received his official copy of the proclamation from England and declared a day of thanksgiving early in August.[6]

There was no peace and no thanksgiving on the frontier. The treaty merely decided ownership of the Ohio Valley between England and France. It failed to resolve the differences between Indians and whites settled in the area. A treaty at Easton in 1758 had promised the Indians that British soldiers would demolish the British forts as soon as the French were vanquished, and in 1760 General Jeffrey Amherst, then in charge of British armies in America, had promised to evict white settlers from Indian land.[7] At treaty negotiations at Lancaster in 1762, Delaware chiefs had expressed a desire for peace but reiterated demands that whites take no more land and remove their forts and soldiers.[8]

When the war ended, the white settlers, the soldiers, and the forts remained. Amherst also curtailed the gifts of ammunition the Indians had become accustomed to receiving. Finding themselves surrounded by armed soldiers and lacking powder, the Indians were afraid the British would enslave them, and an Ottawa chief named Pontiac rallied the Indians against England. On the frontiers of Virginia, Maryland, and Pennsylvania, Indian tribes rebelled in what has been called "Pontiac's Uprising." The rebellion ushered in a period of frontier unrest that would preoccupy the Penns and their appointees until the American Revolution was upon them.

Philadelphia got the first hints of frontier trouble from letters carried by riders called "expresses"—extracts from those letters were published in Philadelphia's two newspapers. News reaching the city could be confusing, because informants at one frontier location often relayed rumors and speculation about what was going on someplace else. A letter from Fort Pitt published in the *Pennsylvania Gazette* early in June 1763 noted: "The Indians have broke out in several Places."[9]

Other issues soon carried more details. By mid-June, Fort Pitt reported

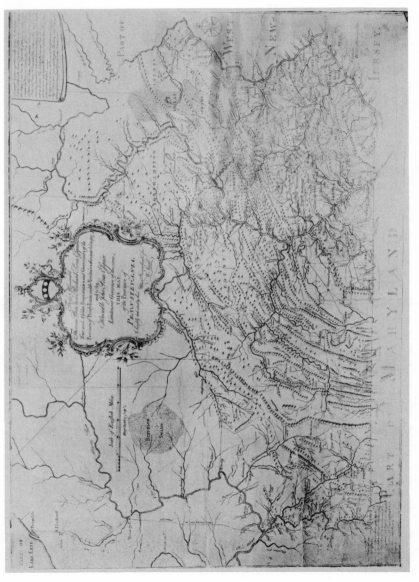

Map 2. Pennsylvania, circa 1770. (Courtesy, The Historical Society of Pennsylvania)

that Indians engaged in trade had warned the British not to remain there, that a nearby mill had been burned, and that Indians had murdered several settlers. The report concluded with ominous news: "Our small Posts, I am afraid, are gone."[10] Settlers seeking protection arrived at the fort, and eventually some five hundred people joined the eight regulars who usually manned Fort Pitt. Soldiers were glad to have the additional men who could help hold the fort and protect the women and children. Fort Pitt adopted a defensive posture, but officials confidently reported that the fort would stand.[11] And from Carlisle came a letter reporting that a friendly Indian married to a white woman had warned them that the rebellious tribes "design to carry the War to as great an Extent as they can." These tribes were later identified as mainly Delawares and Shawnees, but this letter reported that a "great many Tribes" were cooperating. Attacks were expected at harvest time, when the settlers' provisions would be destroyed and the Indians would take no prisoners.[12]

Early in July, news from Fort Pitt told how an Ensign Price had bravely held the fort called Le Boeuf with only six men and was the only one to escape alive, that an officer taken at Venango had been tortured every night until he died, that Presque Isle had fallen when Indians undermined its blockhouse, and that Fort Ligonier was under attack. Detroit was still standing.[13]

By mid-July every fort on the Ohio except Fort Pitt had fallen. Because the British had broken their promises, the Ohio Valley Indians had combined to resolve their grievances and remove the forts and white settlers from their territories on Pennsylvania's northern and western frontiers. In this war, the Indians gave no quarter. Pennsylvanians, long accustomed to good relations with the Indians, were particularly shocked by accounts that women and children were being scalped and mutilated.

Pennsylvania authorities mobilized to defend the terrified settlers who had fled isolated outlying farms for the nearest town or fort. Many had left their crops unattended and all their belongings behind. By the end of July almost fourteen hundred settlers had taken refuge in Shippensburg and were huddled, miserable, in barns, stables, cellars, and sheds.[14] Governor Hamilton called the Pennsylvania assembly into special session, which voted to fund seven hundred fighting men from money in the current treasury, promising additional funds during the next session should this amount be insufficient. Governor Hamilton was pleased by their prompt action.[15]

General Amherst was less pleased. He had expected Pennsylvania to supply a thousand men and complained in England of insufficient manpower. He implied that the entire frontier situation was Pennsylvania's fault because the province had historically contributed grudgingly to its own defense. Although he had also quarreled with the assembly over defense, on this occasion Thomas Penn felt obliged "in honour" to defend Pennsylvania's government from outside criticism. He revealed that the general had made no specific formal requests and could not complain about what the province supplied voluntarily.[16] Thomas was soon able to report that Amherst's complaints had been received coolly: "I have shewn even the Assembly has not refused his applications because he made none to them."[17]

In the meantime, Pennsylvanians supplemented the king's forces with companies of rangers. Rangers might be based at a fort under an officer or might be independent, locally formed fighting companies. Rangers might fight offensively, retaliating for Indian attacks by terrorizing Indian communities. A letter from Carlisle told how rangers had raided an Indian village, forced the inhabitants to flee "leaving their Victuals warm on Pieces of Bark," plundered the village, and sold their loot, dividing the profit among themselves.[18] By September 1763 Northampton County supported some rangers while Cumberland County petitioned the assembly to assist the community in maintaining thirty "intrepid, resolute Fellows" under the command of a man who had once been taken captive by Indians and had lived among them.[19] Perhaps because it saved money, Thomas Penn was glad to hear settlers were organizing to help themselves and hoped Pennsylvania's northern settlers would show as much spirit as the inhabitants of Cumberland and Lancaster counties. He only feared that overzealous Englishmen might harm friendly Indians by mistake.[20]

When Fort Pitt was besieged during the summer of 1763, British officer Colonel Henry Bouquet organized a relief party to provision it with flour, livestock, and gunpowder. Philadelphia newspapers reported the progress of Bouquet's pack train westward across Pennsylvania. The papers noted his arrival at Fort Bedford and Fort Ligonier, stating he had left Ligonier on August 4. Vague news followed that a battle had taken place. Eventually the facts were reported.

At 1:00 P.M. on August 5, Bouquet was ambushed near the stream called Bushy Run. He fought off the Indians who surrounded his men until 6:00 that evening, when both parties disengaged for the night. When the Indians attacked again in the morning, Bouquet feigned retreat. He ordered grenadiers and the light infantry to rush the Indians' flanks while the rest of his men attacked with fixed bayonets "with an Intrepidity that once completed the Rout." Bouquet's companies then united and pursued the fleeing Indians. Out of four hundred Indians, Bouquet's men killed about sixty, but those sixty included some of the principal leaders of the uprising in the west. The Battle of Bushy Run sharply curtailed organized resistance in western Pennsylvania.[21]

Shortly after Bouquet's victory at Bushy Run, John Penn arrived in Pennsylvania. The first Philadelphia newspapers he must have read reported that the western frontier was considerably quieter. The lull continued through the fall, but both settlers and government officials remained wary. Troubled reports continued coming in from the north. In one of John's first letters to his uncle he wrote that the Indians "still continue their ravages in the most cruel manner," vowing not to stop "till they have driven the English into the Sea."[22]

Although John Penn claimed that Indian affairs took up his time from morning to night, he soon had a different kind of uprising to deal with. A letter arrived telling the new governor that a small company of Indians who had settled on a reservation called Conestoga Manor near Lancaster had been attacked.[23] Before dawn on December 14 some fifty unknown armed and mounted white men, believed to be from the communities of Paxton, Derry, and Hanover, had murdered and scalped six Indians and burned their cabins. Fourteen Indians had survived only because they had been away from the settlement at the time. Lancaster County magistrates rounded up the survivors and locked them in the Lancaster workhouse for their own protection.

John Penn and the Pennsylvania assembly were equally shocked. These Indians were believed to be the last remnants of the Conestoga tribe, descendants from Indians who had made early treaties with William Penn. As Sheriff John Hay later sorted through their belongings, he found letters and peace agreements, including an agreement made with William Penn in 1701.[24] These same peaceful, partially Christianized Indians had congratulated John Penn on becoming governor and begged for clothing and provisions because they no longer hunted for their food.[25]

John Penn informed the assembly that the fourteen survivors of what came to be called the Conestoga Massacre wanted to come to Philadelphia, where they would feel safer. And another group—Nanticokes who had settled in the north at a place called Wyalusing and who also wanted peace and were caught in the middle while the Indian uprising continued—made a similar request. The governor and his council recommended that both groups be brought to Philadelphia, in hopes that such overtures would incline the more hostile tribes toward peace.[26] The assembly readily agreed to fund their removal and upkeep.[27]

Before the Indians could be moved, John Penn received another letter from Lancaster. On December 27 between two and three o'clock in the afternoon, more than a hundred men had ridden into town. They stopped at Mr. Slough's Inn to leave a few men behind to guard their horses, then they swooped down on the workhouse, broke in, and killed the fourteen Indians who had survived the previous massacre.[28] The men hurried back to their horses and rode out of town without threatening or insulting Lancaster's other inhabitants. The sheriff later reported that both he and the coroner had tried to stop the men but could not do so "without Danger of Life to the Person attempting it."[29]

The Conestoga Massacre rudely introduced John Penn to frontier sentiment regarding the Indians. Largely Scots-Irish and German settlers fighting for their lives and their farms were furious that Pennsylvania's pacifistic Quakers and pietistic German sects offered Indians they considered friendly provisions and gifts while white refugees were starving. It seemed to them that the Quakers in Pennsylvania's assembly cared more for Indians than for white settlers and just didn't understand the terrifying situation in the west.

Since September 1763, Lancaster leader and minister John Elder had been urging Governor Hamilton to remove the Indians from Conestoga Manor, but his advice had been ignored, perhaps because government officials had not realized just how much the Indians were resented. Perhaps Philadelphians failed to believe newspaper accounts like the story of a dying man in Carlisle whose last words to a friend were, "Here, take my Gun and kill the first Indian you see, and all shall be well."[30]

Many years later a man named Matthew Smith admitted to being a leader of the Conestoga Massacre. He justified the attack by alleging that the Indians at Conestoga Manor were not as peaceful and harmless as Philadelphians assumed—like other previously friendly Indians, they might have been corrupted during the French and Indian War. An Indian known to be hostile had been tracked to their village. Smith and several others had crawled unseen through the woods and observed the Indian settlement, noticing many strange, armed Indians harbored there. On the night Smith and his friends decided to clean the village out, an Indian had fired on them and attacked them with a tomahawk—the same Indian, one of Smith's men claimed, had killed his own mother.[31]

Although frontiersmen did not distinguish between good and bad Indians, John Penn knew there were friendly tribes and that Pennsylvania could be heading for even more serious trouble. On hearing about the Conestoga Massacre, he wrote crown Indian agent Sir William Johnson and asked him to tell the chiefs of the powerful, allied Six Nations that the Conestoga Massacre did not represent Pennsylvania's official policy. Pennsylvania wanted peace and continued friendship.[32]

The governor tried to apprehend the murderers, instructing magistrates in Lancaster, York, and Cumberland counties to order authorities to capture them and offering a generous reward of £200 for any three massacre ringleaders.[33] Although these men must have been known to local residents, John Penn found no one willing to betray them. He only received messages like the one from Colonel John Armstrong in Carlisle tersely informing him that no one in Cumberland County had been involved.[34] The governor was forced to report to Thomas Penn that even ten thousand British soldiers could not round up the murderers.[35] Although Thomas was convinced that his nephew had done all he could, the largely Quaker assembly argued that John Penn's attempts had been lax and halfhearted. Assembly leaders wanted western county officials brought to Philadelphia for interrogation, but Penn's council, sensing legal and constitutional problems, advised against this, and the investigation was kept on-site.[36]

John Penn's crisis was far from over. Westerners were also indignant that the government was housing more Indians in Philadelphia. Popularly known as the "Moravian Indians," this Christianized group had been supported by pietistic Germans called Moravians. The assembly had supported their removal to Philadelphia in November 1763 because Northampton County residents threatened to kill them. Originally housed in the city barracks, the Indians had been moved to an isolated place of quarantine, called "the pesthouse," on Province Island at the mouth of the Schuylkill River because certain Philadelphia residents had also grown hostile and insulted the soldiers who had been guarding them.[37]

When John Penn heard about the Conestoga Massacre, he also learned that settlers on the western frontier were contemplating a march on Philadelphia to wipe out the Moravian Indians, and the council learned that western farmers were collecting money to furnish volunteers with horses. Penn wrote General Thomas Gage, who had replaced General Jeffrey Amherst, seeking the help of soldiers wintering in Carlisle in case there was further trouble.[38] Penn made a proclamation that the Moravian Indians were not to be harmed, and threatened that rioters and murderers "will answer the contrary at their peril."[39] Realizing their danger, the Indians at Province Island asked for safe conduct to Sir William Johnson's lands in New York, where they could put themselves under his personal protection. John Penn prevailed on a group of Royal Highlanders marching from Philadelphia to New York to escort the Indians, and they left on January 5, 1764.[40]

Governor John Penn had duly made all plans known to General Thomas Gage, Sir William Johnson, Governor Cadwalader Colden of New York, and Governor William Franklin of New Jersey, but the Moravian Indians got no farther than Amboy before they heard that Governor Colden had ordered ferrymen not to let them cross into New York.[41] There was nothing to do but march them back to Philadelphia with Captain Schlosser and the Royal Americans that General Gage had decided to send to Philadelphia on receiving John Penn's earlier letter. The Indians reached the city on January 24, and the governor, his council, and the assembly all agreed that they should now be housed at the city barracks, where they could be more easily protected.[42]

Frontier fury had cooled as soon as the Moravian Indians left Philadelphia. Now there were new threats on the lives of these Indians and those who dared to protect them. In Benjamin Kendall's deposition, taken on January 28, this Quaker merchant said he had met an acquaintance on the road between Lancaster and Philadelphia who told him that within ten days some fifteen hundred men would descend on Philadelphia to destroy the Moravian Indians. If fifteen hundred proved to be insufficient, five thousand more were ready to join them. Quakers would be spared unless they interfered. The private houses of those hiding Indians would be burned.[43]

On February 4 Governor Penn received an oral report from a witness named Wayne (or Waine) that a large body of rioters was indeed en route from the west.[44] The news was frightening but the city was not helpless. Gage had sent the governor three battalions plus orders he could use to send for the troops in Carlisle. The council had already advised that the Carlisle men be sent to Lancaster, which was closer to Philadelphia and might have seemed a potential trouble spot in light of the Conestoga Massacre.[45]

The governor realized this crisis was also a constitutional crisis. Could the king's troops be ordered to fire on the king's subjects when it was the duty of civil government to maintain order? Turning to the Pennsylvania assembly, John Penn asked them to "furnish [him] with full powers to repel those bold Invaders of Law and Justice."[46] In a rare display of solidarity, the assembly acted quickly to pass a riot act, forbidding groups to assemble and disturb the peace, and they also assured the governor there was money in the treasury to fend off the invasion.

Governor Penn told the troops guarding the Indians what the procedure would be. If armed men approached the barracks, a civil officer would read them the riot act and demand that they disperse. If they did not, the troops would shoot. Rioters would not be pursued if they broke and ran. He also asked the citizens of Pennsylvania to protect the city. He summoned Philadelphians to a meeting at the statehouse at 4:00 P.M. on February 4, where in a driving rain the governor warned three thousand curious or frightened citizens of the danger and informed them of the riot act.[47]

Many citizens heeded his call by forming voluntary militia associations, and the city sent out scouts and dug redoubts. Many Quakers took up arms, abandoning the pacifistic principles of their founder George Fox and embarrassing the stricter members of their sect.[48] Quakers were later accused of having turned their meetinghouses into armories and arsenals. A Philadelphia wit described the panicked situation in rhyme: "The Paxton Boys are coming down / To kill us all, and burn the Town. / To Arms, to Arms with one Accord, / The Sword of Quakers and the Lord! / Let no one stand with hands in Pocket / Each meeting door—quick, quick, unlock it!"[49] Red-faced Quakers protested that someone had merely allowed some volunteers to take refuge in a meeting house from the rain.

Rumor had it that thousands were on the march. To reach Philadelphia they would have to cross the Schuylkill River, so orders were given to bring all ferryboats to the Philadelphia side. Unfortunately, Philadelphians forgot about the Swedes' Ford farther upriver—it was too late when someone was finally sent to secure it and reports reached Philadelphia that a great many men had already crossed.[50] Before dawn the following morning, Philadelphians heard church bells ringing—signaling an impending emergency—and homeowners put candles in their windows to light the way for volunteer defenders.[51]

About two hundred and fifty rebels finally arrived in Germantown. Before the epithet "Paxton Boys" stuck, the marchers were called the "Hickory Boys." A number of more courageous or more curious Philadelphians traveled to Germantown to gape at them, and what they saw was a contingent of men dressed in the rough clothing of frontier Indian traders. To amuse or perhaps intimidate the city folk, the Paxton Boys yelped Indian war cries, knocked a few Philadelphians down, and pretended to tomahawk and scalp them.[52]

Governor Penn sent a special delegation to Germantown—choosing men who could represent the forces of law and order in Philadelphia. They included Benjamin Franklin and Joseph Galloway, both assembly members; Benjamin Chew and William Logan of the governor's council; Philadelphia's Mayor Thomas Willing; and Dr. Carl Wrangel of Gloria Dei, the Lutheran church in Philadelphia.[53] The delegation rode out of Philadelphia at 5:00 A.M. on February 7 and met representatives chosen by the Paxton Boys at Coleman's Tavern in Germantown. Philadelphia officials informed the insurgents that the Indians at the barracks were under the protection of His Majesty's troops sent to Philadelphia by General Gage at the governor's request. Apparently the Paxton Boys had not expected to encounter so much organized opposition, and they agreed to suspend hostilities if Pennsylvania officials would formally consider their grievances.[54]

Before the rebels left, the city was alarmed anew when about thirty Paxton Boys marched into Philadelphia proper the following day, saying they wanted to see whether they could identify any known murderers among the Indians at the barracks. Philadelphia's citizen soldiers again took up arms, but the governor merely thanked them and dismissed them, declaring a false alarm.[55]

The Paxton Boys had come armed with a document called the "Declaration" in which they justified their march, proclaimed their loyalty to the king, and condemned the government for treating Indians better than the king's subjects. James Gibson and Matthew Smith were appointed to remain behind and state specific grievances in a document called the "Remonstrance," which turned out to be considerably more legalistic and deferential in tone. It suggested that Pennsylvania expel all Indians from inhabited parts of the province, offer settlers a bounty on Indian scalps, and suspend trade with the Indians until all white captives were released. It also complained strongly of unequal representation in Pennsylvania's assembly and implied that the government was not responsive to frontier concerns in the west because the west had insufficient voice in government.[56]

The assembly wanted to dress down the rebels. Assembly members suggested a joint session of the assembly and governor's council that the governor would also attend. This meeting would largely point out to Smith and Gibson that they were wrong and that the government was united against them.[57] Had John Penn agreed completely, this would still have been too unorthodox a move for his conservative nature. He advised the house to treat the Paxton Boys' documents like any other petition. If they drew up any legislation in response, he would consider their bills in the usual way.[58]

Although the Paxton Boys uprising demonstrated that some citizens felt entitled to make demands on government, the Penn family did not treat it as an assault on their governing powers. Both John Penn and Thomas Penn may have been wondering whether the rebellion could be used to proprietary advantage, as more ammunition in an ongoing struggle with the largely Quaker assembly. The Penns might have welcomed more representation for the western frontier in order to balance Quaker power in the legislature. Before Smith and Gibson left Philadelphia, the governor met with them privately and gave them assurances that seemed to satisfy them. While he never justified the rebellion in letters to his uncle, John did acknowledge that the west had suffered much,[59] but he scoffed at the idea that the assembly would ever voluntarily allow the west more legislative representation: "I am of opinion they [the west] will never come into [it] as it will be a means of lessening the power of the Governing few in this Province."[60] Thomas Penn agreed that the backcountry was underrepresented[61] and that westerners might be justifiably provoked to see the assembly maintain and defend certain Indians.[62]

While the Quaker assembly was not privy to the letters that passed between John Penn and his uncle, they sensed that the proprietors were showing an ominous forbearance toward the suddenly unruly west. The governor, they observed, had done little to ferret out the Conestoga Massacre murderers, and now he had met with Smith and Gibson in private negotiation. Was he allying himself with the Presbyterian west against them?

Quakers were also alarmed by the riot because it seemed to demonstrate that western Presbyterians might indeed have the power to organize and overrun the province if they chose to. Even worse, many Philadelphians had sympathized with the rioters. City Presbyterians had not taken up arms, and some Philadelphia Germans had identified with their frontier compatriots. Quakers had every reason to develop a siege mentality during the course of 1764 as pamphleteers took up their pens and waged a war of words against them.

Actually, Ben Franklin started the war with his *Narrative of the Late Massacres,* describing the murders at Conestoga Manor from the perspective of the Indians. In order to make the victims seem human and familiar, he used the Indians' English names and noted family relationships among the men, women, and children who had died on their knees begging for mercy.[63] He characterized one elderly Indian who had spoken with William Penn as what later authors would call a "noble savage." Thomas Penn, initially horrified at news of the massacre, liked Franklin's narrative. He wrote, "I was very well pleased with a small pamphlet wrote by Mr. Franklin for this purpose."[64] Many people were less complimentary. Franklin's pamphlet made enemies as well as friends and further alienated many Scots-Irish Presbyterians.

Pamphlets written in response blasted the governing Quakers for leaving the frontier defenseless, a situation that was particularly reprehensible because the recent riot had shown they had no religious scruples against bearing arms to protect themselves. One pamphlet justified the massacre by calling its Indian victims a "drunken, debauch'd, insolent, quarrelsome Crew."[65] Another pointed out that at least these Indians had died quickly; frontier victims of Indian violence often suffered more.[66] Several writers reiterated the old complaint about Indians being maintained at public expense.

Quakers, thrust on the defensive, argued that they also contributed money for the relief of frontier refugees. A pamphlet entitled *A Looking Glass for Presbyterians* pointed out that Quaker settlers had had no problems with Indians during the province's earlier days, before the Scots-Irish began to dominate the frontier.[67] The Presbyterians were as little swayed by Quaker invective as the Quakers were persuaded by pro-Presbyterian writings. The two sides became increasingly divided.

Assembly leader Benjamin Franklin claimed an important role in the city's defense against the Paxton Boys. In a letter to England, Franklin penned a quite partisan account of the city's frenzied state the night of the western invasion. According to Franklin, Governor John Penn had been unable to deal with the emergency and had essentially turned over control of the city's defenses to him. Franklin wrote that at midnight, with alarm bells ringing, John Penn had run to his house "with his Counsellors at his Heels, for Advice, and made it his Headquarters for some time." Virtually every historian describing the march of the Paxton Boys has quoted Franklin and credited him with taking charge.[68] Franklin had experience in forming voluntary militia associations, so it is logical he might have been consulted. And either the governor himself or one of his councillors must have called on Franklin at some time to invite him to join the governor's delegation to meet with the rioters in Germantown. But did John Penn really throw up his hands and let Franklin take command?

Contemporary accounts don't mention Franklin's role. The *Pennsylvania Gazette* specifically states that the governor called on citizens to form militia associations and sent selected men to go to Germantown. Even a farce written after the invasion places a comically agitated governor clearly in charge, ordering the city bells rung and the watch and constables alerted.[69] The letter John Penn wrote to his uncle describing the riot does not mention Franklin at all. Actually, Franklin was already at loggerheads with the Penn family and had his own reasons for wanting to make the colony's government appear weak and helpless. It is possible he exaggerated his own role in the affair.

While pamphleteers did verbal battle in Philadelphia, frontier settlers were again faced with physical violence in 1764. Early that year many settlers hoped to return to their farms and plant crops in the spring, but many changed their minds on hearing more stories of murders and scalpings.

Unlike the attacks on the frontier forts the previous year, the Indians now avoided armed soldiers and preyed on isolated and relatively helpless individuals. John Penn's information stated that Indians would attack only when certain of success, then melt into the forest where patrolling troops would be unable to find them.[70]

Once again Philadelphia newspapers carried horrifying tales of violent death. In February two men cutting wood just one and a half miles from Fort Pitt had been fired on. One was injured but managed to fight off three Indians and escape; the other was killed. When his body was found it was discovered he had not only been scalped—the skin had also been removed from his entire head, his torso ripped open, and his heart torn from his body.[71] Near Fort Bedford that summer a group of white men reported chasing some Indians who had taken a young boy prisoner. While fleeing their pursuers, the Indians quickly beheaded the boy after he fell from his horse. They took his head and "carried it about forty yards, there scalped it, and left it on the Road for our people to see."[72] From Carlisle came news that a pregnant woman had been attacked while walking alone to a neighbor's house two miles away. Indians murdered and scalped her and "most horridly abused her," slashing open her abdomen and leaving her unborn child beside her.[73] Both Philadelphia newspapers carried stories about the July attack on an isolated school near Fort Loudon—Indians killed the schoolmaster and nine young students.[74]

In light of such reports, Pennsylvania again mobilized against the Indians. The governor and his council considered offering rewards for Indian scalps, as the Remonstrance made by the Paxton Boys had suggested, but before taking this step a cautious John Penn wrote Sir William Johnson asking whether scalp bounties would affect any of Johnson's diplomatic plans.[75] When Johnson sent his approval, Penn issued a proclamation declaring Pennsylvania's rebellious Delawares and Shawnees "Enemies, REBELS and TRAITORS." Pennsylvanians were encouraged to pursue and kill them and could collect a reward for their scalps. Citizens were not to harm peaceful Indians of the Six Nations or Indians under government protection.[76] Sir William Johnson also helped by organizing some four hundred friendly Indians of the Six Nations. John Penn was able to report that mixed parties of white rangers and friendly Indians were patrolling the backwoods together. Johnson's treaties with the Senecas and other tribes farther west were also expected to help bring rebellious Indians to heel.[77] In the late summer and early fall of 1764, there was news that volunteers were forming under Colonel Bouquet to mount an offensive campaign in the west. Fort Pitt reported that the army would consist of 400 regulars, 100 light horse, 400 Pennsylvanians, and 250 volunteers from Virginia and another 60 from Maryland,[78] and their mission was to destroy Indian villages and settlements in order to dishearten and demoralize the enemy.

Even before these troops were deployed, news that the Indians were suing for peace was coming in. By September, representatives from the Delawares, the Shawnees, and the Hurons met with a Colonel Bradstreet at Presque Isle. At first, westerners questioned the Indians' sincerity. A report from Fort Loudon noted that Indians were begging for mercy in their "usual abject manner" but, it went on, "at the same time those Savages continue skulking on the Frontiers and murder every defenseless person they can catch in an unguarded Minute."[79]

Bradstreet's treaty was followed by the good news that Bouquet's offensive had been successful. The *Pennsylvania Gazette* reported that the Indians were convinced "that even their Woods could not protect them, when followed by so brave and judicious a Commander, at the Head of a gallant, though but small army."[80] Leaders of the Shawnees, the Delawares, the Mingoes, and the Senecas submitted to Bouquet and agreed to send representatives to conclude a formal treaty with Sir William Johnson. John Penn acknowledged his debt to Bouquet, writing his uncle that "by his wise & spirited Conduct he has happily put an end to the most cruel war that ever was carried on."[81] The governor's proclamation of peace appeared in Philadelphia papers in December 1764.

The war had been expensive. In 1765 Governor Penn and assembly debated whether to evacuate Fort Augusta or reduce forces there, because the treasury was exhausted. The war had been equally costly for frontiersmen.[82] Those who had suffered most petitioned the assembly for charity. One man wrote on behalf of Dorothy and Magdalen Snyder, two girls who had been orphaned, seriously wounded, and scalped during an Indian attack. They had survived, but they owed a physician a good deal of money for their care. The assembly voted to cover their doctor bills.[83]

Thomas Penn considered the costs of Indian war from another perspective. As long as Indians were harassing outlying settlers, Pennsylvania would not be as profitable for the Penn family as it could be. Although he never complained about the money he had been receiving, he did urge Edmund Physick to continue collecting quitrents, except on the beleaguered frontier.[84] He also advised Richard Hockley to get good prices on already surveyed and located lands, because he did not expect frontier land to sell well until there was peace with the Indians.[85]

Peace and good relations with the Indians were in the Penn family interests, and Thomas Penn wanted a long-term solution that would prevent the turmoil of 1763 and 1764 from ever occurring again. To this end, he wanted the British to be generous and just with the Indians, he wanted to see trade regulated and carried on through licensed traders at standard exchange rates, and he wanted all Indian affairs to be regulated by centralized Imperial policy, not on the whim of provincial assemblies or local communities. Sir William Johnson had been extremely successful at treatymaking, and Penn wanted Johnson in charge of all Indian affairs in America. He spoke of Johnson's merits to British ministers who did not know Johnson, and he offered to do any necessary favors.[86]

Thomas Penn recognized that much frontier trouble stemmed from squatters on unpurchased lands. To one Pennsylvania official he wrote that such people "run themselves into Danger, and are not to be pitied."[87] Thomas hoped that the Proclamation Line of 1763 officially dividing white and Indian areas would be modified to name more easily identifiable natural boundaries so that Indians would have a definite and inviolate hunting preserve. He believed the king's troops had a responsibility not only to defend the frontier forts but also to keep white squatters off unpurchased Indian territory. If such a plan could be adopted, it would preclude the need for westerners to take the law into their own hands, as they had during the Conestoga Massacre and the march on Philadelphia.

Unaware of their proprietor's objectives, frontiersmen again took up their guns in the peculiar incident at Sideling Hill in 1765. An injunction against trade with the Indians had existed since 1763, and officials hesitated to lift it until formal treaties were made through Sir William Johnson. Early in 1765, Philadelphia merchants John Baynton and Samuel Wharton conspired to sneak trade goods to Fort Pitt, hoping to get a jump on competition as soon as the ban was lifted. Somewhere en route a barrel was opened, revealing to local residents that it was full of knives—pruning knives, the carriers claimed, but the frontiersmen feared they were scalping knives and organized to overtake the large train of packhorses. When the carriers showed them they had nothing but trade goods, most of the armed citizens who had stopped the pack train turned back, but a few followed the train to Sideling Hill, where they fired on the drivers, shot some horses, and burned the goods.

The owners of the trade goods had failed to secure a special license from John Penn, but they claimed that the goods were official government property being sent to crown Indian agent George Croghan to be used as gifts for upcoming treaties. John was quite concerned because a great deal of money was involved—it was rumored that the goods destroyed at Sideling Hill had been worth about £20,000.[88] On further investigation, however, the governor was relieved to learn that the goods were privately owned. The covert nature of the shipment was confirmed by the fact that the pack train had been moving over roads that avoided the frontier forts[89]—good news, because the Penn government could not be blamed for having failed to protect government property. Thomas Penn rationalized that the merchants had deserved their loss since they were acting contrary to His Majesty's express proclamation.[90]

John Penn was dismayed that, like the Conestoga murderers, the perpetrators of the Sideling Hill incident were impossible to capture. Robert Allison and some men from Fort Loudon rounded up suspects, but Allison was intimidated into releasing them on the demand of other armed citizens. The party that had attacked the train was sufficiently organized to call its members the "Black Boys." Others called them the Paxton Boys, a name that had come to identify those who had marched on Philadelphia in 1764. The name "Paxton Boys" would later be used by John Penn and other Pennsylvanians to designate various extralegal groups. The intrepid, irresponsible, and mysteriously unidentifiable Paxton Boys would haunt the Penn family for the remainder of their proprietorship.

British officials voiced anxiety about continued frontier lawlessness. In June 1765 General Gage wrote that Indians were well disposed toward peace "unless interrupted by the Riotous and Lawless proceedings of the people upon the Frontiers"[91] and was concerned that Cumberland County citizens "appear daily in arms."[92] Sir William Johnson complained to John Penn that peaceful Indians traveling from North Carolina had been well treated everywhere except in the Pennsylvania communities of Paxton and York County.[93] The governor of Virginia complained in England that men calling themselves "Paxtang Boys" were killing Indians in Virginia and claiming that those who murdered Indians were safe from arrest in Pennsylvania.[94]

Law and order were in the proprietary interest. John Penn and Thomas Penn consistently did what they could to maintain law and order both in the city and on the frontier. If John appeared undynamic, it was because he used only conventional means placed at his disposal in completely orthodox ways. Like his uncle, he saw no particular threat to the proprietorship or to British government in the brief uprising of the Paxton Boys. Like other British figures of authority, both John Penn and Thomas Penn believed the major challenge was to keep peace with the Indians, keep the frontier safe for legitimate settlers, and prevent another Pontiac's Uprising. The frontier would claim so much Penn attention that the family and their supporters would often fail to grasp the significance of other events leading up to the Revolution. The Penns would have agreed with General Gage, who wrote in the summer of 1766: "The people settling themselves upon the Lands belonging to the Indians, it is greatly to be feared . . . will soon involve us again in all the misery of an Indian war."[95]

4

"Contentions and Squabbling"
The Movement for Royal Government

More than a month after the Paxton Boys marched on Philadelphia, John Penn finally wrote his uncle about the disturbance. The governor had a few other things on his mind, and in his letter he complained that he had been "kept prisoner" for three months by the Pennsylvania assembly. "Their Inveterate Malice," he wrote, was "more violent than ever against the Proprietary Family." He spoke of assemblymen plotting their own rebellion—a more formal and legalistic one than the frontiersmen's assault on the city. There had been no physical violence, but tempers were flaring. At the State House, enemies insulted and symbolically challenged Penn authority. John Penn reported: "Some of the members the other day, were for pulling down the [Penn family] Arms over the Speaker's Chair and putting up the King's Arms in their place."[1] The same members would later learn that His Majesty would not have thanked them. In England their attempts to unseat the Penn family would be considered an uprising against the crown.

Leading the assembly in their attempted rebellion was Benjamin Franklin, hero to the common people but bitter enemy to the Penns. His animosity toward the proprietors was a relatively recent development, dating from after John Penn's first visit to the province. Ironically, Franklin had previously received favors from the Penns. Thomas Penn's friend William Allen had helped get him a job as deputy postmaster of North America.[2] In 1754 Franklin praised the proprietors for their "generous and benevolent Designs and Desires of making [the] Province and People flourishing and happy."[3]

During the French and Indian War, two incidents may have begun to turn Franklin against the proprietary family. Franklin distinguished himself during the war by arranging transport for Braddock's expedition to drive the French from the Ohio Valley—he persuaded Pennsylvania's backwoods farmers to lend their horses and wagons to General Braddock. When Braddock was surprised and defeated, the horses and wagons were lost and Franklin faced financial ruin, having pledged his own fortune to guarantee the safety of the farmers' property. Although British General William Shirley eventually paid for the lost property, it is possible that Franklin resented the Penns for not having indemnified him.[4] Not long afterward Thomas Penn's governor, Robert Hunter Morris, blasted the assembly for generally having failed Braddock. Thomas had personally thanked Franklin through another Penn officer, but Franklin might have resented the general reproof after having provided such personal, material assistance.[5]

The French and Indian War had also helped Franklin emerge as a leader in the Pennsylvania assembly. Franklin had held a seat in the assembly since 1751 and had also served as its clerk. In April 1756, bowing to popular will but violating Quaker principles of pacifism, the Quaker assemblymen had asked their governor to declare war on the Delaware tribes and offer bounties on Indian scalps. Some conscience-stricken Quakers began resigning from the assembly, and important London Quakers visited Pennsylvania and urged further resignations to strengthen the Quaker commitment to pacifism.[6] This Quaker exodus from politics created new opportunities for new leaders. In the fall of 1756 Richard Peters wrote Thomas Penn about the upcoming assembly election, saying, "I do not understand what the Quakers will do, I suppose they mean to lye by and not meddle in the ensuing general Election, the Consequences of Which will be that the Assembly will be composed next year of the hot headed of all Denominations, and that as far lyes in Mr. Franklin's power who will have the Rule over them, they will do all the hurt they can to the Proprietaries."[7]

It was probably Thomas Penn's attitude on proprietary instructions that really repelled Franklin. Franklin saw nothing wrong with the assembly's steady assumption of power and proprietary prerogative and resented Thomas's instructions that his governors should veto bills that gave the governor no say in expenditures or taxed the Penn estates. He agreed with the assembly members that the proprietors were dodging taxes and exercising a form of foreign dictatorship that only hindered the progress of government.[8] In 1757 Franklin went to England to talk, persuade, or force Thomas Penn into giving up much of his clout by ceasing to instruct his governors, but Franklin soon learned that Penn had no intention of tolerating further encroachments on what he knew the crown and the Board of Trade considered his legitimate proprietary prerogative. Their few encounters cemented a growing enmity between these two men.[9]

Thomas Penn had gained the first advantage. He had requested that Franklin draft the assembly's complaints against him, so Franklin produced a document called the "Heads of Complaint," an agenda for discussion. But Penn did not use it for that purpose. Instead, his lawyer took the document to England's attorney general and solicitor general, thus enlisting advance opinions from the very men who would rule on the matter should it actually come before the King in Council. Penn refused even to discuss the complaints until he was sure he had the backing of these influential men.[10]

Franklin and Thomas Penn clashed again over the powers of the Pennsylvania assembly. In one of their discussions, Thomas Penn asserted to Franklin that the assembly could not claim as "rights" those powers it had assumed contrary to English law. Even those precious rights guaranteed by William Penn's "Charter of Privileges," written in 1701, were not inviolate should it be determined in England that William Penn had granted powers he had no authority to grant. In a letter, Franklin reported that Penn had uttered this sentiment "with a kind of triumphing, laughing Insolence, such as a low Jockey might do when a Purchaser complained that He had cheated him in a Horse,"[11] and when Thomas learned of this insult he retaliated by making sure that important people on the Board of Trade and the Privy Council shared his own opinion that Franklin was a dangerous schemer. This disarmed Franklin, but it also ended Franklin's attempts to negotiate with Penn.

In 1759 Franklin and his colleagues in the assembly tried to get the king to see the horrors of proprietary instructions and the need to tax proprietary estates. The assembly manipulated Pennsylvania's Governor William Denny into passing a money bill that taxed the Penn estates—Denny was told that Franklin would be able to get the King in Council to uphold the bill, and the governor would therefore not be liable to Thomas Penn for disobeying proprietary instructions.[12] In England, Penn sought the counsel of prestigious lawyers and prepared a petition to disallow the bill, arguing that the assembly wanted to make Pennsylvania a complete democracy for which the Penn family would have to pay the bills. If such a law was upheld, he contended, there would be nothing to stop the assembly from taxing the Penn estates exorbitantly and spending the money however it suited them.[13]

The assembly's search for a royal ally against the Penn proprietors failed. Thomas Penn accurately judged that the idea of pure democracy and the accompanying challenge to legal and proper authority would be frowned on in England, but even he underestimated British sentiment on the issue. The King in Council equated the assembly's tendencies toward popular government to assaults on the crown and the bill was judged an encroachment on royal prerogative as exercised by the Penn proprietors. Far from being thought tyrants, the proprietors were berated for not having adequately protected their authority, and Thomas Penn was instructed to uphold his rights.[14] Although the King in Council declared the assembly's bill unjust, it was not repealed outright because the paper money needed to pay for soldiers and supplies had been issued and was already in circulation in Pennsylvania. Instead, the bill was confirmed conditionally. In 1760 the King in Council decreed that six amendments be adopted to ensure that proprietary rights were upheld and that the Penns were not taxed higher than other Pennsylvania inhabitants.[15]

Thomas Penn planned to see that these royal directives were carried out by his appointees; the Penns would henceforth protect royal prerogative by insisting on their own. When John Penn was sent to America as Pennsylvania's governor, Thomas firmly warned him that the secretary of state for the Northern Department, the Earl of Halifax, would prefer that Pennsylvania contribute *no* money for defense than sacrifice more power to the assembly. "By no means," Halifax had stipulated, should the governor pass a money bill unless it conformed with the 1760 decree of the King in Council.[16] Thomas Penn reiterated his sentiments to Richard Peters, who was expected to assist the new governor in making decisions. Peters was to see that no legislation that might weaken proprietary power was passed, lest the "Constitution will be changed to a perfect Democracy, which must not be." It was "not safe" to deviate from these objectives—doing so would be a breach of duty to the king.[17]

During Pontiac's Uprising, when General Amherst requested that the assembly fund one thousand fighting men Governor John Penn made it clear he would stand by the 1760 decree. In February 1764 the assembly passed a bill it believed complied with the spirit of the decree. The bill stated that the highest tax on surveyed, uncultivated Penn estates would not be higher than the lowest tax on a settler's surveyed, uncultivated land, but the assembly added a clause—"under the same Circumstances of Situation, Kind and Quality"[18]—which implied that valuable Penn lots in the city would be taxed at the same rate as other town lots, not at the much lower rate of frontier farmland. Early in March, John Penn rejected this bill, stating that he was no stranger to disputes between governor and assembly and reiterating his plan to be strictly guided by the 1760 decree.[19] He wanted to see the exact wording of the pertinent amendments reflected in the bill—without the assembly's qualifying clause.

The assembly began a lengthy argument that their bill *did* comply with the decree. Several members went to see the governor and suggested that he should publicly explain how he understood the decree's wording. When John Penn again insisted they simply adopt the exact wording used in 1760, other legislators paid him a visit—surely he did not expect the Penns' best lands to be taxed at the same rate as the meanest, most barren land in the province. At first the governor refused to debate the point and continued to insist that the assembly's bill reflect the wording adopted in 1760. "The English language," he avowed, "does not afford Words more forcible, clear and explicit."[20] The assembly continued to contend that their bill expressed the intent of the King in Council. John Penn was finally goaded into explaining his own understanding of the pertinent part of the 1760 decree. He declared, "If Five, Ten or Fifteen Pounds is the lowest at which *any* such lands of the Inhabitants are assessed, *none* of the located, uncultivated Lands of the Proprietors shall be assessed higher."[21]

John Penn's statement clearly implied that the governor did intend to have the Penn family pay the province's lowest rate for the best of their own land, and it left the governor wide open for a most insolent reply from the house. The assembly maintained that they had not dared to "put so iniquitous a Construction on their Lordships' words—Respect and Decency [forbade] it." Because the province could not vote funds for defense, "but upon terms of great Addition to Proprietary Power," the people would have to depend on local ad hoc efforts.[22] After issuing this message the assembly promptly adjourned.

John Penn was forced to wait several weeks before he could reply. By mid-May, when the house was again in session, he sent the assembly a message in much the same tone. "I am very sorry," he wrote, "that the unwarrantable Freedom with which you have treated not only my Character, but those of the Proprietors themselves . . . will not, now, suffer me to let that Message pass unnoticed." Representatives from the assembly, he observed, including Benjamin Franklin, had been present at the meeting in 1760 and had agreed to the wording of the amendments at that time. If the wording was so ambiguous, why had they not objected then? Why had they waited until a time of crisis? John Penn called for a bill that his instructions would enable him to sign.[23]

The issue was resolved to the advantage of no one. The assembly finally backed down and passed a defense bill that included the exact wording of the pertinent 1760 amendments. John Penn sent back this version also, with the new request that the same amendments be applied to the money bill passed in 1759. The assembly had previously failed to do this by charging that the 1759 legislation had not hurt the Penns in any way. The house objected but eventually capitulated. On May 30, 1764, Governor John Penn signed their defense bill, but Benjamin Franklin, back in Pennsylvania and serving as speaker of the house, got the last word. He drafted another message to the governor, arguing that the assembly had given in to the unworthy demands of an unjust governor rather than ignore the urgent request of the king's general. According to Franklin, the only solution was a public movement that would make Pennsylvania a royal colony and free the province from its enslavement to the Penn family. Franklin concluded: "Such a government we now hope is not far distant, and that an End will thereby be put to these disagreeable and mischievous Proprietary Contentions, and the People of this much injured Province restored to their Privileges, which they have been long deprived of; Proprietary Will and Pleasure expressed in their Instructions, being now our only Law, which through public Necessities, and the Distresses of War, we have been and are compelled to obey."[24]

On the same day that John Penn signed the defense bill, Thomas Penn's lawyer took his own pen in hand to give the chief proprietor his opinion on the governor's late conflict with the assembly. Henry Wilmot believed the governor was technically correct in his interpretation of what the council had intended in 1760, but he now advised Thomas to adopt the assembly's seemingly more equitable interpretation on the taxation of Penn lands. Should the issue come before the King in Council again, Wilmot believed, the assembly's version was more likely to prevail.[25] Proprietors Thomas Penn and Richard Penn quickly sent John Penn word that they consented to their property being taxed at the lowest rate for the same kind of land.[26] To the former governor, James Hamilton, Thomas Penn explained: "We have determined rather to sacrifice our private Interest than keep up the contention any longer."[27] John Penn sincerely regretted that he had not been given the option to compromise sooner—much time might have been saved, and much embarrassment avoided, and the governor could have shown the people "what they had always been industriously taught to disbelieve," that the proprietors were fair and just and had Pennsylvania's best interests at heart.[28]

Because John Penn had refused to give ground, Franklin began actively seeking public support for royal government in Pennsylvania. He and fellow assemblyman Joseph Galloway had already been part of an assembly committee formed to draw up resolves denouncing proprietary instructions. Franklin followed up by writing *Cool Thoughts,* a political polemic in the format of a letter to a friend justifying the movement for royal government. Proprietary instructions, the pamphlet claimed, caused disputes with the people, which were "clogging and embarrassing all the Wheels of Government."[29]

In *Cool Thoughts* Franklin tried to capitalize on Pennsylvania's recent problems. The march of the Paxton Boys had many Philadelphians worried about law and order. Franklin charged that Pennsylvania's proprietary government had been too weak to challenge the mob that had murdered the Indians at Conestoga Manor, or the unruly Paxton Boys who had threatened the safety of Philadelphia. He contended that law and order would best be upheld by an honest royal governor who would have the king's troops at hand.

More than one Penn official had warned Thomas Penn there would be trouble should Franklin return to Pennsylvania. William Allen was among those who believed Franklin's real intention was to get the Penn family out of the way and to become governor of Pennsylvania himself. Allen later commented that Franklin's friends had long since divided up the posts Franklin would be able to hand out as Pennsylvania's royal governor.[30] Thomas Penn remained as calm as he had been in 1757. To James Hamilton, he wrote, "We are not in fear of your mighty Goliath . . . who may lose the Government of a Post Office by grasping at that of a Province."[31]

When the assembly adjourned in March 1764 its members were determined to persuade Pennsylvanians to sign petitions demanding royal government in Pennsylvania. John Penn had cautioned his uncle, "Many people are very busy and very much in earnest about it."[32] At the end of March, Franklin and his former partner in the printing business produced one hundred copies of their petition and circulated them at mass meetings at the State House and at smaller gatherings in taverns where partisans dispensed free liquor. Another two hundred copies were printed in April and circulated by other assemblymen in their counties. Yet when the assembly reconvened some weeks later, their petitions had been signed by only 3,500 Pennsylvanians. Most signers were from Philadelphia, and most were Quakers dutifully following the Quaker leaders in the assembly. In a province whose population was estimated at 250,000, this was a significant defeat for Franklin's movement.[33]

Petitions protesting the movement for royal government, although they came later, fared much better. These counterpetitions claimed that, except for the late Indian problems (which were hardly the fault of the Penn government), Pennsylvania had always enjoyed "most perfect internal tranquility."[34] The petitions were mailed to Thomas Penn, but they addressed the king, asking him to disregard the assembly's call for royal government. Eventually Penn gathered 15,000 signatures. He duly thanked the Penn officers who had exerted themselves and referred to the receipt of such petitions as a "most acceptable Cordial."[35]

Relatively few Pennsylvanians signed Franklin's petition, because they feared a change in government might unnecessarily risk civil and religious liberties granted by William Penn's Charter of Privileges of 1701. This sentiment was articulated well by assemblyman and lawyer John Dickinson. In a speech delivered in the house and reprinted in a newspaper, Dickinson asked that the assembly give up the movement for royal government because their petitions had been signed by "so inconsiderable a number." He claimed the movement was nothing less than a surrender of Pennsylvania's existing constitution and that the house had no right to do this without the consent of all Pennsylvanians. While Dickinson was not uncritical of the Penn government, he contended that royal government was no blueprint for freedom and happiness—the request itself might incur the king's anger. Instead of siding with Franklin on the tax issue, the king might believe "that the Governor, in his late Controversy with this House, has discharged his Duty to the Crown by strictly observing Stipulations approved by his Majesty."[36]

Thomas Penn was favorably impressed. The speech was no accolade for Penn government, but it showed impartial good judgment and that Dickinson had a better feel for the sentiments of British authorities than many of his colleagues in the assembly. Dickinson was not really a member of Thomas Penn's organization, but the chief proprietor was willing to welcome him into the fold. Penn had Dickinson's speech reprinted in England and suggested that his officers be on good terms with Dickinson. To one official, Penn wrote, "I make no doubt but as he shews a good disposition notice is taken of him by the Governor & his Friends."[37] In a letter to Thomas, John Penn explained that, although Dickinson was a good man, Attorney General Benjamin Chew believed Chew had been ill-used by Dickinson and that Dickinson therefore could not be rewarded as openly as Thomas Penn might like.[38]

The Penns were fortunate in having nonpartisan support from men like Dickinson. In the spring of 1764 several key Penn officers were in no position to do political battle with Franklin in Philadelphia. William Allen, their powerful voice in the assembly, and William Smith, provost of the College of Philadelphia, were both in England. James Hamilton was ill and had retired to his country estate, and the ailing Richard Peters was planning a trip to England to regain his own health.[39] Throughout the conflict, both John Penn and Thomas Penn commented on the struggle, but neither the governor nor the chief proprietor took an active part in it. The proprietorship legally belonged to the Penn family, and the Penns depended on the established system to uphold their rights. The proprietorship was not a political party; the Penns were not in the habit of running for office.

As soon as William Allen returned to Pennsylvania, he took his seat in the assembly and began telling its members how British officials viewed what they had heard about the movement for royal government. Assembly members, he said, were very wrong to think they could get any sympathy from British authorities. Lord Halifax considered their rebellion against a legally constituted colonial government nothing less than rebellion against the crown, and even English Quakers opposed it.[40] According to John Penn, however, Allen's warnings had little effect. Assembly members did not believe his reports on British sentiment, and they laughed and told him their own contacts informed them differently.[41]

Penn family sympathizers cooperated to mobilize the province's numerous Germans against the movement for royal government. When William Smith returned, he got church leaders Heinrich Muhlenberg and Carl Wrangel to rally the church Germans against Franklin's movement.[42] A man named William Young and his father also helped motivate Germans to oust Franklin from the assembly in the upcoming election.[43] Proprietary supporters widely publicized the fact that Franklin had once made the mistake of calling Pennsylvania's Germans "boors." Antiproprietary forces made fun of the proprietary supporters in a "Burlesk." In this rhymed narrative, two comic Penn officers discuss how to smear Franklin: "I know an easy way to do it, / Let's blast his Credit with the Dutch; / Shew how in Print he has abus'd them, / Here he has call'd them *Boors,* that's *Hogs,* / If they chuse one that so has used 'em, / They must be worse than stupid Logs." In the burlesque, "Hans" correctly translates the word "boors" as "peasants" without confusing the term with boars or hogs, and the Germans are not offended.[44] In reality, many church Germans sympathized with the proprietary cause, which made Franklin deeply regret having once insulted the Germans.

Pennsylvania's Presbyterians were also organized on the proprietary side. William Smith enlisted the support of Presbyterian ministers Francis Allison and John Ewing, who warned their flocks against Franklin's movement.[45] Although Scots-Irish Presbyterians on the frontier might resent Penn land policies, they were suspicious of the prospect of royal government largely because the Quaker assembly, which had been so recalcitrant in voting money for their defense, was behind it. They suspected the whole movement was a plot to deny them the equal legislative representation they had recently demanded through Smith and Gibson's Remonstrance in the wake of the Paxton Boys march.

The issue came to a head in the elections for assembly members held during the fall of 1764. Voters were asked to choose between an "old ticket" and a "new ticket"—colloquial names for the old assembly faction and the proprietary supporters. John Dickinson was on the "new ticket" with others who wanted to replace Franklin and Galloway and, it was hoped, thereby to end the movement for royal government. Franklin and his friends issued pamphlets comparing the Penns to avaricious slave masters and accusing John Penn of deliberately misconstruing the decree of his just and noble king for his own self-interest.[46] Voters were asked not to endorse proprietors who were protecting vast, rich estates from reasonable taxes and abandoning the province to rioters like the Paxton Boys.[47] In a letter to his uncle, John indignantly related the unseemly politicking of Franklin's son, the governor of New Jersey, who had left his province "to keep open house" in Germantown, soliciting votes for his father through lies.[48] William Allen complained that many Germans in the north had been tricked into believing that if they voted for the "new ticket" and changed the composition of the assembly, they would automatically be voting to change the government, not to retain the proprietary system.[49]

As the heated election grew closer, however, the tide seemed to be turning against Franklin. In September 1764 John Penn wrote his uncle: "The whole Province seem determined to turn out Franklin & Galloway, the Quakers excepted, they never will agree to give up that great *Patriot,* as they call him."[50] John might not have been aware of it, but even some Quakers were turning against Franklin. Many rural Quaker candidates, aware of the unpopularity of the movement for royal government in their areas, were ready to relinquish their support of the movement rather than lose their seats. Franklin must have been aware of his plight. A few days before the election, William Allen gleefully wrote Thomas Penn that Ben was not in his usual good mood: "I am sure he is much chagrined, and seems to have lost his usual spirits."[51]

When the votes were counted, the "old ticket" had lost five out of ten Philadelphia assembly seats. Franklin, Galloway, and several other supporters of royal government had been voted out of office. As William Allen put it, the "great incendiarys" had been turned out. According to Allen, the "new ticket" had found support among the church Germans, about half the members of the Church of England, and the Presbyterians "to a man."[52] It was a stunning victory for the proprietorship.

The witty, canny Franklin had seriously misjudged the people of Pennsylvania. While his own personality and his supporters' mass meetings and propaganda had been able to influence many in Philadelphia, the issue of proprietary instructions was not important to most voters. Proponents of royal government also failed to point out clearly the advantages of the system they advocated. Their campaign literature had simply damned the Penns. To most voters, the prospect of royal government seemed too unknown a quantity and too drastic a solution for current problems.[53]

Despite public opinion as expressed in the election, the assembly members did not let the movement for royal government die. Although Franklin and Galloway lost their seats, both John Penn and Attorney General Benjamin Chew observed that Franklin's "creatures" were still in the majority.[54] At private meetings held at night, Franklin and Galloway were kept informed of all legislative proceedings. Rather than forsaking the movement for royal government, the house instructed its agent in London, Richard Jackson, to present their petition for royal government to the king at an appropriate time. Even more perturbing was the house's vote to send another agent to London to assist Jackson. This assistant, they decided, would be Benjamin Franklin.[55]

Before Franklin departed, the assembly received a "remonstrance" signed by "a Number of the Inhabitants of the City of Philadelphia" protesting his appointment to go to England. Franklin, they accused, was a poor choice to represent the province in England—he hated the proprietors, many important ministers did not like him, and he would work only to further his own ends.[56] Franklin publicly replied that all enmity between himself and the Penn family had arisen because he rightly championed Pennsylvania's causes. Were the proprietors fair and honest, there would be no rancor between them.[57]

John Penn and the *Pennsylvania Gazette* both noted early in November 1764 that Franklin had set out for Chester, where he would embark for England. The newspaper said he was accompanied by "a great Number of the reputable Inhabitants, from both City and County."[58] Penn estimated their number at about five hundred.[59] The governor even more sourly recorded the city's reaction when news arrived that Franklin had safely landed in London. There was more thanksgiving than had been shown at the end of the recent war. People shook hands and wished each other joy. "The bells rang almost all night and the whole town seemed to be in motion upon it, especially the Quaker part of it, they ran about like mad men to acquaint such of their crew of the joyfull Tidings."[60]

In returning to England, Franklin hoped to lobby among ministers who might have previously voiced their own condemnations of proprietary governments. Franklin was on good terms with the Earl of Bute, a powerful politician and a friend of George III. Although Bute had technically resigned from politics, he retained his influence over the current prime minister, George Grenville. Bute had secured for Franklin's son an appointment as governor of New Jersey.

Thomas Penn wrote, "Franklin is certainly destined to be our plague and we must deal with him here as well as we can,"[61] but Penn did not fear for the proprietorship. He had been sending his Pennsylvania officers encouraging messages since the summer, when he had written to Benjamin Chew: "Neither my brother or myself will be intimidated by any thing Franklin and his faction can do."[62] Franklin might have powerful friends who did not like the concept of proprietary government, but Thomas Penn knew they would do Franklin no good. England would not dismantle a legitimate government simply because the people's elected representatives asked their king to do so. Government was something created for the people, not by them. To William Peters at the land office, Thomas Penn wrote: "Those that have the honour of serving the Crown I well know will abhor such a dishonest method of proceeding, however well pleased they would be to get the Government from us in an honourable way."[63] To Receiver General Richard Hockley he added, "I know the people they think they will oblige are astonished at the wickedness of their proceedings."[64] Thomas reiterated what William Allen had told the assembly and assured the governor that Franklin's movement was being viewed as an attack on the crown rather than on the Penn family.[65] He added, to Chew, that it was considered "as little less than rebellion."[66]

William Allen had warned Thomas that Franklin would use his petition to gain certain concessions.[67] English Quaker leader Dr. John Fothergill offered to act as mediator and acquaint both proprietors with the assembly's articles of complaint. In addition to the issue of proprietary instructions, the proprietors were informed that the assembly did not like the way the

Penn family appointed justices, that they wanted a new inquiry into the Conestoga Massacre, and that they believed the governor's income from tavern licenses had created far too many public houses in Pennsylvania. While Thomas Penn might have negotiated on the tavern licenses, he refused to budge on the issue of proprietary instructions. Negotiations broke down by July 1765.[68]

During this period, Thomas Penn expressed his certainty that Franklin had been doing "all the mischief he could privately."[69] Some of that mischief might have included furthering a harebrained scheme Allen had already warned about in December. There had been some talk of luring Springett Penn, a descendant of William Penn by his first wife, to Pennsylvania. Franklin hoped to induce him to sue Thomas Penn in Chancery, thus reopening the ancient argument of whether the proprietorship properly belonged in the senior or junior branch of the Penn family. While it seemed unlikely that Chancery would reverse its own decision, Allen believed the real plot was to cause so much confusion in Pennsylvania that the crown would assume the government just to keep civil order.[70] In February 1765 Thomas learned that Springett Penn was in Ireland and probably not likely to be persuaded to go to Pennsylvania.[71] All such hope ended for Franklin when Springett died a little over a year later.

Since the summer of 1764, Thomas Penn had been working his own mischief through Lord Hyde, Franklin's superior in the post office. He had convinced Hyde to concur that a crown servant, such as Franklin, should not be involved in plotting rebellion against a legal colonial government and to write Franklin advising him to "pursue another conduct."[72] Thomas Penn also asked John Penn not to gloat publicly that Franklin was being reprimanded by his boss. Thomas would have preferred that Hyde's letter induce Franklin to quietly give up his cause.[73] John Penn accurately foresaw that the message would have no effect and advised his uncle to try having Franklin removed from his office altogether so that everyone could clearly see he was in disfavor in England. "As long as this vile fellow continues in power & credit, so long will this Province be torn to pieces by contentions and squabbling," John Penn predicted.[74] The governor was right. The letter from Hyde merely prompted another famous Franklin witticism when Franklin commented to friends that he would not be "Hyde bound."[75]

The real blow to Franklin's cause was inflicted not by Thomas Penn but by the fall of the Grenville ministry early in July 1765. Grenville was replaced as prime minister by Lord Rockingham, and any friends Franklin might have had high up in the old ministry were gone from office. As for the new ministry, Penn modestly observed: "I stand as well with this ministry as I need to."[76] Indeed, the new southern secretary in charge of American affairs was Lord Shelburne, who was married to a niece of Lady Juliana Penn. Thomas confidently reported he need fear no injustice to the Penn family.[77]

Franklin's situation seemed hopeless. He might have given up except for the election results of 1765. The polls were kept open for three days, and Franklin's supporters recouped the losses of the previous year while the proprietary coalition disintegrated. Franklin's friend Galloway became speaker of the house, and Franklin interpreted the overall result as a vote of confidence. Within a month, on November 4, 1765, Franklin presented his petition for royal government to the King in Council over the objections of fellow colonial agent Richard Jackson.

Thomas Penn immediately began sounding out his friends, looking for the earliest indication of what the royal reaction would be. During November, he informed Pennsylvania contacts that all seemed well for the proprietorship. By the end of the month, Penn was able to report the fate of Franklin's petition to his nephew. The King in Council had regarded the petition as unworthy of further consideration. It had been "by his Majesty's order postponed, sine die, that is (to use my Lord President's own expression) for ever & ever."[78] According to Thomas Penn, this kind of postponement was just a less harsh way of rejecting a petition. The *Pennsylvania Journal* repeated his interpretation of the decision and commented, "Thus we hope we have got rid of this unhappy bone of contention."[79] The movement for royal government was officially over.

Despite its failure, the movement may have prompted an important change within the Penn organization. Perhaps to portray an image of fairness and honesty, Thomas Penn reorganized the land office, replacing William Peters (Richard Peters's brother) at William Allen's suggestion with James Tilghman, a lawyer from a Maryland family. Penn acted when he heard that William Peters had been taking advantage of his office and accepting bribes to forward certain land applications at the expense of others.[80] The chief proprietor discreetly allowed Peters to resign. The Board of Property, which consisted of the governor, the provincial secretary, the surveyor general, and the receiver general, was also created at this time. New procedures were instituted to guard against land speculators and to speed up the land acquisition process for legitimate settlers.[81]

With the movement for royal government officially dead, those who looked to the crown for sympathy, justice, and protection might have been greatly disheartened, but Franklin refused to believe that the king had dismissed his petition. He stubbornly deluded himself and his cronies into believing the King in Council had actually postponed it and would consider it another time. The Penns ignored him, believing his real object was to get the assembly to continue paying him a salary so he could live comfortably in England.

Although everyone knew Franklin had gone to England to destroy the proprietorship, technically he had been sent for another purpose. He was supposed to help Richard Jackson protest new legislation imposed by the crown and designed to raise revenue in the colonies. In fact, Franklin's movement for royal government failed so spectacularly in part because England's gracious king was not in the mood to grant any colonial petition while much of America was aroused in noisy protest over the proposed Stamp Act.

5

"To Prevent a Stamp Duty Being Laid on America"

Pennsylvania and the Stamp Act

The Remonstrance signed by "a number of the Inhabitants of the City of Philadelphia" was received by the assembly in October 1764. It protested Benjamin Franklin's imminent departure for England and showed that at least some citizens were concerned about several recent revenue-raising measures Parliament was trying to implement in the colonies. The Remonstrance voiced the novel idea that the new legislation was more important than the movement for royal government and that cooperation would be necessary to protect American liberties. The anonymous Philadelphia "Inhabitants" suggested that proprietary assistance would be needed "in preventing, if possible, any unnecessary burthens being laid upon the Province." And the proprietors were the very people "against whom Mr. Franklin entertains such a rooted Enmity, that they cannot take joint Council for the public Good."[1] While Franklin's followers in the assembly sought crown protection from the perceived oppression of the proprietors, the Remonstrance indicates that its authors saw the proprietors as potential defenders against oppression by the crown.

British legislation affecting life in the American colonies was nothing new. The British mercantile system was regulated through the Navigation Acts, laws stipulating that certain colonial products could be shipped only to England or other British colonies, while European manufactured goods were expected to come to America through England on English ships with English crews. The regulations also discouraged Americans from manufacturing products that would compete with established British industries but encouraged the manufacture of noncompetitive products through bounties. On the whole, Americans had never considered the mercantile system oppressive. It had not yet prohibited growth, and because it was not strictly enforced it had allowed the colonists to do much as they pleased.

In the wake of the French and Indian War, England was faced with a huge national debt in addition to vast new territory on the American continent that required military protection. The Grenville ministry endorsed the idea of extracting funds from America to defray the cost of troops to be stationed there and also sought stricter enforcement of existing trade regulations in the colonies. This changed the nature of the British system. Legislation would be used not only to regulate American trade but also to treat America as a source of revenue for the British Empire.

Thomas Penn was aware of the change in policy and made some moves to look after Pennsylvania's interests as he saw them. In 1763 he warned Governor James Hamilton that companies of regulars would be maintained in America through revenue to be raised by the Sugar Act, which taxed sugar, molasses, wines, and other articles. Early in 1764 Thomas and Richard Penn appeared before the Board of Trade with William Allen and Richard Jackson to give their opinions on another proposal, which became the Currency Act and would prevent the colonies from issuing paper money as legal tender. Thomas Penn testified that the colonies needed a certain amount of paper money and suggested that the legislation be deferred to let the colonies consider its impact.[2]

Although Pennsylvania merchants were already complaining about poor trade and scarce hard cash, the Sugar Act and reports of other possible revenue measures failed to arouse much early protest in Pennsylvania. In September 1764 Massachusetts wrote the Pennsylvania assembly to warn of a threat to American rights and suggest that the other colonies join Massachusetts in remonstrating against this new posture. The Pennsylvania assembly merely instructed Richard Jackson to work with other colonial agents in trying to get the recent legislation repealed.[3]

During the fall of 1763 and the winter months of 1764, Thomas Penn's letters to his nephew commented on Grenville's latest proposed revenue measure, soon to become the Stamp Act. This legislation would require many legal and public documents to be printed on stamped paper that could be obtained only through distributors or agents when certain taxes had been paid. In principle, Thomas liked the idea of a general, centrally administered tax to fund defense, because it would make it unnecessary for the Pennsylvania assembly to raise money and would thus prevent contentions between the governor and the house. He wrote, "This will entirely put an end to disputes about raising Money for the public Services, as an Excise will answer all the purposes of civil Government."[4] Although to Thomas Penn the Stamp Act seemed "the most easy of a general tax,"[5] he foresaw opposition in America and correctly predicted: "I believe it will be opposed, as an internal Taxation rather to be done by Act of Assembly."[6] He stopped analyzing the matter when the issue was postponed for a year while Britain tried to collect the needed money through the Sugar Act.

As the time drew near for the Stamp Act to go into effect, Thomas Penn began actively lobbying against it, but his correspondence does not mention exactly why. Although he might have harbored some Whiggish or liberal principles himself, he probably viewed the Stamp Act as something certain to cause more trouble in America than it was worth. Early in 1765 he reported that he and "every one concerned for America has been employed in conceiving measures for the alteration of the [Sugar Act] . . . or in using their endeavors to put off the Bill for laying a Stamp Duty."[7] He did not name specific allies even when he abruptly announced defeat to John Penn: "We have been much employed in endeavoring to prevent a Stamp Duty being laid on America, but have miscarried, as it was valid on Wednesday."[8] The chief proprietor then turned his attention to getting the Stamp Act modified to the advantage of the northern colonies. To William Allen he expressed the hope that he could get the tax lowered or altered to cover fewer documents.[9]

Few Americans would ever hear of Thomas Penn's opposition to the Stamp Act, but readers of the *Pennsylvania Gazette* might have noticed some brief reports on assemblyman William Allen's attempts to halt the Stamp Act's progress in 1764. At the time, Allen was in England, where he was seeing much of Thomas Penn. "Mr. Allen, of this Place," the *Gazette* noted, "was indefatigable, in remonstrating to many of the Members with whom he was acquainted on the Illegality of an internal tax, and had Influence in preventing it."[10] A June 1764 issue of the *Gazette* reported that without Allen's opposition the Stamp Act would have passed in that session.[11]

The same Mr. Allen expressed his indignation to Thomas Penn when he learned his efforts had been in vain. "We are thereby virtually disfranchised," he wrote. If Parliament could tax the colonies, "we never had the rights of freemen."[12] Allen speculated Parliament had reasoned that the more money they could extract from America, the less their voting constituents would have to pay. Thomas, whose estates had long been eyed by a revenue-hungry assembly, must have found this sentiment ironically familiar.

Pennsylvanians who shared Allen's view were mobilized by William Bradford, the man who printed the *Pennsylvania Journal* and ran the London Coffee House at the southwest corner of Front and Market streets, a gathering place for city businessmen. In the days before office buildings dominated the cityscape, taverns and coffeehouses were the scenes of many important business meetings and trade transactions. The London Coffee House became the spot where Philadelphia merchants and government officers shared their views on the Stamp Act, making the thought of resistance increasingly acceptable and widespread.[13]

John Dickinson, who had warned of the dangers of royal government in 1764, urged resistance to the Stamp Act. He protested that revenue raised through the Stamp Act would go to defend territory from which Americans derived no benefit[14] and that Americans would also have problems coming up with silver to pay the tax. Dickinson urged resistance, suggesting all Pennsylvanians follow the example of the province's German settlers, who lived off their farms and required few imported items. England's dependence on the American market would soon make the Stamp Act a thing of the past.[15]

Pennsylvania's Germans, Presbyterians, and many of its Anglicans agreed with Bradford and Dickinson. Many Quakers failed to protest, or protested in a lukewarm way. Writing under the name "Americanus," assembly leader Joseph Galloway defended Parliament's right to raise money in the colonies and suggested that Americans accept the Stamp Act on principle and merely protest that they had little hard money to pay the tax.[16] Unknowingly, he shared the sentiments of Thomas Penn, who did not understand how Americans could insist they could not be taxed by their king and Parliament.[17]

Benjamin Franklin never anticipated the amount of rancor the Stamp Act would incur in America. Wrapped up in his movement for royal government, he decided to make the best of it and hoped the Americans would do the same. It has been suggested that Franklin was willing to accept the Stamp Act as a necessary price for royal government. Perhaps he thought that once Pennsylvania was rid of Thomas Penn and the proprietorship he could help remodel Great Britain's imperial structure to the advantage of both America and the mother country.[18]

Franklin managed to get his friend John Hughes appointed to the potentially lucrative post of stamp distributor for Pennsylvania. Grenville had been seeking advice about these appointments, and no doubt Thomas Penn could have named Pennsylvania's stamp distributor had he wanted to. Yet the chief proprietor confided to the governor, "I did not choose to ask for any Person lest it should be thought I was a favourer of the Bill."[19] When Thomas heard Hughes had received the commission, he warned Grenville that Hughes was a close friend of Franklin and his supporter in the movement for royal government. Grenville agreed to make it clear to Hughes that his appointment was no reward for plotting rebellion.[20] Thomas Penn later denied a Pennsylvania rumor that there had been a contest between himself and Franklin over who would become stamp distributor. To receiver general Richard Hockley he explained that the position had not been considered important in England: "Any one that had been named first would have been appointed."[21]

News that the Grenville ministry had fallen reached Pennsylvania in mid-September 1765. For those against the Stamp Act, reports that Stamp Act promoters were no longer in power was good news indeed. On September 16 the *Journal* noted that joyous Philadelphians rang church bells, drank toasts, and lit bonfires.[22] A crowd gathered at Bradford's London Coffee House, where those who were still resentful about the Stamp Act made angry threats to destroy the houses of Pennsylvania's stamp distributor and of the man who had appointed him. Franklin's friend Joseph Galloway knew Franklin was still trying to sell his movement for royal government in Britain. Galloway feared that riots over the Stamp Act might make the king think twice about becoming directly responsible for Pennsylvania. To quell the threat of violence, Galloway organized seven hundred to eight hundred supporters, who posted themselves at the threatened properties, intimidating potential troublemakers. Leading Galloway's volunteers were the city's "White Oaks," probably an organization of ship's carpenters. Other mechanics joined their ranks, and Franklin's wife described her protectors as "honest good tradesmen." Throughout the Stamp Act crisis, these men would act as constables, discouraging violence and upholding civil order. They might have been inspired by their admiration for Franklin (who had started his career as a tradesman himself), but they were consistently loyal to Hughes and Galloway, who came as close to being Stamp Act advocates as anyone in America.[23]

Just a few days after the October election in 1765, Philadelphians learned that their local supply of stamped paper was on its way. Bradford's *Pennsylvania Journal* reported the "melancholy news" that ships bearing the stamped paper had reached New Castle. "Rage, resentment and grief appeared in every countenance," the paper read, "and the mournful language of one and all our inhabitants seems to be farewell, farewell liberty!"[24] When ships carrying the stamped paper rounded Gloucester Point on October 5 and came into view of the city, vessels docked at Philadelphia wharves lowered their flags to half mast. Muffled church bells rang, and several citizens roamed the streets mournfully beating muffled drums.[25]

By the afternoon of October 5, thousands had gathered at the State House to prevent the stamped paper from arriving by forcing stamp distributor Hughes to resign. Hughes had recently sidestepped the issue in a message to Dickinson stating he could not resign his post before he received his formal commission, but because his commission was arriving together with the stamped paper, the assembled public sent another delegation to Mr. Hughes. Hughes still refused to resign, but he compromised by swearing he would not execute his commission until the stamp distributors in the other colonies did so. Hughes confirmed this in writing on October 7. Once more there were threats to destroy Hughes's house, but the stubborn stamp distributor was again saved from the angry mob by Galloway's White Oaks and other city mechanics, plus the fact that he was very ill at the time.[26]

Many prominent Philadelphians took part in the effort to force Hughes's resignation. Dickinson was one of the protest leaders. Charles Thomson and Robert Morris, who would be increasingly important during the later revolutionary movement, were also involved. Both John Hughes and Deborah Franklin accused William Allen's son James of rousing the mob.[27] Thomas Penn was sorry to hear that James Tilghman, then under consideration to head the Penn land office, had been instrumental in pressuring Hughes.[28] Between October 5 and October 7, Hughes had sought the help of the governor, but he received no satisfactory reply. His own account bitterly complained that neither the governor, the chief justice, the attorney general, the mayor, or even a single magistrate had been on hand to help him.[29]

Pennsylvania's reaction to the Stamp Act Congress might have convinced the other American colonies that Pennsylvania's spirit of liberty had taken a similar holiday. A letter from Massachusetts prompted the Pennsylvania assembly to identify delegates for the Stamp Act Congress meeting in New York, October 7–24, 1765. The assembly, however, instructed its delegates to address England loyally and dutifully, taking care to offer no offense to

Parliament or the king. That winter, the assembly read and approved the resolves adopted by the congress, which affirmed that the colonies were essentially beyond the reach of Parliament and subject only to taxes levied by their own elected representatives. Other than this, the Pennsylvania assembly ignored the Stamp Act crisis.[30]

John Penn warned his uncle that Pennsylvanians "seem determined rather to die, than to suffer the law to take place,"[31] but when the Stamp Act technically took effect on November 1, little actually changed in Pennsylvania. The province's courts and ports closed temporarily, but by December Pennsylvanians were conducting business as usual by disregarding the law and printing official documents on unstamped paper. On October 31 both the *Pennsylvania Journal* and the *Pennsylvania Gazette* published editions banded in black with news that they would cease publication rather than comply with the law—but, they too were soon doing business as usual. Instead of going into circulation, most of Pennsylvania's stamped paper remained on board the British ship *Sardine,* where John Penn had ordered it stored for protection against angry mobs.

Widespread protest against the Stamp Act quickly evaporated in Pennsylvania. Charles Thomson organized another attempt at a mass meeting in mid-November and again tried to rouse the public into forcing Hughes to resign formally. This time, however, only two hundred people attended his meeting, during which White Oaks in the audience showed their disapproval by hissing. Galloway took credit for the city's apparent lack of interest, boasting that his loyal supporters in the White Oaks and another group of mechanics called the Hearts of Oak would keep peace in the city through the rest of the crisis. He claimed that his friends outnumbered those who were against the Stamp Act, stating that he could muster "ten men to their one." Pennsylvania became the only province in which a stamp distributor was *not* forced to resign.[32]

Protest was confined to smaller groups. When the *Charming Nancy* arrived from Halifax, it was rumored that stamped paper was aboard. This turned out to be no more than half a sheet, "with eighteen pence worth of oppression" (as the *Journal* put it),[33] and the ship's captain swore he was concealing no more. The *Gazette* reported that this half sheet "was purified with fire at the Coffee-House, in the Presence of a full Company, who all expressed their Satisfaction therewith."[34] Groups of merchants and traders also met and resolved that they would import no manufactured goods until May 1, 1766, or until the Stamp Act was repealed. Committees would enforce their agreement. Prominent Pennsylvanians approved this peaceful use of economic pressure—with the notable exception of Galloway and Hughes.

In May the brig *Minerva* docked opposite the city. A Philadelphian went on board and was the first to learn that the Stamp Act had actually been repealed. News raced through the city, and soon the *Minerva*'s captain was summoned to the Coffee House, where a punch bowl had been prepared. The captain drank to the prosperity of America and thanked the cheering gentlemen for compliments on his new gold-laced hat, which he said he had purchased on first hearing news of the Stamp Act's repeal. The city was illuminated that night, and the *Gazette* reported that the governor had hosted a dinner at the State House for three hundred. A royal salute was fired when the governor's guests drank to the king's health.[35]

A few days later the governor received official documents from His Majesty's officer Henry Conway, which he forwarded to the assembly with his congratulations. A letter from Conway to Penn cautioned that the controversial legislation had been repealed, thanks to the leniency of Parliament, and that any display of ingratitude would seriously damage Anglo-American relations.[36] Thomas Penn reinforced this message. Repeal, he told the governor, was due to the "tenderness" of Parliament "towards a People that have shewn their love of freedom in a very improper manner."[37] The chief proprietor informed William Allen that he had promised important people in England there would be no public rejoicing over this victory, writing that he had "pawned [his] own honour" to that effect. According to Thomas, many lords and gentlemen were friends of liberty but enemies of "riotous methods of shewing it."[38] Respectful gratitude, the chief proprietor suggested, was the appropriate attitude for this occasion.

Philadelphia celebrated, but the city's theme was warmth and loyalty. Both the assembly and the governor's council penned messages of thanks. The assembly's version thanked the king for his "Condescension and Goodness" and commended Parliament for its "Justice and Tenderness . . . manifested in their good Dispositions and Lenity to us, in our late distressed Situation."[39] On the king's birthday the assembly dined with the governor "by particular invitation" at the State House. Galloway staged another celebration with parades and bands.[40] The White Oaks built a boat they named the *Ben Franklin* and dragged it through the city streets. Loyal toasts were drunk, including toasts to Franklin.[41]

In Thomas Penn's not unbiased opinion, Franklin's efforts to fulfill his mission and lobby against the Stamp Act had had little effect. Early in 1765 Penn noted that Franklin had met with Grenville and other colonial agents, and he expressed annoyance that Franklin had been set in "a conspicuous point of light" when the other agents chose him as speaker.[42] In any case, the meeting had no effect. People like Franklin who were most active in America's assemblies were generally out of favor in England at the time. The British were alarmed at the powers such people claimed to possess and argued that a province's elected assembly was "little more than the Common Council of a Borough." No one had listened to anything Franklin then had to say.[43]

Once the movement for royal government had been indefinitely postponed and Franklin realized how seriously he had misjudged America's reaction to the Stamp Act, he and his friends moved quickly to save his reputation in America. Although Franklin had published nothing himself, his supporters in Pennsylvania obtained some letters from London that stated he had been working diligently in Pennsylvania's behalf all along. Extracts from the letters were printed in Pennsylvania's newspapers in the late winter and spring of 1766, after repeal was already certain. One letter said Franklin had served the assembly ably, meeting with important ministers and attempting to stop passage of the Stamp Act.[44] Another letter speculated, "Had his salutary Advice been followed, all this uproar . . . would have been avoided."[45]

Franklin's political career was actually saved by his so-called "examination" at the bar before the House of Commons on February 18, 1766. The Rockingham ministry, which had succeeded the Grenville ministry, also wanted to repeal the disastrous Stamp Act but could not afford to appear to give in to rebellion in the colonies. Franklin provided cool, logical reasons for repeal that could save face for British authority, clearly showing that the Stamp Act ran contrary to custom and would be impossible to administer. It was particularly ill-suited to America's frontier areas, whose residents would have to send for stamped paper through the post at a cost to themselves of £3 to £4 for every sixpence the British government would collect. Franklin also mentioned that, prior to 1763, America's attitude toward the mother country had been the "best in the world." Good relations had been threatened by the specter of internal taxation.[46]

Franklin's examination bolstered his sagging reputation in America. A copy of the examination was sent to Philadelphia, where it was published, widely read, and praised. John Penn observed that Pennsylvanians were eagerly handing copies around and mentioned to Thomas Penn his suspicions that the whole thing had been fabricated.[47] Thomas had not heard the examination himself or seen anyone who had been present, but he confirmed that it had indeed taken place. He apparently did not consider it very important. "I was told he [Franklin] was very bold in his answers," he wrote

John, and he offered to inquire further if he ran across anyone who had heard Franklin speak.[48]

While some praised Franklin, others attempted to discredit Franklin and his friends. A rumor circulated in both England and America that Franklin had originally proposed the Stamp Act. In the Pennsylvania assembly, William Allen publicly called Franklin "the greatest Enemy to the Repeal of the Stamp Act, of all the Men in England."[49] Franklin's enemies in America acquired and published some letters Franklin's friend Hughes had written to superiors in London describing his attempts to function as a loyal stamp distributor despite popular pressure to resign. Franklin's other friend, Galloway, was revealed as the author of the unpopular "Americanus" advice. His work was reprinted in the *Pennsylvania Journal* in September 1766, together with a letter to Franklin praising Hughes's refusal to resign.

Many historians have blamed proprietary officers for this smear campaign. If any Penn officers or friends of the Penn family were involved, it was not at the direction of Thomas Penn or John Penn. Thomas wrote the governor that he was sorry to see Hughes's letters reprinted in the papers.[50] Throughout the Stamp Act crisis, Thomas had been fearful that Franklin or his friends would find a way to blame the proprietors for any violent protests in Pennsylvania. The Hughes letters strongly accused the Penn administration of having condoned what little protest had taken place and having failed to help the stamp distributor execute his commission.

Many historians say that, once the Stamp Act crisis was over, John Penn got undeserved credit for the relative peace in Pennsylvania. Citing the Hughes letters, they contend John and the proprietary officers looked the other way when violence threatened, hoping an unruly province would make a poor candidate for royal government. Galloway and his White Oaks are generally credited with having kept the peace, but the proprietary faction was hardly in a position to benefit by Stamp Act riots. By the fall of 1765, Penn officers had already heard Thomas Penn's opinion that the movement for royal government had no chance. From December 1765 through March 1766, Thomas had been telling his contacts in America that repeal of the Stamp Act was expected shortly. In the meantime, John Penn had received specific instructions from Henry Conway to prevent violence. His Majesty, Conway wrote, did not want his subjects endangered yet would not permit his authority to be trampled.[51] In November 1765 Thomas Penn anxiously wanted to hear from his nephew about any violence that had so far arisen.[52]

The Penns and Franklin's supporters were separately working toward the same end. While they saw no particular threat to the proprietorship in either the Stamp Act or provincial opposition to it, the Penns did want to protect themselves from official censure in the wake of Franklin's movement for royal government. John Penn's correspondence indicates that he kept a close watch on Stamp Act protest and did all he could to preserve peace in Pennsylvania. In December, John Penn wrote his uncle that there had been little violence so far, "though many of the good people called Quakers were desirous of it and endeavored to promote it," hoping royal government would be seen as a solution. The governor's own house had been threatened with fire in an anonymous letter written, Penn speculated, "by the advice of Governor [William] Franklin who has been used to that work and has made it his business this year past to do every thing that lay in his power to create disturbances in this Government."[53] John Penn's countermeasures are suggested in one letter to a William Smith and a John Reynolds enjoining magistrates to preserve the peace and calm turbulent spirits.[54] In February 1766 John Penn wrote Conway that the "giddy Magnitude" had so far been restrained from doing violence.[55] To Thomas Penn he elaborated that there had been only two mass meetings, to which the council had sent some "prudent persons" to be present among the mob to keep order. The governor could do no more. Had he attempted to disband or forbid the mass meetings, he "should have been obliged to flee for [his] life."[56]

Once the crisis was over, John Penn promoted Pennsylvania's relatively good behavior by making sure the king's ministers heard about it. The assembly thanked him for having done "that Justice to the good People of this Province, which their credit merited, by representing to his Majesty's Ministers the Moderation & Decency with which they have behaved."[57] The assembly also attempted to placate the English ministry by complying with the Quartering Act of 1765, which required colonists to supply British troops with housing and necessary items.[58] Few remarks were made in Pennsylvania about the Declaratory Act, which affirmed that Parliament had the power to make laws binding all Englishmen. Pennsylvanians, like most Americans, saw this as a kind of retreat by Parliament.

Since John Penn's arrival in America in 1763, there had been many changes on the political scene in Pennsylvania. By election time, 1766, Penn reported that the Quakers seemed tired of politics[59] and ready for rapprochement with the proprietors, who shared their desire for an end to contention between England and America. The church Germans, who had briefly rebelled against Quaker leadership, again supported their assemblymen, but the Scots-Irish had established themselves as a political force. They dissolved their temporary alliance with Thomas Penn's officers as people began calling them the "Presbyterian Party," defining them as an opposing party to the still largely Quaker assembly. Thomas Penn did not like these labels, and he advised John not to use the terms "Quaker party" or "Presbyterian party."[60] This group would soon become known as the Whig party, with John Dickinson and Charles Thomson at the helm.

The Stamp Act crisis had exposed many Pennsylvanians to Whig (or opposition) thinking, and some began to question the validity of the mercantile system and Parliament's power to legislate for America. Perhaps even Thomas Penn's early opposition to the Stamp Act had not been entirely motivated by self-interest. Yet the Penns did not sanction the small amount of public protest that had taken place in Pennsylvania. While Thomas had worked conservatively through established channels to get the Stamp Act repealed, John had dutifully followed orders issued by the chief proprietor and the British government and acted to preserve the peace in Pennsylvania. No one was yet ready for the next logical step.

In January 1766, at the height of the Stamp Act crisis, Thomas Penn had written Benjamin Chew that in England "the common cry is that the Colonies want to throw off all dependence on the Mother Country."[61] The governor's councillors must have discussed this point, for John Penn soon replied that independence was "not at all the Intention here at present, nor do I believe such a thought has entered any man's head." Repeal of the Stamp Act, John predicted, would win back America's affection for England—and Pennsylvanians did indeed emerge from the Stamp Act crisis with their patriotism intact.[62] When Thomas Penn wrote John about the Declaratory Act, he expressed little concern about how Pennsylvanians would react. Although Parliament thus declared it had the power to legislate for America, Thomas confidently predicted "it will be many, many years before it is attempted again."[63]

6

"Greatest Confusion"
The Personal Trials of John Penn

Thomas Penn had no illusions about John Penn's background and experience when he appointed him governor, and the chief proprietor was probably dismayed that his nephew was so quickly tested by a series of crises unequaled in Pennsylvania's recent history. Within a year of John Penn's arrival in Pennsylvania late in 1763, Thomas confided to another official that he had unintentionally appointed his nephew to serve during what he considered the period of "greatest confusion ever known in Pennsylvania."[1] John Penn would have agreed. In the same letter in which he first told his uncle about the Paxton Boys and the movement for royal government, he mentioned that he had been quite busy. "My house is more like a Coffee house than a Private one," he wrote.[2]

Thomas Penn was counting on the governor's councillors to provide a consensus of wise advice, but unfortunately even John Penn's younger brother Richard could see the council was "poorly Man'd & scarcely equal to the weighty matters that often come before them."[3] John observed that members Lawrence Growden and William Till were not capable and that Thomas

Cadwalader, Benjamin Shoemaker, and William Logan did not attend meetings. Richard Peters suffered from poor health, Lynford Lardner was wrapped up in his family and business, the trusted former governor James Hamilton wanted to be bothered only for emergencies, and loyal Benjamin Chew was often out riding the circuit in his capacity as attorney general. Many meetings were attended by only two councillors, and twice the governor called meetings that no councillors attended.[4]

When the council did get together, members often quarreled among themselves. Cadwalader was at odds with Chew.[5] The governor himself miffed William Allen by appointing a supreme court justice Allen did not like. John Penn was promptly called on the carpet by the chief proprietor but told his uncle he had not intended to offend Allen. He had consulted with Allen's friends Benjamin Chew and Edward Shippen and was acting on the best advice he could get.[6] Thomas Penn urged his men to settle their differences and cooperate.

Thomas Penn could have reorganized the council, but he was extremely cautious and reluctant to replace people once they had been appointed. To provide the governor with an assistant he could count on, Richard Penn Jr. was sworn in and seated as a council member early in 1764. Thomas wanted Richard trained as a potential successor to the governor and advised him to become "acquainted with every branch of our Affairs" should he ever need to take control himself.[7] While this added a person to the council, it did not infuse new life into the group. Both the governor and his secretary reported that most meetings were attended only by John and Richard Penn, their uncle Lynford Lardner, and Benjamin Chew. During that time of "greatest confusion" John Penn admitted he often relied on his own judgment.[8] It was not until 1766, when the crisis appeared to be over, that Thomas Penn finally agreed that the governor could appoint James Tilghman to fill the first council "vacancy."[9]

Although Thomas Penn wanted the council and all his appointees to protect proprietary interests in Pennsylvania, he often left little to their judgment. The council might have complained as loudly as the assembly when it came to absentee direction from Thomas, who might veto appointments that seemed perfectly logical to his officers. Chew was ready to resign as attorney general to make room for Chief Justice William Allen's son Andrew, who had read law under his direction. Thomas Penn stepped in to prevent the abdication, pointing out that the appointment would smack too much of personal friendship, because Andrew Allen had had little opportunity to practice law, and that it might further antagonize the Quakers, with whom Thomas wanted his officers to function more harmoniously.[10]

Thomas Penn also fretted over the actions of his two nephews. He chided councillor Richard Penn for not writing often enough to describe important public events. Wanting Richard to have "some particular business under [his] direction," he suggested that his younger nephew manage some land the proprietors wanted to sell in Jersey.[11] Two years later he commented to Richard Peters: "I admire at Dick's not taking a great deal of trouble who has nothing to do."[12] Fearing that John Penn was reverting to the spendthrift habits of his youth, Thomas warned the governor to keep "a constant attention to your Expences in order to form a Scheme of living so as to make the best appearance at the least Expence."[13] It is not known whether Thomas was aware that in February 1765 the *Pennsylvania Gazette* had commented favorably on the governor's liberality. Penn had donated some forty cords of wood to the poor, also having paid to haul the fuel to the city.[14]

From 1764 through 1766, while John Penn juggled local crises and followed his uncle's orders, the governor also survived a period of personal trial. William Allen had returned from England with his two daughters the previous summer. Early in September, John had reported that the family was at Mount Airy, their country house, still receiving "welcome back" calls. John did not note how many times he himself visited the Allens, but by the following year he confided that he wanted to marry William Allen's daughter Anne.

Haste and passion may have played a part in John Penn's first marriage, but he downplayed his emotions when he made this revelation to his uncle. He mentioned he had been thinking for some time of matrimony, a state that was "rational & wise . . . fitted for the proper enjoyment of this world." Unlike his first experience, he now felt his affections were properly placed on the eldest Miss Allen, who was "mistress of many valuable accomplishments, with the best of Tempers, and an understanding equal if not superior to most of her Sex." But John was not going to marry in haste again. The lady had no inkling of his intentions, nor would she until the governor was assured of William Allen's consent, his own father's "concurrence," and Thomas Penn's "approval." His cool facade cracked only a little when he concluded, "I own the prospect is a pleasing one to me & I am too much interested to think of it with Indifference."[15]

Anne and Margaret Allen had impressed the chief proprietor and Lady Juliana Penn most favorably when they visited England with their father William Allen. Thomas Penn had written their uncle James Hamilton that he had never met any young ladies "that prejudiced [him] more in their favor."[16]

To Richard Peters he added: "Their good sense and good nature will gain them many friends."[17] Their brother John Allen heard that the Misses Allen were being noticed for "their pleasing modest address and engaging behavior. They have the esteem of every body they are acquainted with, and very much deserve it."[18] Anne Allen became Thomas Penn's favorite. He wrote James Hamilton: "Your eldest niece has given great marks of her prudence and good Sense . . . and must make some Man of good understanding and good disposition very happy."[19]

Nevertheless, Thomas Penn hesitated to make his nephew that happy man. John had asked for his uncle's advice, and Thomas quickly provided it, treating the prospect of Anne Allen as the governor's wife like any other Penn appointment. While he had a high regard for the lady, he feared that a Penn-Allen connection might beget "very injurious Consequences to our affairs." Supporters of the movement for royal government complained that the proprietors exercised too much control over the province's justices. What would people think if the governor married the chief justice's daughter? Other people complained that William Allen already directed too many Penn affairs behind the scenes. A Penn-Allen marriage would make it appear that his power had increased. Members of William Allen's large family would hound the governor for appointments, and his wife would no doubt use her influence to get posts for her many relatives. The connection was *not* proper—the two proprietors had deliberated on the matter and agreed.[20]

It was perhaps a lucky accident that before John Penn received his uncle's letter he again wrote Thomas Penn. His second letter betrayed a good deal more emotion. John was in love and in considerable torment, which prevented him from giving his full attention to Penn business. He apologized for having failed to answer other letters due to "the uneasiness and anxiety of mind I am under with regard to an affair that particularly regards myself" and stated flatly: "The whole happiness of my life depends upon my success in this affair. I never had any thing so much at heart in my life." But because he did not have approval from his own family, Anne was still ignorant of his feelings, and he knew nothing about hers. To make matters worse, a wealthy rival had just arrived in town from Carolina.[21]

Thomas Penn had always had a warm spot in his heart for his nephew, and the second letter may have caused him to reconsider and withdraw his objections. Thomas must have written another letter—which does not survive—for in October 1765 John Penn wrote on consecutive days, thanking his uncle for setting his mind at ease. The problem remaining was "how to accomplish what I have been happy enough to [be] given my father's and your approbation of."[22]

John Penn's love life illustrates how ideas of marriage were changing among the British in the eighteenth century. When John married for the first time, around the middle of the century, propertied classes in England still considered the choice of a spouse an economic decision that should be handled by one's family. The Penns considered John's first marriage inappropriate and had been instrumental in dissolving it. By the end of the eighteenth century, however, public opinion had changed, and marriage for romantic love had become somewhat more acceptable. John's second letter to his uncle revealed his real feelings and prompted his father and uncle to reverse their decision and let him pursue the woman he loved.

In October 1765 John Penn hinted that he was likely to meet with "many difficulties" in winning Anne Allen's hand.[23] In March 1766 he told Thomas about some of the difficulties he had been encountering. John admitted he was "naturally bashful" but protested, "I have not been so upon this occasion." He had secured William Allen's consent and had spoken to Anne about his regard and esteem to be sure she understood he was in earnest. The problem? Anne was "ten times" more reserved. He had asked to speak to her privately, but she had refused, hinting she would not encourage his attentions. John persevered and reported that friends were working to forward his suit. Despite the lady's initial reaction, John's March letter stated, "I am now in a fair way of succeeding."[24]

The practical and businesslike Thomas Penn inquired of John, "Has Mr. Allen had conversation with you about a settlement?" and advised him to delay the marriage until he knew just how much the wealthy William Allen would bestow on his eldest daughter.[25] John waited little longer than it took to get Anne to accept his proposal. Perhaps one of the governor's friends was able to influence Anne. Late in 1766, after the couple were married, John Penn's father included a strangely used metaphor in a letter to Richard Peters. He commented that he was "glad to find you have been the Instrument by your Gordian knot of Conveying my Son into a state that makes him truly happy."[26]

On June 5 the *Pennsylvania Gazette* reported that the governor had recently wed Miss Allen, "a young lady adorned with every Accomplishment requisite to render the married state happy."[27] The new spirit of harmony between the executive and legislative branches of government prompted the assembly to send the governor a cordial message: "Give us leave to congratulate your Honour upon your Marriage, and to offer our sincerest wishes for your future happiness."[28] Thomas Penn added his own congratulations, informing his nephew that he had dined with Richard and Hannah Penn, who also wished the couple happiness.[29] To another Penn officer Thomas added his hope that the governor could now "apply himself to Business and to an oeconomical management of his own affairs."[30]

Although Thomas Penn had called it a period of "greatest confusion," Pennsylvania's problems between 1763 and 1766 had not seriously challenged the Penn proprietorship. With the Penn councillors and appointees divided, proprietary interests relatively isolated, and an inexperienced governor considerably distracted by his pursuit of a wife, the proprietorship had managed to survive Pontiac's Uprising, Franklin's movement for royal government, and protest against the Stamp Act. At the end of this period, the Penn administration stood well with the British government, and there was every indication that future Anglo-Pennsylvania relations would be good. Pennsylvania's sedate behavior during the Stamp Act crisis had won compliments in England. The address to the king written by the governor's council on the repeal of the Stamp Act had been well received. In July 1766 William Pitt replaced Lord Rockingham as prime minister while Thomas Penn's friend and relative Lord Shelburne continued as southern secretary in charge of American affairs. Thomas looked forward confidently to exerting more political influence in the future. No new crises arose as the year progressed, and in December a Pennsylvania newspaper quoted a London letter reporting a "dead calm" in politics.[31]

Late in 1766 Thomas Penn also complimented Richard Hockley on the amount of cash he was collecting[32] and recommissioned John Penn as governor of Pennsylvania.[33] In December the governor, his council, the mayor, the city recorder, and many others arrived at the city courthouse, where John Penn's new commission was read.[34] William Allen told the chief proprietor that his new son-in-law was spoken of with "great esteem." People approved of the governor's appointments and considered him an honest man.[35] John Penn perhaps learned that fame and success had a price when, less than two weeks later, his house was burglarized. Even in this unfortunate incident, luck was with the governor. On hearing strange noises, the servants were alarmed and seized the two thieves who had tried to make off with His Honour's silver candlesticks.[36] John Penn seemed to be leading a charmed life.

7

"Ungovernable Spirit of the Frontier"
The Incident at Middle Creek

On January 10, 1768, six Indians arrived at Frederick Stump's house on Middle Creek in the Pennsylvania wilderness near Fort Augusta. Their visit triggered an act of violence resulting in their own deaths and ending the relative calm that had existed in Pennsylvania ever since John Penn's marriage.

The Indians were known to Stump. They were Senecas and Mohicans, and two had brought their wives. One, a local Indian leader and considered friendly, was called White Mingo and also known by the English name John Cook. On this particular day all six Indians were drunk, and they entered Stump's house demanding more rum. Unable to get the Indians to leave, Stump later contended, he had feared for his life. Alone except for John Ironcutter, his servant, Stump waited until the Indians had all fallen into a drunken sleep, then he killed them one by one. To conceal his crime, he dragged their bodies to the frozen creek, made a hole in the ice, and plunged them into the frigid water.[1]

Stump feared the Indians' revenge, perhaps because he had also mutilated the corpses. About one month later a Cumberland County coroner and magistrate held an inquest concerning an Indian corpse that had washed up within the high-water mark of the Susquehanna. They believed the body had floated downstream and was that of one of Stump's victims. The Indian had died from several blows to the skull apparently delivered with the pole end of a tomahawk and had also been scalped savagely enough to have lost both ears.

To prevent the Indian community from missing and seeking their friends, Stump and Ironcutter had committed a second atrocity. The following day, Stump and Ironcutter had traveled fourteen miles up Middle Creek to two other Indian cabins, where they found the wife of one of the murdered men. Stump and Ironcutter killed both her and the two girls and female infant they found there, burned the cabins over their remains, then fled to George Gabriel's mill, a local gathering spot at the mouth of Penn's Creek.[2]

Stump was apparently not unwilling to talk about the incident to local whites, and word reached John Blyth, who had been an officer in the French and Indian War. On January 12 Blyth visited the mill and heard Stump's story firsthand. To confirm the tale, he sent four men to the burned cabins on Middle Creek, where they found human remains blackened by fire. On January 19 John Blyth went to Philadelphia and told Stump's story to the governor and other Pennsylvania officials.[3]

The Penns and their appointees had long been concerned about the frontier, where white squatters on Indian land had been arousing Indian discontent ever since the treaties that had officially ended Pontiac's Uprising. Thomas Penn was still promoting new policies in England for better Indian relations overall, but at the end of 1767 he had made little progress. In the meantime, John Penn had been at a loss when squatters settled on land where the border between Pennsylvania and Virginia had not been firmly established. These intruders ignored the proclamations of both colonial governors and dealt with the Indians however they pleased.[4] Just over a month before, John Penn had received yet another letter from General Gage, informing him that squatters were provoking Indians everywhere. Once driven off illegal settlements, they simply reestablished themselves elsewhere. Gage called for more effective punishment of squatters,[5] and John Penn had replied that his appointed civil officers could not really "exert their Authority in so distant and extensive a Wilderness."[6] But Governor Penn also sent Gage's letter to the assembly, asking for legislation to permit more severe punishment and, it was hoped, to remedy the situation. The governor knew that news of the Stump murders was not going to make the already restive Indians any happier.

John Penn quickly filled his uncle in. Ironically, Stump himself had been one of Pennsylvania's troublesome squatters. In 1766 this Pennsylvania German from Heidelburg Township had been driven off land that the Indians called Shamokin, an area between the northern and western branches of the Susquehanna. At the time, Stump insisted that he had paid for the land—an obvious lie because the Penn land office was not selling property in this area. John Penn remembered the incident and described Stump to his uncle as "one of the greatest Villains in the Country." His letter also suggested that the governor believed the Stump murders had been somewhat premeditated in that Stump himself might have supplied enough liquor to make the Indians pass out. "Stump must have made the Indians he murdered, at his house, dead drunk," Penn wrote. "Otherwise he could not have done the business alone, as any one of the men were an equal match for him had they been sober."[7]

The Penn government took steps to capture Stump and placate the Indians. Chief Justice William Allen issued a warrant for Stump's arrest and ordered his delivery under guard to Philadelphia for a special hearing. John Penn announced a reward and wrote the sheriff and magistrates of Cumberland, York, Berks, and Lancaster counties urging the apprehension of Stump and his servant.[8] The governor then notified General Gage and Sir William Johnson and asked Johnson to convince the Indians with whom he treated that Stump's actions had not been sanctioned by the Pennsylvania government.[9] The governor and council also made attempts to conciliate Indians locally. John Penn wrote the chief of the Delawares, assuring him that Stump would be punished.[10] A Delaware who happened to be in Philadelphia was summoned and given a similar message.

When Sheriff John Holmes delayed in obeying Governor John Penn's orders, a privately organized posse captured Frederick Stump. The orders had arrived on court week, when the sheriff's absence from Carlisle would have seriously impeded official business. Sheriff Holmes sent word to the coroner asking that he follow the matter up. Meanwhile, William Patterson, another former officer of the French and Indian War, personally paid about twenty local farmers to accompany him to Gabriel's mill on January 21. They circled the building, only to find that, at their approach, Stump and Ironcutter had fled into the woods. Patterson used a ruse to flush Stump out of hiding, saying he and his men were going to nearby Great Island to kill all the Indians settled there. When this message was relayed to Stump, he agreed to join their party. Patterson's men then bound and chained both Stump and Ironcutter and took them to Carlisle, arriving on Saturday evening, January 23, just as Sheriff Holmes and the local magistrates were setting out to arrest Stump themselves.[11]

Sheriff Holmes intended to transport Stump and Ironcutter east to Philadelphia but was forced to delay. Ice was breaking up on the Susquehanna,
making crossing dangerous. While the sheriff waited for better weather, local
magistrates who had been in Carlisle for court sessions pressured him not to
carry out his orders. The magistrates prevailed on Senior Magistrate Colonel
John Armstrong to see that Stump was not turned over to Philadelphia
authorities. They suspected that, once removed to Philadelphia, Stump would
be tried there, thus setting a dangerous precedent that would deny frontiersmen
a local trial by a jury of their peers. When the sheriff refused to dismiss the
guard organized to take Stump to the city, the magistrates dismissed it for
him and kept Stump in the jail at Carlisle.[12] Outlying frontiersmen soon
marched on Carlisle to make their own opinions known. On January 27
about forty armed men came into town, threatening to free Stump en route if
he was taken to Philadelphia for trial. Once they were convinced there were
no plans to try Stump in the city, they dispersed.[13] Sheriff Holmes, by then
suspicious of other rescue attempts, kept Stump where he was and wrote
John Penn about the situation.

John Penn got news that Stump was still in Carlisle on January 29. The
governor had been concentrating on averting Indian war and was shocked to
have to defend his orders to those who were appointed to carry them out. In
a letter to Armstrong, he expressed his astonishment at the "impertinent
insolence" of those who suggested or supposed that the Penn government
would illegally attempt to try Stump in Philadelphia.[14] He quickly wrote
back ordering both prisoners to Philadelphia unless there was definite knowledge that a rescue attempt would be made.[15] In all his correspondence with
Thomas Penn, the governor contended the trip to Philadelphia was for
questioning only. William Allen also insisted that questioning would be more
responsibly accomplished in Philadelphia, but he expressed doubts about
exactly where the crimes had occurred.[16] County boundaries were still
uncertain on the frontier, and perhaps Allen was hoping such confusion
would lead to trial by a Philadelphia jury, which would be more likely to
convict Stump and thus appease the Indians.

On January 29, while the governor fumed over frontier impertinence,
Pennsylvania frontiersmen again took the law into their hands and freed
Stump and Ironcutter. Late that morning James Cunningham was having
breakfast with John Armstrong across from the Carlisle jail when they saw
through a window a large number of armed men ride into town and
surround the prison. Suspecting foul play, they abandoned their meal and
forced their way up the steps to the jail door. The commotion alerted

Reverend Steel, the sheriff, and two other magistrates, who joined them. These representatives of law and order pleaded for a parley with the leaders of the raid, but they could not reason with the mob or dislodge the four strangers who kept their muskets crossed before the jail door. One of these men shoved Armstrong down the steps. Armstrong picked himself up and shouted, "Gentlemen, I am unarmed, and it is in your Power to kill me, but I will die on the Spot before you shall rescue the Prisoners!"[17]

Unknown to Armstrong, the rescue was already well under way. The mob had quietly sent a few advance men to the Carlisle jail who were already inside. They had asked the jailer for a dram—a short drink—which the jailer provided. The jailer did not become alarmed until he noticed that the men were heavily armed with concealed weapons. At that point he tried to shut the jail door against other intruders, but it was too late. Three more men rushed in and seized him, forcing him into another room. They bullied a servant girl into giving them a candle and the keys to the dungeon where Stump and Ironcutter were being kept. They drew pistol and cutlass and swore that the jailer was a dead man if he resisted or made any noise.[18]

Once the intruders released the prisoners and brought them out of the jail, Carlisle officials tried to retake their former captives. The sheriff tried to grab Stump, but someone thrust a cutlass at him, narrowly missing his throat. The magistrates were jostled into the street, where the mob cheered, "Make way—here are the prisoners! We have them! We have them!" Then they rode off with Stump and Ironcutter, stopping only briefly at a blacksmith's shop to get the men's handcuffs removed. Sheriff Holmes later organized a posse and rode to Sherman's Valley, from where it was thought many of the rescuers came. He spoke with some of these men but failed to learn where Stump and Ironcutter were. The governor offered generous rewards for their recapture, but to no avail. The prisoners were never retaken.[19]

The daring rescue of Frederick Stump soon forced the Penn government to defend the proprietorship against renewed attack from the assembly. Assembly speaker Joseph Galloway still harbored hopes for royal government in Pennsylvania. In 1768 he continued trying to exploit current events to further those ambitions. Governor John Penn had lately requested legislation specifying death without benefit of clergy for squatters on Indian lands. In making preparations to pass this bill, the assembly tried to revive indignation over the Conestoga Massacre—they contacted Indian agent George Croghan, who had observed lingering Indian discontent over the murders. John Penn had been forced to reply. On January 25 he reminded the assembly that "every vigorous Step was taken by me on that melancholy Occasion." The problem? "No one could be found who had Virtue or Resolution enough to give the Officers of Justice any Information in the Matter; to which it is owing, and not to the Debility of the Government, that Justice has not long since overtaken the Murderers."[20]

Once the assembly members learned of Stump's escape, they shot back with sarcastic messages about frontier magistrates on February 2 and again on February 5. Justice, they implied, was administered by the proprietors through the magistracy. If the magistrates could not be made to do their jobs, neither the proprietors nor their executive were doing theirs. The Penn government had clearly lost control on the frontier.[21]

Again John Penn was forced on the defensive. He replied that their latest message was "not only indecent and unbecoming, but indicates a Spirit prevailing among you, very ill suited to the present critical situation of our public Affairs." According to him, the Conestoga Massacre was a closed issue to everyone except the assemblymen. And now, just when the governor had to deal with the Stump murders, he was "called upon by [them], in a Manner most extraordinary, to vindicate [himself], and, as it were, arraigned by [them] for neglecting the Duties of [his] Station." He concluded, "I shall expect that you will not dictate to me in Matters which relate to the executive Powers of Government."[22]

The assembly replied by accusing John Penn of having done little to bring the Conestoga murderers to justice—he had merely written orders to minor officials, who disobeyed them with impunity. "Every impartial Person," they concluded, "must be convinced that the Powers of Government, vested in the feeble Hands of a Proprietary Governor, are too weak to support Order in the Province, or give Safety to the People."[23]

In their private correspondence the Penns and their chief officers expressed more indignation and concern over the assembly's behavior than over the frontier's defiance of their government's orders. The assembly, John Penn feared, was using the distress of their country to advance their own ends. The assembly housed "a Club of the most obstinate & inveterate opposers the Government has."[24] James Hamilton also warned Thomas Penn that "malignants here, together with their Agent in England," would exploit this problem "to do you a prejudice." The agent he meant was of course Ben Franklin.[25] Thomas was furious with the frontier magistrates and dismayed that "the Assembly have behaved so very unjustly in their messages." He was not concerned about Franklin, however, and reassured John Penn: "I cannot think Mr. Franklin's opposition to our Government will continue long."[26] A previous letter related the precautions Thomas had already taken to ensure that news of the murders on Middle Creek reached the king through the chief proprietor's own communication with Lord Hillsborough. Thomas already had assurances that both the king and the secretary of state believed the Penn administration had acted properly in every respect.[27]

The Stump murders failed to reanimate the movement for royal government. Indeed, in 1768, London suffered strikes and riots that made Pennsylvania's frontier lawlessness seem insignificant. Although Franklin did make some attempt to renew his petition by speaking to Lord Hillsborough, Hillsborough advised Franklin in no uncertain terms to give up. Franklin finally relayed this information to his friend Galloway in a letter dated August 20, 1768. Long before Galloway received this news, the assembly had backed down and was acting more in accord with the governor's wishes. Perhaps sharing the Penn administration's fear of renewed Indian war, the assembly appropriated public funds to appease the Indians for the Stump murders. By the end of March, John Penn was able to inform Thomas Penn that an Indian conference would soon be held at Fort Pitt.

Attending the conference were men representing both the proprietors and the assembly. George Croghan had been the assembly's choice to organize and lead the conference. The assembly felt that the Indians trusted Croghan, but Richard Peters feared Croghan might somehow use the incident to turn the Indians against the Penn government. Peters remembered rumors that Croghan was involved in land speculation deals with Franklin and Galloway. Due to Peters's suspicions, the Penn organization made sure that their interests would be represented by their own trusted officers; John Allen and Joseph Shippen would accompany Croghan to Fort Pitt.[28]

No one had been appointed to represent the point of view of frontiersmen like those who had rescued Frederick Stump. In fact, it was reported that some frontiersmen wanted no reconciliation with the Indians. A treaty might establish the law in clearer terms of white and black and leave less room for their kind of Indian diplomacy. Croghan had heard he might be attacked on the way to Fort Pitt, but the party was not deterred and reached its destination safely.[29]

The Fort Pitt conference opened April 26, 1768. Croghan spoke first. Addressing the assembled Indians from various tribes as "brethren," he spoke of their relationship in the colorful metaphors appropriate to Indian treaty-making in the eighteenth century. Presenting an Indian representative with wampum, he said: "With this String of Wampum I clear your Eyes, and wipe away your Tears that you may see and look on your Brethren the English, with Pleasure." He presented other wampum strings and belts to symbolically cleanse the Indians of sweat, remove their evil memories, and clean their ears so they could listen to what the English had to say.[30]

Although John Penn did not go to Fort Pitt, those who did attend delivered the governor's messages to the Indians. Croghan delivered a message from John Penn asking that the Indians not let the Middle Creek murders disturb their peace. Several days later, Allen and Shippen followed up with a second message from the governor, who wrote that he wanted to take the Indians "by the Hand, and sit down and condole with [them]" and asked that the Indians speak freely to his agents instead. John suggested that the Indians view the Stump murders as an isolated incident caused by a specific person, not as a general threat. To give himself bargaining power, he told the Indians to remember "the Number of People I have lost in the Indian Country by some of your foolish young Men." Through his agents, the governor offered more presents and said, "I, with this String of Wampum, gather up the Bones of all our dead Friends, and bury them in the Earth that they may be no more seen."[31]

On May 1 the Indians replied, saying they believed John Penn and would assume the Middle Creek murders had been caused by the Evil Spirit working through a wicked man. As for John Penn's murdered white settlers, an Indian representative replied: "I now gather the Bones of your deceased Friends, and bury them in the Ground, in the same Place with ours." The Indians had been asked to air any other grievances at the conference, so they mentioned the squatters settled on their lands. The conference adjourned on May 6 with all parties agreeing that the symbolic "chain of friendship" had been renewed.[32]

The conference may have reaffirmed the uneasy peace between Pennsylvania's government and Pennsylvania's Indians, but no treaty had been made with the ideological successors of the Paxton Boys, who had engineered Stump's escape from justice. Four years after the Paxton Boys had marched on Philadelphia to defy the assembly, frontiersmen were defying their proprietary governor's express orders and getting away with it. It was obvious the Penns could no longer effectively exert their authority on the frontier. They seemed to realize this and blamed the nature of the frontiersmen. As John Penn reported to his uncle in March 1768, "The turbulent and ungovernable Spirit of the Frontier inhabitants . . . will continually be counteracting the Efforts of the Government to establish a lasting peace with the Indians. They think it meritorious to murder the Heathen, . . . nor have they any Idea that they ought to suffer for it."[33] The conference at Fort Pitt may have temporarily placated the Indians, but that fall William Allen also showed concern about what would happen if newly opened frontier areas were settled by what he termed "the scum of America."[34]

That summer and fall, however, lingering concerns about the frontier situation were overshadowed by events in Philadelphia as the British government once again tried to exert the authority it claimed in America.

8

"The Storm Gathering"
Pennsylvania and the Townshend Duties

At the end of July 1768, John Penn wrote his uncle about a mass meeting that had just taken place at the State House. Attendees protested the new Parliamentary legislation known as the Townshend Acts and neglected to express the eternal loyalty almost universally pledged to the mother country when the Stamp Act had been repealed. The governor spoke ominously of a "gathering storm" and warned, "It is my firm opinion that the Submission required by the Government at home of the American Colonies, can never be obtained but by the Sword."[1]

By that time Pennsylvanians had known about the Townshend duties for about a year, and a few had already protested these taxes. Protest had swelled suddenly after the governor received a letter from Lord Hillsborough that appeared to threaten the province's most cherished liberties. His Lordship's letter had turned countless Pennsylvanians uncharacteristically against their mother country. The governor reported that the letter was being treated "with the utmost contempt from the highest to the lowest."[2]

Although the warmth of such protest may have seemed sudden, events had long been leading up to the meeting at the State House. Shortly after the Stamp Act was repealed in 1766, Rockingham had been replaced as prime minister by William Pitt. England still needed the cash the Stamp Act had failed to raise, and the feeling persisted that America was not carrying her fair share of the empire's debts and ongoing expenses. Charles Townshend, then England's Chancellor of the Exchequer, thought he knew a way to get more real income out of America, and in May 1767 he unveiled the "Townshend formula." Unlike the Stamp Act, the Townshend Acts established duties that would merely be "external taxes," or further regulations of America's trade. The acts called for taxes on such items as glass, painters' lead, paper, painters' colors, and tea and also shifted the customs bureau headquarters to America to ensure more efficient tax collection and better control over smuggling.

Americans got news of the Townshend duties in September 1767. While the new taxes seemed straightforward and unexceptionable to British lawmakers, they further complicated the British regulatory system, which had already created a huge customs bureau and a bewildering mass of regulations that even some of its own officers failed to understand. It soon became clear—at least to the people of Boston—that the new customs officials empowered by Charles Townshend's plan were out to manipulate a confusing system for quick profit. They played games with merchants and ship owners: They would be lax for a time in enforcing a certain regulation, then suddenly crack down and seize vessels just when everyone thought *that* particular regulation would not be enforced. Politically minded Americans also noticed that the Townshend duties specifically raised revenue to pay the salaries of the royal governors of Virginia and Massachusetts, threatening to put them in a position where they did not have to answer to the people.

By February 1768 the Massachusetts assembly published its "circular letter" to the other colonies' assemblies, seeking help in forming a united resistance. Many Americans responded by proposing boycotts. In December 1767 John Dickinson publicly advocated nonimportation, or a boycott of imported British goods, in his *Letters from a Pennsylvania Farmer,* which stated that the Townshend duties were unconstitutional and that they set a dangerous precedent. The "Farmer's Letters" were widely read, but they made Dickinson more of a hero in neighboring colonies than in Pennsylvania.

The Townshend duties had renewed Joseph Galloway's hopes for royal government in Pennsylvania, and his influence prevented many Pennsylvanians from taking up Dickinson's cause. Galloway reasoned that if revenue generated by these new taxes was earmarked for the salaries of royal governors, perhaps England was ready to consider a royal governor for Pennsylvania.

When the Stump murders occurred at the beginning of 1768, Galloway began his campaign to use the incident at Middle Creek to reactivate the long dormant movement for royal government. Once again Galloway needed Pennsylvania to appear submissive and dutiful toward the British government, and the city's artisans and mechanics followed his lead just as they had during the Stamp Act crisis. Galloway also ensured that the assembly would essentially ignore the Massachusetts circular letter and merely instruct its agents in London to lobby against the new taxes.[3]

Even Galloway could not stifle all the voices that would be raised in Pennsylvania against the Townshend duties. By March, Philadelphia's newspapers had gotten hold of the Massachusetts circular letter, and the Townshend duties became a topic for intense discussion in the taverns. Conservatives opposed precipitate action, but in April 1768 one group of Philadelphia merchants roundly denounced the duties in an address reprinted as a broadside. The taxes, it suggested, threatened the liberty of Americans. "As then we cannot enjoy Liberty without Property, both in our Lives and Estates; as we can have no Property in that which another may of Right take and dispose of as he pleases, without our Consent; and as the late Acts of Parliament assert this Right to be in them, we cannot enjoy Freedom until this Claim is given up, and until the Acts made in Consequence of it be repealed."[4]

William Allen voiced some less lofty and more practical concerns in his letters to Thomas Penn. In October 1767 he observed that America's ports were "so clogged with duties, and restrictions, that no foreigners will come nigh them." Nor were the duties they already paid insignificant to a cash-poor society. People couldn't find enough silver to pay the customs houses. Allen had been using his connections with Thomas Penn to solve some other problems he saw in America's business environment. He was a major manufacturer and exporter of iron and had asked the chief proprietor for help in getting restraints removed from iron exportation. The Iron Act of 1750 had "in a manner knocked that branch of business in the head." He also wanted to know how America could get more paper money when its use had been curtailed in 1764.[5]

Thomas Penn's reply was sympathetic. Having started out as a businessman, he sided with Allen. Although he held out little hope for paper money (the powerful Lord Hillsborough was immovably opposed to it), he promised he would see his friend Lord Shelburne on the iron issue. In his letter to Allen, Thomas again displayed Whiggish sentiments, making it clear he opposed the Townshend duties just as much as he disliked any scheme to restrict America's trade. His opposition was more practical than philosophical—he predicted that "great inconveniences will arise, and losses even to our mother country."[6]

Only a few days after Thomas Penn had written William Allen, Lord Hillsborough heard about the Massachusetts circular letter. He was so angry he delayed the regular packet boat's departure until he could prepare instructions for the colonial governors. Hillsborough demanded that the governors order their assemblies to ignore the circular letter, and to prorogue or dissolve the assemblies if they disobeyed.

Thomas Penn managed to get a letter to John Penn on the same ship as Hillsborough's instructions. The chief proprietor strongly exhorted John Penn to stay on the right side of the British government. Despite his personal opposition to the Townshend duties, Thomas instructed John to see that Pennsylvania did *not* unite with other colonies in petitioning for repeal of the new taxes. Pennsylvania was welcome to send her own petitions, but a joint petition would create an illegal "combination." Moreover, such a combination would be resented by the ministry and was therefore useless. Thomas Penn wrote: "Use your utmost endeavors to prevent our assembly joining with [the other colonies] in such petitions, and if possible engage them to refuse [the Massachusetts circular letter], as being a very improper act; and not legal." The governor was to confer with William Allen and other moderate assemblymen to get the Massachusetts circular letter rejected or at least "put it off, without giving a reason, for six month."[7]

Before Thomas Penn's letter even arrived, the assembly had complied with his wishes. On May 10 Galloway had the Massachusetts circular letter read. No comments were noted in the minutes, and the next day the assembly adjourned their spring session. John Penn wrote Thomas, "I believe there is no danger of [the assembly] coming in to the New England Measures, but this I shall be sure of at their next Session. I know they have not yet taken any notice at all of the letter from Boston and Mr. Allen tells me he is sure they will not."[8]

While the governor and chief proprietor warily watched the assembly, protests against the Townshend duties were voiced in the streets and taverns of Pennsylvania. Before the assembly came back into session, the contents of Lord Hillsborough's letter became widely known. To those who still shared Galloway's hopes for royal government, Hillsborough's sentiments were poor reward for Pennsylvania's dutiful obedience. The situation indicated that royal officials were prepared to be far more dictatorial than Thomas Penn had ever been. Hillsborough's orders that royal governors dissolve disobedient assemblies threatened a privilege Pennsylvania held dear: the right of the elected assembly to sit on their own adjournment. John Dickinson and Charles Thomson fanned the flames at the meeting held on July 30 at the State House. Someone read a stirring address reinforcing the idea that the Townshend duties posed a clear threat to liberty. Those attending the meeting drew up instructions for the Pennsylvania assembly ordering it to unite with the other colonies in the common cause.

John Penn wrote his uncle the day after this mass meeting and noted that the Hillsborough letter "so far from having the desired effect has only served to forward the intended purpose of the general Petition from the Several Colonies [the Massachusetts circular letter]." Those instructions to the assembly had been signed by "great numbers, many of them men of the best understanding among us." He added, "Even those persons who were the most moderate are now set in a flame and have joined in the general Cry of Liberty." They were saying that if Englishmen could not petition for redress of grievances they were worse off than slaves.[9]

Hillsborough's letter also forced a response from the assembly. On September 13, 1768, the assembly had its first quorum of its fall session. Although John Penn was out of town, a secretary brought a message from the governor together with the dreaded Hillsborough letter. The message may have been purposely vague. Governor Penn urged the assembly to "conduct yourselves on the Occasion in such a Manner as to confirm our gracious Sovereign in the favourable Opinion he is pleased to entertain of you."[10] The assembly considered these documents and came up with several resolutions. They were most concerned with making it understood that Pennsylvania's Charter of Privileges stipulated that they could not be prorogued or dissolved at the whim of their governor or anyone else. Next they resolved that they *could* correspond with the other colonies if they chose to.[11] However, they sent their own petition to the king and to both houses of Parliament, a purposely tactful gesture influenced by Galloway, who had not yet received Franklin's letter informing him that all hope for royal government was lost.

William Allen reported the assembly's sentiments to Thomas Penn and said his fellow assemblymen considered Massachusetts's request very modest. Whether united or individually, "we are of all men the most Miserable," if the colonies could not petition. In a more practical vein, he added, "It will, in the end, be found an Utopian Scheme to lay dutys, and taxes on America." Why? There was simply no silver to pay. In New York they were "hammering up their old plate" to pay the customs house. Americans would become so cash-poor they would be unable to purchase British manufactured goods and be reduced to manufacturing their own inferior products.[12]

A few weeks later William Allen vented more frustration to Thomas Penn: "Every act of Parliament of late, Though made, as it is said, for the benefit of the Colonys, is attended with so many provisions, and restrictions, that trade is rather injured by them than otherwise." Allen was still annoyed that England had encouraged the American iron industry and then restricted its exports. He had lost money on this deal. He seconded John Penn's opinion that forcing Americans to pay taxes would cost more than it gained. Americans were united in opposition to the Townshend duties—they differed only on exactly how to oppose them.[13] In December 1768, after Pennsylvania's individual petitions protesting the duties had been dispatched, William Allen warned Thomas Penn that if the new taxes were not repealed "then . . . shall we begin our Constitutional war with our Mother Country."[14]

Because of the detailed information he received from his officers, Thomas Penn had a perspective on the Townshend duties that Lord Hillsborough lacked. Thomas believed Hillsborough was wrong in thinking that opposition to the duties was the "cabal" or conspiracy of a factious few.[15] He also believed Parliament was misguided. To one contact he wrote: "We have too many violent people in that House, that I fear, will endeavor rather to shew their power by taxing, than their wisdom by giving encouragement to trade, to get ten times the Sum."[16]

Nevertheless, because he also dealt frequently with the British government, Thomas Penn could see that the American colonies were not using the best means to gain their ends. He could see that a joint petition was a tactical error—it would only confirm the ministry's belief in a nonexistent cabal.[17] By December 1768 he resignedly informed the governor that the Townshend duties might have been repealed already if it had not been for all the American protest that made the British government unwilling to give up their presumed right to tax the colonies.[18] In the fall of 1768 Thomas Penn echoed his nephew's sentiments of the previous summer, ironically using the same metaphor to describe the growing rift between America and Britain: "I am clearly of opinion, that the Storm gathering will be full as injurious to this Country as to America in the end."[19]

The storm did not burst until February 1769, when it became obvious that the American petitions had failed to get the Townshend duties repealed. As for Pennsylvania's modest individual petition, Thomas Penn reported that it "gave great offense and was not necessary and so was not received."[20] Lord Hillsborough wrote John Penn that the petition to His Majesty that he had received from Ben Franklin was "irregular and disrespectful." It had been received but was not approved.[21]

Philadelphia's merchants renewed the outcry of the previous summer. On February 4, 1769, a broadside appeared: "The Merchants of this City are earnestly requested to meet at the CoffeeHouse, on MONDAY next, at Nine o'Clock, to consider a Matter of great Importance, that will then be laid before them."[22] The next month, Philadelphia's dry-goods merchants agreed to boycott British dry-goods from April 1 until the majority of the agreement's subscribers voted otherwise.[23] To enforce the agreement's terms, the merchants chose twenty-one men to serve as a committee of inspection that would seek out infractions and meet and reprove violators. At first the committee had a good enforcement record and there were few problems.[24] The committee ensured that goods ordered after February 6 were returned, and perishable goods were confiscated and put to public use. Imports were severely curtailed for a year.[25] The economic "constitutional war" was on.

Political changes that had occurred during the previous months had created much new popular support for nonimportation and had increased the level of protest against the Townshend duties. Galloway finally received Franklin's letter informing him that the movement for royal government was officially dead. This further angered Quaker leaders, who were already alarmed at the implications of Hillsborough's letter. Their incentive for obedience was gone, and the Quaker party was left without a program. The mechanics' hero, Franklin, who had at first remained silent about the Townshend duties, began supporting nonimportation early in 1769. He wrote letters to Charles Thomson, which Thomson published. City artisans and mechanics, still loyal to Franklin, drifted toward that body of men Thomas Penn did not like to call the "Presbyterian party." Their support made John Dickinson and Charles Thomson generals *with* an army.[26]

What Allen had called Pennsylvania's "constitutional war" was not without its casualties. By the summer of 1769 merchants who had little capital were suffering. Dry-goods merchants were perturbed to see wet-goods merchants, whose imports were not proscribed, doing business as usual in wine and molasses, which were covered by other taxes. Dry-goods merchants were also annoyed to see Maryland and Albany still importing dry-goods supposedly for the "Indian trade." These goods had a way of getting into the hands of many people who were not Indians.[27] That summer, farmers as well as merchants suffered economically when they found they were expected to pay steep prices for leftover shop goods while the prices they received for produce were not rising proportionally.[28] At the same time, Quakers became alarmed that the committee of twenty-one was revealing the names of nonimportation violators to the press. These unhappy violators were being visited by mobs, who hustled them out of their homes, covered them with tar and feathers, and paraded them around town. Such un-Quakerly violence was shocking, and the Philadelphia Quaker Monthly Meeting condemned members who were involved in the nonimportation committee.[29]

In England, Thomas Penn was doing what he could to return trade to normal. He informed William Allen, "I have made frequent applications to the Secretary of State for the repeal of the Laws." He was hoping for good news in the next session of Parliament but warned John Penn that Pennsylvania should not expect too much from its boycott. While England certainly did not want Americans to manufacture their own goods, the American market was perhaps not as crucial to British trade as Americans might like to think.[30] While he waited, Thomas replied to Pennsylvania merchants who had appealed to the merchants of Great Britain and their own proprietors for help. He informed them that Parliament would not be "forced by the Colonys," urged them toward more conservative behavior, and assured them the taxes would be repealed in 1770. Wait patiently, he advised, and be assured that we, the proprietors, will use "our utmost endeavors to serve you."[31]

In March 1770 Thomas Penn finally had good news for his contacts in America. A new ministry now headed by Lord North had been formed early in 1770. Lord North proposed that the Townshend Acts duties be repealed except for the tax on tea. This, Thomas Penn supposed, "will be much more acceptable to the Americans."[32]

American opinions on whether this move was acceptable varied. Many merchants whose inventories were by then depleted were in favor of ending their boycott, but the mechanics and artisans of Philadelphia had discovered that nonimportation had produced new demand for their own products. The mechanics and artisans were by then fully allied with Charles Thomson, who had gained control of the nonimportation enforcement committee. Thomson and his supporters tried to prevent Pennsylvania from abandoning its boycott. In June, Thomson packed a meeting of merchants with mechanics and prevented those present from voting to end the boycott. In July, despite news that New York had ended its own boycott, Thomson organized a meeting at the State House, where it was resolved that the remaining tax on tea still threatened America's liberties. It was further resolved that anyone hauling goods from New York would have his name published in the papers. The threat of tar and feathers could be read between the lines.[33]

Suffering merchants fought back. In September a broadside invited "every subscriber to our nonimportation agreement who wishes well to the liberties of his country" to a meeting at Davenport's tavern.[34] Such meetings were usually held at Bradford's London Coffee House, and conservative merchants were later accused of winning their point by holding their meeting in a tavern too small to be packed with mechanics. In any case, the merchants voted to alter their agreement. Only tea would now be proscribed. The merchants touted this as an "alteration" to their agreement, not an end to it.[35]

Throughout the crisis period, the Pennsylvania assembly had cooperated with the Penn government, but neither body could control those who were protesting the Townshend duties. In fact, after Quaker assembly leaders abandoned the movement for royal government, the Penns experienced few other problems with the assembly throughout the rest of their tenure as proprietors. But while the assembly had formed no cabal with the other American colonies, Philadelphia merchants had initiated the same sort of boycotts being mounted elsewhere in America.

During the nonimportation movement, the city's artisans and mechanics had mounted public protests, challenged their merchant neighbors, and tarred and feathered their way to political consciousness. Galloway lost what control he had had over this group, and in 1770 Galloway wrote that they had "left the old Ticket and 'tis feared will go over to the Presbyterians."[36] As their Presbyterian party became known as the Whig party, the Penn government drifted further away, despite any Whiggish thinking Thomas Penn or his appointees may have once had. As proprietors of Pennsylvania, the Penns were duty bound to support crown interests. Unfortunately, they had been helpless to carry out their duty and stop protest in the streets of Philadelphia.

Both John and Thomas Penn had seen the threat of war in America's resistance to the Townshend duties, yet once the crisis was over the Penns seem to have forgotten the danger. As America resumed trade with England and business picked up, there was no more talk of the gathering storm.

9

"More Vexation and Uneasiness"

The Connecticut Yankees in Pennsylvania, 1763–1773

"A Number of Persons, chiefly of the Colony of Connecticut, have lately, as well as at different Times heretofore, in a forcible Manner . . . possessed themselves of, and settled upon a large Tract of Land on the River Susquehanna," proclaimed James Hamilton, president of the governor's council in 1771. His proclamation went on to say that resulting problems and violence had forced the assembly to pass a riot act, this one specifying that any group of twelve or more that did not disperse on official orders "shall be adjudged Felons, and shall suffer Death . . . without Benefit of Clergy."[1] Although the Penn government had done little more than observe and comment on the protests over the Townshend duties, the Penns and their appointees were ready to take strong measures to quell what they believed was a much more immediate problem. Pennsylvania was on the verge of war with Connecticut.

The dispute between these two colonies focused on land now in upstate Pennsylvania: the rich Wyoming Valley and the area between the forks of the Susquehanna River, which the Indians called Shamokin. William Penn's charter appeared to include the disputed area, but Connecticut had an earlier charter stipulating that, except for Dutch lands in the Hudson River valley, Connecticut's western boundary was the Pacific Ocean. Back in the early 1750s the inhabitants of rocky, infertile eastern Connecticut had heard tales about Shamokin from returning adventurers and explorers. Pennsylvania frontiersmen were even more familiar with the territory. Men like Frederick Stump had already settled there illegally on unpurchased land. The lush river valleys were so tempting that squatters like Stump were willing to risk being driven off their farms by Penn officials intent on keeping peace with the Indians.

In 1753 several prominent Connecticut citizens formed the Susquehanna Company to buy the Wyoming Valley directly from its Indian owners. At the Albany Congress in 1754 both Pennsylvania and Connecticut acquired Indian land. On July 6 the Indians sold to the Penns land west of the Susquehanna and land between the Kittochtinny hills and the province's southern boundary, but they specifically reserved the Wyoming Valley and Shamokin for themselves. A few days later a group of warriors from the Six Nations sold the Wyoming Valley to John Henry Lydius of the Susquehanna Company. Some of the same Indians signed both purchase documents. Penn officials suspected that the Susquehanna Company had manipulated the Indians with bribes and liquor and believed their suspicions were confirmed when the Indians later denied that the Lydius purchase was valid. Nevertheless, the Susquehanna Company acted quickly on its presumed ownership. By 1755 the Connecticut assembly authorized settlements in their new territory, and surveyors began to lay out land.

The Penn government also acted quickly to halt early trespassers in the north. As early as 1753, even before the Connecticut purchase, Richard Peters had been alerted that New Englanders had crossed the Delaware and seemed to be spying out land. Penn officials in Easton foresaw trouble and urged the governor to take action against potential disturbers of the peace. By 1760 Philadelphia heard that twenty families from Connecticut had erected houses, a mill, and a blockhouse west of the Delaware at a place the Indians called Cushietunk. The Indians protested, and both the Penns and crown Indian agent Sir William Johnson complained to the Board of Trade. Johnson specifically warned that such an illegal settlement could lead to Indian war, and Governor Hamilton issued proclamations against the Connecticut settlers.[2]

By 1762, people from Connecticut had established a settlement on Mill Creek at the site of present-day Wilkes-Barre. The Penn government sent magistrate Daniel Brodhead north to find out what was going on. He pretended an interest in buying land, and the Yankees welcomed him, telling him not to worry about the Penn government because Connecticut would soon secure the territory with a thousand armed men and artillery.[3]

The Indians also valued their hunting grounds in northeastern Pennsylvania and were determined to keep them. The powerful Indian leader Teedyuscung was a formidable obstacle to white settlement in the area until his death in 1763, when Indians more or less abandoned the area to whites. Indians made one final assertion of their rights in October 1763, during the height of Pontiac's Uprising, when they swooped down on the Connecticut settlers, killing men, women, and children, carrying off prisoners, and plundering houses and farms. After the few survivors returned to Connecticut, rangers from Paxton Township in Pennsylvania discovered the bodies of the Connecticut victims. It made little difference to the white rangers that the Yankees had established themselves where they had no right to be. It has been suggested that the Conestoga Massacre later that year was meant to avenge the Indian attack on the Connecticut settlers.[4]

Connecticut first disavowed responsibility, then seemed willing to have the matter settled by a higher authority. In 1763, after Connecticut issued its own proclamations against the Yankee invaders, Connecticut lawyer Eliphalet Dyer traveled to London to work with Connecticut's colonial agent in getting the British ministry to recognize the Susquehanna Company and grant it land. This suited Thomas Penn perfectly—he believed that if the British ministry ever really considered the matter the Susquehanna Company would cease to exist at all. Early in 1764 he confidently reported to Richard Peters, "I expect this business will be settled here this winter."[5]

If Connecticut really desired a formal settlement, their timing was poor. An official grant to Connecticut that recognized their charter claims in any way would have defeated the purpose of Britain's Proclamation Line of 1763, which technically separated Indian and white lands throughout the colonies. Dyer's petition was pigeonholed indefinitely. Ironically, this worked to the Yankees' advantage. While the matter remained formally unresolved, Connecticut settlers kept drifting into the area. In the long run, they would have squatters' rights on a very large scale.

Pontiac's Uprising and the Connecticut invasion both prompted Thomas Penn to seek a new boundary between British and Indian lands and attempt to purchase the disputed territory formally. In 1767 he dined with his friend Lord Shelburne and showed him supporting letters from crown Indian agent George Croghan and Pennsylvania's Chief Justice William Allen. Penn warned his nephew that once he had won over the right British officials he would immediately require Sir William Johnson to negotiate purchases with the Indians.[6]

Thomas Penn got his wish when Lord Shelburne authorized Johnson to negotiate with the Indians for a new boundary on January 5, 1768. Thomas rushed this message to William Johnson, John Penn, and virtually every Penn agent likely to be involved in the transaction. He made it clear he wanted the land along the Delaware as far north as the Indians would sell. He also wanted Shamokin, or at least a promise that the Indians would sell it to no one else. He wanted large tracts of land west of the Alleghenies as far as the Ohio River.[7] In Thomas Penn's mind, the Ohio would make a good natural boundary for Pennsylvania's white settlers. And natural boundaries were more difficult to dispute than unsurveyed lines.

John Penn organized the party that would attend the treaty-making session. During the summer of 1768 he reported that planning for the treaty occupied his "principal attention."[8] As soon as Johnson made final arrangements, Attorney General Benjamin Chew, Land Office Secretary James Tilghman, and Governor John Penn all traveled to Fort Stanwix (present-day Rome, New York), above Albany at the head of the Mohawk River. They were accompanied by one of William Allen's sons and Richard Peters. This was news to Thomas Penn, who had recently heard that Peters was at death's door. Thomas was pleasantly surprised to have the trusted Peters involved in the treaty.[9]

The party reached Albany on September 15 and arrived at Fort Stanwix by September 22. According to William Allen, they were "in good health, Though all lodge in one room upon the floor." As for Peters, the rough journey seemed to revive him.[10] They had to wait several weeks for the Indians to assemble, and by October 15, before the treaty-making process had formally begun, John Penn and Benjamin Chew were forced to return to Pennsylvania on business. John Penn had Johnson's assurance that his presence was not absolutely required, and Chew seemed anxious to return to civilization. "The governor and I took our Leaves of that disagreeable Country & came home," he wrote Thomas.[11]

The Fort Stanwix treaty gave Thomas Penn the land he wanted, but at a price that shocked the frugal chief proprietor. Although commissioners from New England and Connecticut failed to attend, the Indians repudiated the Susquehanna Company's claim to the Wyoming Valley. Johnson purchased Wyoming, Shamokin, and more land in the west. The price was £10,000 payable in installments, far more than Thomas had anticipated spending. Thomas had also assumed that the crown would actually pay the Indians, while he reimbursed the treasury for Pennsylvania's new territory. Still, he approved the arrangements and fondly hoped that the new land would bring the Penns lots of revenue.[12]

The Penn government's primary objective became selling and settling the new territory. Thomas Penn wanted to reward loyal officers, such as William Allen, James Tilghman, and Colonel Turbutt Francis, a county official who had proven useful and happened to be the man who had chased Frederick Stump off his illegal settlement in Shamokin. Thomas also wanted his own family to profit through their proprietary right to establish manors. He had already instructed John that as soon as the new land was purchased he "must instantly survey for us about fifty thousand Acres there. . . . Pray lose no time in this."[13]

John Penn wanted to settle the area in a way that would stop the Connecticut invasion. There were rumors that Eliphalet Dyer was gathering a force of four thousand men to seize the Wyoming Valley as soon as the Indians sold it to the Penns. The governor made a pact with Colonel Amos Ogden (an Indian trader already established in the area by William Johnson's permission), Northampton County Sheriff John Jennings, and Charles Stewart, a speculator from New Jersey. These men were to lease the Penn manors to settlers who could drive off any Connecticut Yankees who dared to intrude.[14]

Differences of opinion over land-sale procedures created a breach among Thomas Penn's appointees. At the Penn land office, James Tilghman advocated preventing further Connecticut intrusions by filling up the area quickly. He advocated reducing quitrents and accepting late payment of purchase prices for speedy sale of the land adjacent to the Penn manors. Ostensibly these measures favored land-hungry farmers and frontiersmen, but they were also most welcome to money-hungry speculators in the city. Tilghman's policies put him at odds with receivers Richard Hockley and Edmund Physick (a new man in the Penn organization). Hockley and Physick both believed that the Connecticut intruders were less of a threat than resentment among Pennsylvanians over land jobbers. The receivers wanted to delay opening the land office until old accounts could be paid off and the surveyors better regulated, also allowing backcountry frontiersmen more time to travel to Philadelphia.[15] Tilghman finally closed the land office until April 1769, but only after having accepted applications from certain individuals in February. Physick indignantly reported that between February and April 1769 *no* land was surveyed for farmers or real settlers. The land office was open to "none but favorites," who had hurried all the surveyors out of town.

These favorites, he feared, would establish a dangerous land monopoly and give the westerners additional cause for complaint.[16]

While Thomas Penn's appointees argued over how to sell the new land, squatters from Connecticut continued to occupy the area. As early as January 1769 a number of Connecticut men organized by John Durkee planned an expedition headed for the new territory. Lewis Gordon of Easton warned he had heard from the Minisink Indians who lived along their route that forty or fifty invaders were on their way; Charles Stewart and Sheriff Jennings estimated the number at over a hundred.[17] The Connecticut settlers arrived at Mill Creek only to find a number of Pennsylvanians established in the old buildings. They traveled north to present-day Pittston, but Sheriff Jennings quickly rounded them up and sent them to the jail in Easton. There were no grounds for incarcerating them for long, however. When they were released, some returned to Connecticut and others explored the Pennsylvania back-country seeking help. There they encountered disgruntled Pennsylvania frontiersmen who were annoyed with Penn land policies and still believed the Penn government had intended to abrogate their rights by trying Frederick Stump in Philadelphia. When told they might be able to buy valuable land and live in a Connecticut township, many were willing to listen.[18]

The settlers who had returned to Connecticut were soon back in such numbers that the Penn government could not resist them. In May 1769 Charles Stewart reported that 146 New Englanders had passed his way on horseback while 500 more were expected to follow. Even worse was the news from James McClure, whom he had met at the mouth of Fishing Creek. McClure identified himself as the advance man of a party of one hundred Pennsylvanians who intended to join the New England squatters.[19] John Penn was furious to learn that his own province's citizens were willing to join "a parcel of Robbers, who are come to seize upon their Lands by violence," but his practical nature prevailed. He replied to John Jennings, "Their numbers, I am afraid, are too great to resist." He advised his contacts to avoid resistance and bloodshed while the Penns pursued an official solution in England.[20]

During the summer of 1769, the *Pennsylvania Chronicle* actually welcomed the invaders, who were then peacefully engaged in erecting cabins and a stockade and tending new farms. Of course, this newspaper had been founded by Penn enemies to further the movement for royal government. Perhaps its founders took pleasure in announcing in June 1769 that more than three hundred Connecticut settlers had about two hundred acres under cultivation. The paper reported: "They treat everyone who goes among them with so much Friendship and Hospitality and appear so upright and humane and their Tempers, as engage the Esteem and Respect of all their Visitants." The writer wished them every success.[21]

After Colonel Francis made one more unsuccessful attempt to drive the Yankees off in June, John Penn ordered him to gather a party and join forces with the Northampton County sheriff.[22] By November, Penn officials were finally able to raise a posse big enough to surround the Connecticut fort and call for its surrender. The capitulation agreement stipulated that most of the Yankees would go home but that fourteen would be allowed to remain in their fort to await a final decision by His Majesty, whom both sides believed was the only person who could really resolve the affair.[23]

Throughout the summer of 1769, Thomas Penn had sought help from the British government. After failing to get Lord Hillsborough to prod General Gage into sending an army to remove the Connecticut settlers, he asked John Penn to apply to Gage personally. To more clearly define the trouble for legal minds in England, Thomas requested that John get the Connecticut governor to state definitely whether the settlers had his support. If they did not, "They must be treated as a Banditti settling in defiance of all Law."[24] Thomas Penn also lobbied to get Dyer's old petition heard, certain that it would be summarily dismissed. He optimistically wrote his solicitor, "I hope tho' Connecticut Disclaims any right, we shall recover some Damages of 'em, for presuming to assign our Property as their right."[25] The following summer the Board of Trade finally came to a decision that seemed like a victory for the Penns. The board decided that the New Englanders had settled "in Pennsylvania"—but this meant it was up to the Penn government to evict them or receive them as tenants, which was much easier said than done.

In early 1770 violence erupted again, and this time the Yankee invaders had allies. In January, John Penn had written his uncle that he believed the backcountry Pennsylvanians who were joining the New Englanders were more of a problem than the Connecticut people themselves.[26] In March he reiterated his fears, reporting, "The Paxton Boys have joined themselves to the New Englanders."[27] These were probably not the same Paxton Boys who had marched on Philadelphia in 1764, but in the Penn organization the name had come to designate any rebellious frontier rabble. This particular crew was led by Connecticut settler Zebulon Butler, who had joined forces with Pennsylvania outlaw Lazarus Stewart. They reclaimed their fort and harassed Pennsylvania leaseholders by pulling their houses down and stealing their horses and cattle.

That spring the governor wrote his uncle describing the alarming audacity of the Yankee invaders and their Pennsylvania allies. By then John Penn knew he would receive no help from General Gage, who had refused to interfere in what he considered private land disputes, so the governor was powerless to assist his legitimate settlers. Pennsylvanians were abandoning their settlements to the Yankees, who together with their Paxton musclemen now claimed they would take over all Shamokin. The rebels wore white cockades and had set up their own rudimentary government. John Penn heard they had imprisoned nine Pennsylvania settlers in a fort and were slowly killing them by starvation. They took one prisoner out and slashed open the veins of his arms, and after he bled to death they "stript his body & threw it into a small room among the rest of the persons where they left it to rot." Penn sadly concluded that many others of questionable moral character were joining the outlaws. A magistrate from Lebanon told him people were marching north daily, "all armed, with drums beating & colors flying."[28]

Then, late in October 1770, the tide turned again. News came that the sheriff of Northampton County had launched a surprise attack. He had descended on the Yankee fort at night, his attack wounding many. The intruders were ousted, and the rightful settlers could move back. John Penn incorrectly believed the trouble was finally over. He confidently reported to Thomas Penn that Pennsylvania lawmen had three ringleaders in jail. The offensive expeditions had proven expensive, but John promised his uncle that the government had not and would not "expend a farthing more . . . than is absolutely necessary."[29]

Lazarus Stewart tried but failed to regain the lost territory. He gathered a band of followers from Hanover in Lancaster County, and on December 18, 1770, these outlaws invaded Wyoming, where they broke into dwellings, beat and abused legitimate settlers, and once again drove them from their homes.[30] On January 18, 1771, the Northampton County sheriff raised another posse and forced Stewart and his gang to retreat to a fort. The sheriff ordered them to surrender, but they only replied with threats. At one point Stewart's men requested a parley. Mistakenly thinking they were ready to give up, Nathan Ogden, a member of the posse, approached the fort. There were some reports that he paused to exchange words with a man inside the fort whom he recognized as an old school friend. "I am sorry we are of different parties, I have a regard for you," Ogden told him. The other man replied, "I am sorry it is so, Mr. Ogden."[31] Before they could chat much more, Stewart aimed his musket through a loophole and murdered Ogden "in cool Blood and in the most treacherous Manner," as John Penn put it in his message to the assembly on this subject.[32]

After a shooting match that lasted until dark, Stewart and his men escaped, but only to return in July 1771 with a bigger party that would further torment the Pennsylvania settlers. One of their new victims, a Colonel Asher Clayton, spoke of being warned that Lazarus Stewart and his accomplice Zebulon Butler were on their way to dispossess the Pennsylvania settlers once again. Eighty-two men, women, and children retreated to a blockhouse, sending out scouts and a messenger whom they hoped would reach Philadelphia and bring back help. Clayton parleyed with Butler, who told him the Stewart gang now came on Connecticut's authority and planned to take and keep the land. Clayton suggested that both parties refer the matter to the Penn government, but Butler rejected this out of hand. At midnight on July 27 the Yankees and their allies surrounded the blockhouse, demanding its surrender by morning. If the Pennsylvania settlers refused, "they would blow [Clayton] and the people within to hell." The blockhouse did not surrender, nor did Stewart make good his threat, but the besieged farmers were forced to watch helplessly while their assailants stole their horses, cattle, and possessions.[33]

Because it was harvest time, it proved impossible to raise another posse immediately. Instead, the Penn government sent a party with provisions to relieve the blockhouse. On July 30, at daybreak, about two hundred yards from the fort, the relief party was challenged by a Connecticut sentinel. The party claimed to be friendly, but the sentinel threatened to fire on them. "Fire at your peril!" shouted one of the Pennsylvania men as he raised his firearm. About twenty Connecticut men sprang from hiding, firing muskets and forcing the relief party to dash into the fort under fire. They managed to provision the Pennsylvania settlers for a few more weeks, but on August 15, while a posse was en route only ten miles away, the blockhouse defenders surrendered and were forced once more to leave.[34] The Wyoming Valley was again in Yankee hands, a state of affairs that lasted only until September, when a Northampton County raid managed to take many prisoners but allowed women and children to remain. The Yankees that were left were gradually joined by more Connecticut people the following year.

The conflict with the Yankee settlers cost the Penn government money. The Penns had been forced to sell good land cheap to settlers, whom they could only hope would remain loyal and defend their territory. Penn manors in Wyoming were sold for a fraction of their value. Settlers bought the choice land, but by the end of 1771 they had lost enough horses, cattle, hogs, and fields of grain to make them destitute and desperate. Some petitioned the assembly for relief, while others thought the Penns should compensate their losses. Receiver General Richard Hockley complained that settlers had applied to the Penn government for up to half their purchase price. One submitted a claim for £2,000 for the loss of his house and forty acres of corn. Until they obtained what they called "quiet and certain possession," these settlers claimed they could not complete payments for their grants or pay the Penns any quitrents.[35]

By this time circumstances had forced John Penn to return to England while his brother Richard had taken over as governor. Richard Penn seemed almost delighted to join Hockley in insinuating that the huge claims were all his brother's fault. He told Thomas Penn that the settlers thought they had had John Penn's assurance that no expense would be spared to drive out the Connecticut settlers.[36] His accusations forced John to justify prior expenses by saying it had been reasonable to expect "that every Removal of the Connecticut people would be the last." He had only advocated just compensation for the colonists and Penn officers who had taken part in posses and expeditions to hold the territory. Furthermore, had the Penn government not underwritten such expenses, there would be many more Connecticut settlers in the north. John Penn thought Hockley's letters to his uncle were "very idle." "Some of his insinuations," John charged, "are only excusable upon a plea of Folly or Ignorance."[37]

By the end of 1773 Connecticut officially claimed jurisdiction over the disputed territory. In October, Connecticut commissioners came to Philadelphia hoping Pennsylvania and Connecticut could resolve the issue in America and apply jointly to the crown. The commissioners wanted a line drawn giving Connecticut jurisdiction over the northeastern branch of the Susquehanna. John Penn, once again governor, disdained to grant them even temporary jurisdiction in a place where the Penns firmly believed Yankee squatters had no right to be at all. He advised the commissioners to apply to the crown immediately and threatened that Pennsylvania would make application if they did not.[38] The Connecticut government began making preparations to substantiate their claim; they published a pamphlet explaining in legalistic terms just why the disputed territory was theirs. The Rev. William Smith countered with a pamphlet explaining the Penn position. The only thing more ludicrous and "chimerical" than the Connecticut claims, Smith wrote, was the fact that people were taking them seriously.[39]

While the conflict rose to a province versus province level, conditions in the north slowly stabilized. Cheap land offers had finally lured sufficient buyers, and Pennsylvania settlements were taking firmer root. Although Yankees remained in control of Wyoming and had even sent for their wives and families, Pennsylvanians established themselves on the west branch of the

Susquehanna and elsewhere in Shamokin. In the summer of 1773 New Englanders also tried to settle on the west branch. They confidently expected the support of frontiersmen like the Stewart gang, but instead found magistrates and farmers armed and ready to oppose them. After a short skirmish, the Pennsylvania forces took some prisoners but were forced to release them—the area as yet had no jails. Thwarted Yankees retreated to their settlements on the northeastern branch, still threatening to blossom into a larger force. William Johnson warned Thomas Penn not to be too encouraged. If these intruders were allowed to increase in number, they could be an even bigger problem in the future.[40]

By 1773 the situation in the disputed territory had been stabilized, but the cost to the Penn proprietorship had been enormous. Disputes over land sales had caused rifts among Thomas Penn's appointees. Their constant efforts to defend the proprietorship had diverted John and Thomas Penn from much analysis of the changing relationship between the British government and the American colonies. Their search for solutions in England effectively bound the proprietorship closer to Britain than circumstances might otherwise have dictated. Pennsylvania frontiersmen, already suspicious over the Penn government's apparent attempts to abrogate their rights by trying Frederick Stump in Philadelphia courts, were further alienated from the proprietors when they found it difficult to purchase land in the newly opened territory. A certain element of frontiersman, which the Penns and their officials alternately referred to as "wretched villains," "a lawless rabble," and "the scum of America," had joined forces with outsiders, enabling about two thousand Yankees to settle on Pennsylvania lands. Such frontiersmen had kept the Penn family from profiting from their proprietary right to sell land and establish manors.

The unrest in the north had failed to gain the Penn government any new allies. Although the proprietors were finally at peace with the assembly, except for passing a riot act in 1771 and granting smaller sums for the relief of individuals, the assembly appeared to ignore the situation. They did not frame legislation to raise enough money to pay a military force to remove the intruders. As a result, the Penns were forced to rely on sheriffs and posses that could only slow down the invasion from Connecticut. Nor did the Penns get much help or sympathy from the British government. Once the Board of Trade had declared the disturbances "in Pennsylvania," the Penns had been hamstrung. They were officially prevented from even appealing to the king—until 1773, when Connecticut officially declared that the Wyoming Valley and Shamokin were covered by their charter.

Perhaps most disturbing was the fact that Pennsylvania and Connecticut had been unable to work the matter out between them. Within a few years this type of situation would make Americans wonder whether the United States could exist as a nation. In a few more years it would raise the question of whether the Articles of Confederation were a strong enough bond between the states.

But by the end of 1773 there was a brief lull in the Connecticut issue, and John Penn had other problems to concentrate on. Still, whenever he reflected on the matter he must have remembered the words he had used to describe it to his uncle in 1771. The Connecticut situation, he had written, "has given me more vexation and uneasiness than anything I ever met with before."[41]

10

"A Fortune in the Clouds"

The Dispute After the Death
of Richard Penn Sr.

In the early spring of 1771 Governor John Penn of Pennsylvania received a letter from his uncle informing him that his father was dead of a "fit of the Spasm." Thomas Penn limited his message of sympathy to eight words: "I sincerely condole with you for this loss." The letter continued: "What now remains for us to do is to provide for the carrying on the Affairs of our Government." Of course, John would take his late father's place as joint proprietor of Pennsylvania. Of course, John would return to England immediately. John's brother Richard would fill his position as governor. This, Thomas Penn wrote, "is what I suppose you would wish to do, if you were on the spot here." The letter gave John Penn no opportunity to disagree. His uncle had efficiently enclosed all the necessary paperwork. Only his signature was required. John was not at all sure he wanted to reside permanently in England, but he started packing. After all, his uncle expected him "by the first conveyance after you are ready."[1]

The news of his father's death must have come as a shock. In 1771 anyone might have expected Richard Penn Sr. to outlive his brother Thomas.

Thomas Penn's health had been poor since September 1769, when he had suffered a stroke of palsy that had disabled him seriously. For many months he could neither walk nor hold a pen to write. Yet even at his worst he had never neglected the proprietorship. His officers in Pennsylvania still heard from him, though he was "obliged to make use of Lady Juliana's pen."[2] Luckily, Thomas was wealthy enough to afford what the eighteenth century considered appropriate therapy: he visited several watering places and slowly improved. By March 1770 he informed his contacts that he was ready to apply himself more fully to business, though he found himself unable to attend to all the details he had formerly overseen. After his stroke Thomas was forced to focus his attention on proprietary matters he considered the most pressing—such as the Connecticut Yankees in Pennsylvania.

John Penn heard more details about his father's death from his brother Richard Penn Jr., who had been in England and was with their father when he died. It seemed that during 1770 Richard Penn Sr. had suffered a relapse of an old stomach complaint, but the Penn correspondence does not dwell on this. Perhaps at first it did not seem serious, but Richard Penn Sr. grew steadily worse and on Monday, January 29, 1771, he died. John's brother wrote a brief account of their father's calm and resignation in the face of death and professed himself "afflicted much more so than I could [have] Imagined."[3]

The bulk of Richard Penn's letter was filled with information about his father's will and other business concerns. "You will find he has left you in a princely Manner," Richard wrote John, "Joint Proprietor of Pennsylvania and Heir to the quarter Part of the Province."[4] He continued with news that their sister's husband had inherited the family's house on Cavendish Square in London and an income of £500 to £600 a year during his wife's lifetime. Their sister was now worth almost £10,000 in cash. Poor Richard did not make out nearly so well. He had inherited his father's lands in the Jerseys and whatever cash was left over—in short, he had no immediate source of income. In a later letter, he described his own inheritance as "a Fortune in the Clouds."[5] Richard Penn Sr. and Thomas Penn, however, had lately planned for Richard Jr. to become governor of Pennsylvania, allowing John to take his father's place in England as junior proprietor. The younger Richard Penn informed John of these plans. Like his uncle, he expected no dissent from John: "I flatter Myself I need scarcely solicit your Voice yet as it is certainly my Duty to do it."[6]

Richard Penn had returned to England in 1768 after a failed attempt to follow in his brother's footsteps and marry another daughter of the wealthy

William Allen. William Allen had discouraged Richard's courtship of his younger daughter Margaret, whose dowry, it seemed, would be mostly real estate. It would prove valuable in time—but not to Richard Penn, who would be forced to sell it immediately to provide the couple with money to live on. Richard agreed to stop pursuing Margaret and left for England later that year, perhaps in a huff, perhaps brokenhearted. The *Pennsylvania Chronicle,* a newspaper never particularly friendly to the Penns, had surprisingly kind words upon Richard's departure in October 1768 and spoke of "the great Regret of those who had the Happiness of his Acquaintance."[7]

Because he had captured no American heiress, Richard's financial situation had remained distressed. Even after his father's death gave him the Pennsylvania governorship, he was smart enough to realize that his short-term income depended on his brother's goodwill. In the same letter in which he told John he was taking over the governorship, he humbly begged his brother's "Interest and Favour" and hoped that, until he actually became governor, John would allow him the "usual Bounty."[8]

By the summer of 1771 an idea arose in the minds of certain lawyers and executors of Richard Penn Sr.'s estate in America that Richard Penn Jr. might have a right to a share of the reserved Penn manors that had been surveyed during his father's lifetime. Richard Hockley wrote Thomas Penn that he hoped young Richard would not actually try to claim this property because that would severely complicate the sale of those lands.[9] About a year later, when the Penn brothers were outright quarreling over the issue, John Penn suspected that the original idea was the brainchild of a certain Mr. Hicks, a lawyer and close friend of Richard Penn Jr.[10] After Richard became governor of Pennsylvania, one of his first acts was to try to get Hicks a profitable position in the Penn organization. Other Penn officers, however, thought little of Hicks's capabilities and prevented his career from being as rewarding as Richard Penn intended. It's possible that Hicks had seen a way to do Richard Penn a little favor that might profit him personally in the long run.

Thomas Penn was shocked at the presumption. All Penn manors were part of the Penn proprietorship and had been jointly owned by himself and Richard Penn Sr. As land had been sold, profits were customarily submitted to each of them according to his share in the proprietorship. Thomas Penn had received three-quarters of the money, and Richard Penn Sr. had received the other one-quarter. As far back as 1732 the Pennsylvania proprietors had made an agreement that their shares of the proprietorship would always go to their eldest male heirs in entail. Unless specific, named tracts had been made over to Richard Penn Sr. as an individual, he could not legally have left his share of the reserved Penn manors to anyone but his eldest son.[11]

As soon as John and Anne Penn arrived in England, John met with his brother to discuss the situation. At that time, young Richard assured his brother that he knew their father had had no intention of trying to separate his one-quarter share from the rest of the unsold Penn manors. Richard promised he would make no such claims and together the brothers visited the Penn family solicitor, Henry Wilmot, and talked the matter over before Richard left for America.[12]

Richard Penn arrived in Philadelphia near the end of 1771, his ship greeted by friends and prominent citizens, who conducted him into the city, where happy Philadelphians were once again ringing the church bells in welcome. Lavish entertainments were staged in his honor, and the usual formal addresses of welcome were offered in the city newspapers.[13] Richard proudly wrote his uncle that he had been welcomed by "a vast concourse of People who seemed to express great satisfaction on the Occasion." He had found "all Ranks of people desirous of living upon good terms with me, which disposition I shall endeavor to cultivate."[14]

Richard Penn had always been proud, so it wounded him to learn that the letter he had written to John after their father's death, begging for his brother's favor and bounty, was well known among John Penn's American friends. One of Richard's first letters home complained that this letter was "the common Topic of Conversation in every Beer House in the Town." John's brother-in-law James Allen could quote it almost verbatim and had related its contents to many people. If Richard still harbored a grudge over his loss of Margaret Allen, James's taunting gave him yet another reason to despise the Allen family. It might be the Allen family that Richard Penn alludes to when his letter to John mentions "a few Enemies who have rose up against me, and who I find have been propagating many many malicious Tales in Order to prejudice me in the good Oppinion of the People."[15]

Angry and humiliated, Richard lashed out against his own family. He made Mr. Hicks a council member without seeking Thomas Penn's approval, and he let John Penn know he had decided to claim his father's share of the Penn manors after all.[16] The Penn cash flow was almost immediately obstructed. Edmund Physick, who was by then receiver general, did not want to end up on the wrong side of a family quarrel and refused to give any money to Richard Hockley, who had been promoted to auditor and whose task it was to remit profits to England. Physick wanted to wait either until the claim was

Fig. 1. Thomas Penn (1701/2–1775), who became proprietor of Pennsylvania with his brothers John and Richard after the death of their father, William Penn. The brothers chose Thomas to oversee the financial affairs of the colony. (Courtesy, The Historical Society of Pennsylvania)

Fig. 2. Richard Penn Sr. (1705/6–1771), Thomas's brother and the father of the future Governor John Penn. (Courtesy, The Historical Society of Pennsylvania)

Fig. 3. The Penn coat-of-arms
(Courtesy, The Historic
Society of Pennsylvania

Fig. 4. John Penn (1729–1795),
who was groomed by h
uncle Thomas Penn to
be the governor of
Pennsylvania. He first
traveled to the colony ir
1752 and was appointed
governor in 1763, holdin
the post until 1771 and
again from late 1773 unt
the summer of 1776. He
was Pennsylvania's last
colonial governor.
(Courtesy, The Historic
Society of Pennsylvania

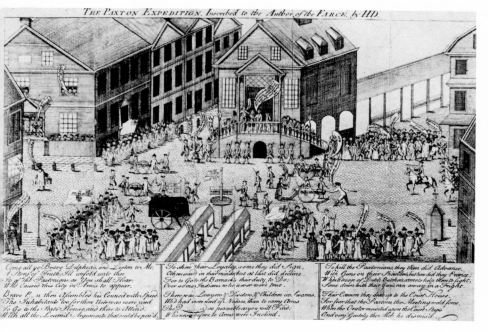

THE PAXTON EXPEDITION, Inscribed to the Author of the Farce, by H.D.

Come all ye Brave Delphia's and Listen to Me, / A Story of Truth, Ill unfold unto thee / ...fo of the Paxtonians, as You shall Hear. / Who Caused this City in Arms to appear. / ... / Brave P....n then Assembled his Council with Speed. / The Inhabitants too, for there Notice was more need / To Go to the State House, and there to Attend / With all the Learn'd Arguments that could be pen'd.

To shew their Loyalty, some they did Sign, / Others won'd in their minds but at last did decline / For to Go to the Barrack's their duty to Do; / Over some Indians who never were true. / There was a Lawyers & Doctors & Children in Swarms, / Who had more need of Nurses, than to carry Arms / She D....so parade as you will Prive: / Who never before to Arms were Inclind.

To kill the Paxtonians, they then did Advance / With Guns on their Shoulders, but how did they Prance; / With whole troops of Dutch Butchers came to help them to fight, / Some down their Guns ran away in a Fright. / Their Cannon they drew up to the Court House, / For fear that the Paxtons, the Meeting wo'ld force. / When the Orator mounted upon the Court-Steps / And very Gentely the Mob, he dismis'd.

Fig. 5.   "The Paxton Expedition," a contemporary cartoon depicting the march of the Paxton Boys in 1764. (Courtesy, The Library Company of Philadelphia)

COOL THOUGHTS

ON THE

PRESENT SITUATION

OF OUR

PUBLIC AFFAIRS.

IN A LETTER TO A FRIEND IN THE COUNTRY.

Fig. 6.   The cover of Ben Franklin's 1764 pamphlet *Cool Thoughts,* in which he advocated the demise of the Penn proprietorship. (Courtesy, The Library Company of Philadelphia)

PHILADELPHIA:

PRINTED BY W. DUNLAP. M, DCC, LXIV.

TO THE
Delaware Pilots.

WE took the Pleasure, some Days since, of kindly admonishing you *to do your Duty*; if per-chance you should meet with the *(Tea,)* SHIP POLLY, CAPTAIN AYRES; a THREE DECKER which is hourly expected.

We have now to add, that Matters ripen fast here; and that *much is expected from those Lads who meet with the Tea Ship*.----There is some Talk of A HANDSOME REWARD FOR THE PILOT WHO GIVES THE FIRST GOOD ACCOUNT OF HER.----How that may be, we cannot *for certain* determine: But ALL agree, that TAR and FEATHERS will be his Portion, who pilots her into this Harbour. And we will answer for ourselves, that, whoever is committed to us, as an Offender against the Rights of *America*, will experience the utmost Ex-ertion of our Abilities; as

THE COMMITTEE FOR TARRING AND FEATHERING.

P. S. We expect you will furnish yourselves with Copies of the foregoing and following Letter; which are printed for this Purpose, that the Pilot who meets with Captain *Ayres* may favor him with a Sight of them.

Committee of Taring and Feathering.

T O
Capt. A Y R E S,

Of the SHIP *P O L L Y*, on a Voyage from *London* to *Philadelphia*.

SIR,

WE are informed that you have, imprudently, taken Charge of a Quantity of Tea; which has been sent out by the *Inaia* Company, *under the Auspices of the Ministry*, as a Trial of *American* Virtue and Re-solution.

Now, as your Cargo, on your Arrival here, will most assuredly bring you into hot water; and as you are perhaps a Stranger *to these Parts*, we have concluded to advise you of the present Situation of Affairs in *Philadelphia*---that, taking Time by the Forelock, you may stop short in your dangerous Errand----secure your Ship against the Rafts of combustible Matter which may be set on Fire, and turned loose against her; and more than all this, that you may preserve your own Person, from the Pitch and Feathers that are pre-pared for you.

In the first Place, we must tell you, that the *Pennsylvanians* are, *to a Man*, passionately fond of Freedom; the Birthright of *Americans*; and at all Events are determined to enjoy it.

That they sincerely believe, no Power on the Face of the Earth has a Right to tax them without their Consent.

That in their Opinion, the Tea in your Custody is designed by the Ministry to enforce such a Tax, which they will undoubtedly oppose; and in so doing, give you every possible Obstruction.

We are nominated to a very disagreeable, but necessary Service.---- To our Care are committed all Offenders against the Rights of *America*; and hapless is he, whose evil Destiny has doomed him to suffer at our Hands.

You are sent out on a diabolical Service; and if you are so foolish and obstinate as to compleat your Voyage; by bringing your Ship to Anchor in this Port; you may run such a Gauntlet, as will induce you, in your last Moments, most heartily to curse those who have made you the Dupe of their Avarice and Ambition.

What think you Captain, of a Halter around your Neck----ten Gallons of liquid Tar decanted on your Pate----with the Feathers of a dozen wild Geese laid over that to enliven your Appearance?

Only think seriously of this----and fly to the Place from whence you came----fly without Hesitation----without the Formality of a Protest----and above all, Captain *Ayres* let us advise you to fly without the wild Geese Feathers.

Your Friends *to serve*

Philadelphia, *Nov.* 27, 1773   THE COMMITTEE *as before subscribed*

Fig. 7.   Broadside from "The Committee for Tarring and Feathering" during the tea crisis, in which Philadelphia's Whigs warn Captain Ayres, and anyone who might help him, not to land any tea in Philadelphia. (Courtesy, The Library Company of Philadelphia)

Fig. 8. "Liberty Triumphant," a contemporary cartoon in which America congratulates herself on her actions during the tea crisis. It is believed to have been published in Philadelphia in 1774. (Courtesy, The Library Company of Philadelphia)

Fig. 9. Lady Juliana Penn (1729–1801), wife of Thomas Penn and mother of the "younger" John Penn "of Stoke." She was the daughter of the first Earl of Pomfret. (Courtesy, The Historical Society of Pennsylvania)

Fig. 10. The "younger" John Penn "of Stoke" (1760–1834). John arrived in Philadelphia in the fall of 1783 to join his older cousin John, the former governor of Pennsylvania, in settling Penn family claims in the aftermath of the Revolution. (Courtesy, The Historical Society of Pennsylvania)

Fig. 11. Lansdowne (the current preferred spelling) was an elegant country estate built by Governor John Penn on the banks of the Schuylkill River in the 1770s. It served as his retreat during much of the American Revolution. (Courtesy, The Historical Society of Pennsylvania)

Fig. 12. Solitude, the mansion built by the younger John Penn during his five-year stay in America from 1783 to 1788. It is still standing on the grounds of the Philadelphia Zoo but is not open to the public. (Courtesy, The Historical Society of Pennsylvania)

Fig. 13.   William Birch's "view" of the port of Philadelphia in the postwar period, first published in 1800. (Courtesy, The Historical Society of Pennsylvania)

resolved or until he was personally indemnified.[17] Both Thomas Penn and John Penn hurried to reassure Physick and got the money moving again.

An exasperated Thomas Penn also tried to explain how Richard Penn might have misunderstood his father's intentions. Richard Penn Sr. had had a deed of trust stipulating that the profit from certain lands was to go to his younger children, but Richard must realize that Richard Sr. could not have left a younger son his own share of the Penn manors. Furthermore, Thomas Penn had double-checked with Richard's mother and sister, and neither thought such a thing had ever entered the mind of his late father.[18]

John Penn was disappointed and distressed at his brother's actions. After John had so willingly handed over his coveted governorship, he had arrived in England to find that his brother had left a trail of debts he was expected to cover. He complained that he would "not be able to discharge [these debts] without living in a garret."[19] John tersely asked Richard Penn to release his claim on the Penn manors. He also wanted assurance that if the matter ever came to a lawsuit, Richard would not enter litigation as governor of Pennsylvania.[20]

Richard Penn answered the letter in July 1772. Since his arrival in America the previous November, his circumstances had changed considerably. He had pursued and married sixteen-year-old Polly Masters, one of the richest heiresses in the province and the daughter of a former assembly member. He proudly informed John Penn, "I have gained a most amiable Woman for my Wife who has brought me a large Fortune." His tone became almost cocky as he informed his brother of his new intentions regarding the Penn manors. "I have not usually been branded with the name of Villain," he wrote. He now insisted that his father had indeed intended him to have his one-quarter share of the Penn manors but that because of his father's "indolent disposition" he had simply never gotten around to changing the agreement of 1732, which he had come to consider unfair to his younger children. Moreover, shortly before his death, Richard Sr. had urged the sale of some reserved manors to convert more of his assets to cash. Hicks was supposed to have been his agent. Richard Penn blamed his brother that no sale had been transacted: "You perhaps can tell why these Orders were not instantly comply'd with." Richard would not give up his claim or resign the governorship. And as for all the furor both John and Thomas Penn had raised about his making Hicks a council member, it "falls short of its aim—he, poor man has paid his debt to Nature." Richard's friend Mr. Hicks was dead.[21]

That same summer of 1772, Thomas Penn must have been doing some careful thinking about the future of the proprietorship and the welfare of the Penn family, and particularly that of his own underage son, also named John.

Remittances in 1769 had been poor, for which Edmund Physick blamed the scarcity of cash, but by fall 1770 they had picked up, and Thomas Penn had been happy to receive "more than common."[22] Sometime in 1771, however, his income level had again been disappointing, although Physick remained hopeful that large sums would be coming in soon. But 1771 had not been a good year in Pennsylvania. The Penn organization had spent heavily trying to remove the Connecticut settlers, and Richard Penn's claim had temporarily stopped the Penn cash flow. By mid-1772 Thomas was almost frantically prodding Richard Penn and Richard Hockley to improve remittances and send more cash. Nor was 1772 a good year for Thomas Penn personally. His health had improved throughout 1771, but in 1772 he spoke of "declining in that bad way in which I was."[23] Anticipating his own death, Thomas foresaw a bleak financial future for his son.

Thomas Penn also began seeing traits in Richard that made him fear Richard would not respect his son's rights as chief proprietor. Richard Penn had appointed his personal friend Hicks to the provincial council without consulting anyone and seemed to be gathering some sort of popular party around himself in Pennsylvania. He had quoted to his uncle a message from the assembly to show that public opinion favored his claim on the Penn manors. When Thomas's son inherited three-quarters of the proprietorship, would Richard Penn join with men like Franklin to further threaten the very existence of the proprietorship? Thomas countered with his own threat: Give up the unfounded claim on the Penn manors, he wrote Richard, or be removed from the governorship.[24]

While his uncle's health suffered in 1772, John became wistfully homesick for America. He wrote his mother's brother: "I am determined not to remain in England, as it neither agrees with my interest or Inclination."[25] To his friend Benjamin Chew he wrote: "Though every thing is higher polished here, yet I cannot help thinking a rational being may enjoy as much or more happiness [in America]. I am so convinced of this, that were I once more landed on your side of the Atlantic, I should never wish to see England again."[26]

It took another year, but by the summer of 1773 John Penn was able to tell Benjamin Chew the happy news that he was on his way back. Thomas Penn had revoked Richard's commission and made John Penn governor once more. Now John was coming home to "extricate [himself] from the difficulties [he] must have been involved in by the Conduct of [his] Brother." Yet for the good of the proprietorship, John Penn did not want to perpetuate the quarrel and had decided to be generous. He offered Richard Penn an income of £500 a year while he, John, continued as governor.[27]

John and Anne Penn reached America in the fall of 1773. Their ship docked in New York and they traveled to Bristol, Pennsylvania, where they were met by ladies and gentlemen who conducted them to town. The following day John's commission was publicly read and the new governor earnestly expressed his desire that "the Ceremony of written Addresses might be dispensed with." He said he did not doubt the goodwill of the people of Pennsylvania.[28] At entertainment at the State House, the merchants of Philadelphia thanked Richard Penn for his administration, saying he had always been a friend to trade. Richard replied that "although [he was] so unexpectedly deprived of the power of being serviceable to [them], in a public manner," he hoped to retain their approval as a private citizen.[29]

John Penn attended the dinner at the State House, and Richard attended another dinner hosted by the mayor of Philadelphia to honor John. Publicly there was no quarrel between the Penn brothers, but privately they were not speaking. John knew all too well that Richard bitterly resented having been replaced as governor. John found him "very violent and . . . determined not to give up his Claim"[30] and unwilling to patch up the quarrel. Richard would not accept the £500 that he feared would make him John Penn's "pensioner."[31] Loyal Penn officers felt threatened by the breach in family solidarity. Richard Hockley wrote Thomas Penn: "God knows how many uneasy hours I have pass'd and the tears I have shed when laid on my pillow, thinking on this unaccountable Ideal Claim."[32]

Even though the Penn family was now torn with internal problems, as proprietors they continued to enjoy their new era of solidarity with the assembly. The *Pennsylvania Chronicle* even mentioned that, shortly after John's arrival in 1773, Lady Juliana Penn sent over a bust of her husband Thomas as a gift to the assembly.[33] The Penns did not pressure the assembly about their border problems because they were still hoping for a long-term resolution in England. Once that was accomplished, it almost seemed that Thomas Penn's worries would be over and he could hand the proprietorship over to his son and nephew with confidence. By the end of 1773 James Tilghman reported that land was once again selling well, and Physick was receiving so much purchase money he hardly had time to manage the rent rolls.[34] The old fears that had risen over the Townshend duties were long forgotten, and it looked as if 1774 would be good financially.

But before the Penn family could ring in the new year, the usually conservative citizens of Pennsylvania surprised them greatly by eagerly joining their fellow Americans in noisy protest over England's new Tea Act.

11

"So Glorious an Exertion of Public Virtue and Spirit"

Opposing the Tea Act in Philadelphia

When John Penn arrived in Pennsylvania in September 1773, his immediate concerns were patching up the quarrel with his brother and finding land on which to build a home so he and Anne could move out of their temporary lodgings in Anne's brother's house. John's initial letters home failed to mention a request the Pennsylvania assembly had received from Virginia, Massachusetts, Connecticut, and Rhode Island to appoint men to a correspondence committee that would investigate Parliament's latest threats to American liberty. Perhaps the governor didn't think this was important, and apparently the assembly didn't consider it too important either. The request had arrived during its summer recess in 1773, and in September assemblymen simply referred it to the new assembly that would be created by upcoming October elections. The new assembly glanced over the request and noted that they considered it "a matter of the greatest Importance to co-operate with the Representatives of the other Colonies in every wise and prudent Measure." Then they ignored the issue until a series of surprising events forced the matter back into the limelight that December.[1]

Unlike in other colonies, neither Pennsylvania's governor nor the assembly saw any reason for concern in Parliament's new "Act to Allow a Drawback of the Duties of Customs on the Exportation of Tea." Unlike the Stamp Act and the Townshend Acts, the Tea Act was not intended as a revenue measure. Ever since the Townshend duties had been repealed, the British government had retained its tax on tea, and many Americans had simply paid it. However, many others bought tea from Holland or drank tea that had been smuggled into American ports. The result was a large inventory of unsold tea for Britain's East India Company. By 1772 the company was having serious financial problems. This crisis threatened other English businesses, and Parliament soon decided to bail out the company with its Tea Act, stipulating that all taxes on tea would be removed except for the modest Townshend duty. The Tea Act was calculated to make the East India Company's tea cheaper than smuggled tea. Several American merchants, commissioned as tea agents to receive and market the tea, would be able to undersell their illegal competition, giving American consumers a favorite commodity at a lower price. From the English point of view, it looked like a good deal all around.

Many Pennsylvanians thought it was a good deal too—except those with Whiggish principles, who saw a danger in meekly receiving the tea and paying the tax that remained due on it. Some merchants tended to agree. Yet they doubted it would be possible to mount a significant protest against something like cheap tea. The Tea Act only promised to hurt the business of tea smugglers, and, besides, the people of Philadelphia were tired of boycotts and the attendant inconveniences.

William Bradford, owner of the London Coffee House and publisher of the *Pennsylvania Journal,* has been credited with rousing Philadelphia's Whigs to action. When merchants told him no one would be interested in protesting the Tea Act, he reportedly replied, "Leave that business to me—I'll collect a town meeting for you—Prepare some resolves;—and,—they shall be executed."[2] Accordingly, prominent Whigs, probably including Thomas Mifflin and Charles Thomson, gathered on the evening of October 14, 1773, to discuss why the Tea Act was such a threat to American liberty. Their argument had far less to do with the tax on tea than with how Parliament planned to raise the revenue. They insisted that the East India Company had no business selling direct to the American public through certain commissioned agents. Commissioned tea agents were the antithesis of healthy competition; they eliminated colonial middlemen and thereby created a monopoly. If England could establish one monopoly, it could establish others. Where would it end? Americans would lose control of their own economy and truly become Parliament's slaves.[3]

Not everyone in Philadelphia shared these sentiments. Those expecting tea commissions did not necessarily agree, and neither did the common people of America. Designated tea agents Abel James and Henry Drinker of the Quaker business firm James & Drinker had heard from a firm called Pigou & Booth in New York that there might be attempts to protest the Tea Act. Yet Pigou & Booth optimistically wrote: "Our private intelligencers inform us that the common people are very slow at apprehending this to be a matter of so much moment as the Smugglers would represent it."[4]

Bradford and his friends realized this too. Without public support the protest would go nowhere, so Whig merchants printed notices inviting Philadelphians to a public meeting on October 16 "to consider what Measures will be necessary to prevent the Landing of a large Quantity of TEA." To encourage attendance, the notice denounced the Tea Act as "a VERY dangerous Attempt to render ineffectual your virtuous Exertions, against the Inroads of Oppression and Slavery."[5] This was the start of an effective propaganda campaign that rallied Philadelphia by stating the problem in the compelling vernacular of popular rights rather than in the dull terms of potential profit and loss to merchants.

The meeting on October 16 was organized by Whig merchants, and Dr. Thomas Cadwalader, from one of Philadelphia's most prominent families, presided. The meeting's resolves were printed in Pennsylvania newspapers. According to their reports, people at the meeting had agreed the Tea Act was "a Tax on the Americans, or levying Contributions on them without their Consent." In short, it was Parliament's underhanded way to get the people to approve taxation without representation. The meeting also resolved that "Whoever shall, directly or indirectly, countenance this Attempt, or in any wise aid or abet in unloading, receiving, or vending the Tea sent . . . is an Enemy to his Country."[6]

This public meeting made Philadelphia the first city in America to oppose the Tea Act, and Philadelphia's tea resolves became the model for other colonies. Even fiery Boston, it seemed, had hesitated to protest. A few days after Philadelphia, Bostonians adopted nearly identical resolves, and years later John Adams admitted that Philadelphia had given them the courage to do so.[7] From New York, Pigou & Booth wrote James & Drinker of their own surprise to find that Philadelphia's protest movement suddenly loomed much larger than New York's.[8]

The meeting on October 16 also established a committee of twelve, which successfully drove a wedge between the Philadelphia tea agents and succeeded in pressing some of them to resign. The committee called at the homes of prospective tea agents, trying to convince these merchants that no good could come of a trade advantage that was becoming so unpopular. They "expressed the united Desire of the City, that they would renounce the Commission and engage not to intermeddle with the Ship or Cargos in any Shape whatever."[9] Quaker merchants Thomas and Isaac Wharton heeded the committee's warning. The Whartons were not sure circumstances would allow them to profit by the advantage their commission promised. They realized that neither Pennsylvania's conservative assembly nor its conservative governor was offering to defend the tea or the tea agents. Thomas Wharton wrote his brother: "It does not seem to me that there is resolution enough in the Executive branch of Government to protect the Property."[10] With no militia or British army troops at his command, there was indeed little John Penn would be able to do if the protest became violent. The Whartons decided it would be better to comply with the committee's demands and resign.

Tea agents who did not comply with the committee's demands quickly became the targets of not-so-subtle threats. Colleagues in New York had advised James and Drinker *not* to resign, lest this strengthen the opposition, so instead James and Drinker equivocated. As yet, no merchant firm had definite proof they had been appointed tea agents, they replied to the committee, so there was really no commission to resign, and should they learn they did have commissions, they would be obliged to perform their duty.[11] To urge them to reconsider, a card addressed to James and Drinker was printed and circulated in Philadelphia. Its ominous wording read: "You have this day received your commission to enslave your native Country; ... WE expect and desire YOU will immediately inform the PUBLIC, by a Line or two to be left at the COFFEE HOUSE, Whether you will, or will not, renounce all Pretensions to execute this Commission? ... THAT WE MAY GOVERN OURSELVES ACCORDINGLY."[12] The tea commissioners may have remembered what had happened during protests against the Stamp Act, when stamp commissioners had been hanged in effigy and their houses and property had been damaged by angry mobs. Eventually all Philadelphia's tea agents resigned, including James and Drinker.

At the end of December the *Pennsylvania Gazette* reported that there had been a second mass meeting that autumn in Philadelphia. Public indignation "rose to such a Heighth," the paper read, that "a great Number of respectable Inhabitants attended; and it appeared to be the unanimous Opinion, that the Entry of the Ship at the Custom-House, or the landing any Part of her Cargo, would be attended with great Danger and Difficulty, and would directly tend to destroy that Peace and Good Order which ought to be preserved."[13]

Everyone wondered what would happen when the ship carrying Philadelphia's consignment of tea reached the city. Exactly how would the committee and the city merchants prevent its captain from landing the tea? The tea ship bound for Philadelphia, the *Polly,* was under the command of a Captain Ayres. The *Gazette* reported that it had sailed from Gravesend on September 27, "having the DETESTED TEA on board." "Americans!" the newspaper cautioned, "be wise—be virtuous."[14] The Whigs echoed this exhortation in a barrage of essays by Mifflin, Thomson, Dr. Benjamin Rush, and later John Dickinson and told the public that all Christendom was watching Philadelphia. One broadside read: "All Europe, nay the whole world, are now attentive to your cause and have, with wonder, heard of the decent, manly and determined conduct of the freemen of America."[15] In his *Pennsylvania Journal* William Bradford promised that the world would see that Philadelphia could not be "frightened, or cajoled out of our Liberty by Nabobs, Ministers, or ministerial Hirelings."[16] Thomas Wharton wrote: "Threats are throw'd out, of destroying the Property, to such a pitch of Zeal are some People rais'd that, I fear the Worst."[17]

Efforts were made to unite Philadelphia against the landing of the tea ship. To ensure that the city's tradesmen supported the Whig merchants, other broadsides and newspaper accounts insisted that this was not just a merchants' issue. If England monopolized America's trade, not only would its merchants fail but so would the trades that supplied the merchants. If "our Merchants are ruined," one broadside warned, "Ship Building ceases."[18] The clergy preached tea sermons. One printed sermon suggested that the only way to evade Parliament's attempts to tax the colonies was to "disuse" the commodities it taxed. It advised Americans to give up drinking tea. Tea drinking, it charged, had always been extravagant and unhealthy and only encouraged women to gather and spread malicious gossip.[19] For those who could not kick the habit, the committee kept the price of Philadelphia's existing tea low by rolling back the inflated prices of some retailers. Citizens were encouraged to report overpriced tea at Bradford's London Coffee House.

Once the tea ship did arrive, everyone knew that the first Philadelphians to have contact with her would be those who operated the pilot boats that brought oceangoing vessels into harbor. Special broadsides were printed just for the Delaware pilots by the self-proclaimed "Committee for Tarring and Feathering." Their first message was relatively tame. "This you may depend on," it read, "that whatever Pilot brings her into this River, such Pilot will be marked for his *treason,* and will never after meet with the least Encouragement in his Business."[20] As the city's emotions rose to a fever pitch, the messages became more strongly worded: "TAR and FEATHERS will be his Portion, who pilots her into this Harbor." This particular broadside continued: "Whoever is committed to us, as an Offender against the Rights of AMERICA, will experience the utmost Exertion of our Abilities, as THE COMMITTEE FOR TARRING AND FEATHERING."[21] The pilots were given a message to forward to Captain Ayres, its language geared to make him sail back to London of his own accord. "What think you Captain, of a Halter around your Neck—ten Gallons of liquid Tar decanted on your Pate—with the Feathers of a dozen wild Geese laid over that to enliven your Appearance?" Ayres was urged to "fly" back to England. Above all, he was advised to "fly without the wild Geese Feathers."[22]

On Christmas Eve the *Gazette* published a special supplement describing what had happened in Boston a few days before. It seemed the "people" had gone to the wharves, boarded the tea ships, hoisted the tea on deck, and tossed it into the harbor.[23] Although they had nobly confined themselves to destroying tea and had refrained from looting the rest of the ships' cargoes, many Philadelphians privately considered such wanton destruction of private property shocking. Thomas Wharton wrote an English colleague that the news had "alarmed the thoughtful Considerate mind."[24]

On Christmas Day the committee, which had been expanded to twenty-four members in the fall, learned that the *Polly* had entered the Delaware River, prompting committee members to make plans to intercept the vessel before it could reach the wharves of Philadelphia. The committee also learned that another commissioned tea agent, Gilbert Barclay, had sailed to America on board the *Polly,* making his way overland to Philadelphia when the ship briefly docked in Chester. Soon after Barclay arrived, committee members called on him. The *Gazette* later reported that Barclay quickly and dramatically resigned "in a Manner which affected every one present." The committee also sent representatives both to Chester and to Gloucester Point, a spot three and a half miles below Philadelphia. Committee members arrived in Chester only to find they had missed the boat, but those at Gloucester Point sighted the *Polly* on December 26, hailed her, and asked Captain Ayres to anchor his vessel at Gloucester Point and come ashore alone to meet with them.[25]

The excitement of the previous months and all the talk of tar and feathers caused a crowd of curious onlookers to gather around the waiting committee members. When the captain complied with the committee's request, this crowd parted solemnly, forming a lane that led Captain Ayres to the waiting committee members. These men carried no buckets of tar or bags of feathers and assured the captain they meant no harm. They asked him to come to the city bringing only the letters he had to deliver and observe for himself that the people had no use for his tea. The captain agreed and went to refresh himself at the London Coffee House. Everywhere he went, the crowd followed. No one wanted to miss whatever drama might unfold. Nevertheless, there was one unpleasant incident: Several boys annoyed the captain with "some small rudeness," but these mischief-makers were quickly silenced by respectable gentlemen.[26]

Captain Ayres called on Thomas Wharton at home and said he would have to register a formal protest if he could not land his cargo. Businessman Wharton understood. When the captain returned to Wharton's house on December 27, he found Wharton had lined up a notary and invited fellow tea agent Jonathan Browne. The captain formally asked whether the agents would receive the tea and pay its freight. Wharton gave a polite answer calculated to give no offense in England: "While the tea belonging to the Hon.ble East India Compy (under your Care) is subject to the Payment of a Duty in America we cannot Act in the Commission which they have been pleas'd to Honor Us with."[27]

Captain Ayres was then invited to a hastily called town meeting. The meeting had been arranged on very short notice, but all the broadsides and newspaper accounts of the previous months guaranteed a good turnout. It was estimated that more than eight thousand people packed themselves into the square near Philadelphia's State House. Some may have come expecting tar and feathers, but the crowd remained orderly. Newspaper accounts reported that the meeting was conducted "with a Decorum and Order worthy [of] the Importance of the Cause."[28] The meeting resolved that Captain Ayres should take the tea back to London. With few other options open, the captain agreed. The Wharton firm and Jonathan Browne generously advanced money for provisions for the *Polly*'s return voyage. Not a thing was to be unloaded from his vessel; other goods that merchants had ordered would be sent back too. Even Thomas Wharton's new carriage, waiting for him on board the *Polly*, would have to be reshipped by another vessel.[29]

Only one day later another crowd followed Captain Ayres to the Arch Street Wharf, where he boarded a pilot boat to take him back to the *Polly*. Tar and feathers were no longer in order. Captain Ayres had proven himself a friend to the liberties of America.[30]

John Penn had arrived in Philadelphia in September 1773 and was in town during all the fervor over the Tea Act. But he apparently ignored it completely. His few letters to England that autumn did not mention the public meetings, the broadsides, Captain Ayres, or the arrival of the *Polly*. Besides his quarrel with his brother and his search for land for a house, he and other Penn officers were deeply involved with the Connecticut settlers and Pennsylvania's other border problems, which must have seemed far more important at the time. In fact, the same issue of one newspaper that carried a detailed account of Captain Ayres's reception also carried news that Connecticut would shortly publish the pamphlet stating that province's claims to lands in northeastern Pennsylvania. Border issues and family problems must have preoccupied the governor to the point where he had no time for what seemed like a tempest in a teapot.

Back in England, Thomas Penn was mystified when he received no word from the governor about the tea affair in Philadelphia. What was worse, Secretary of State Lord Dartmouth was hounding him for information. Thomas's secretary sent John Penn two brief notes: one from Lord Dartmouth to his uncle and the other a reply from Thomas Penn. The note from Lord Dartmouth indicated that His Lordship had stopped by to pay his compliments and was wondering why a ship had arrived from Philadelphia bearing no letter from Pennsylvania's governor on the "late Transactions relative to the Teas." Had Thomas received such a letter by this ship? Thomas Penn's letter apologized for having missed Lord Dartmouth and explained that he had been out taking the air for his declining health when His Lordship had called. He was equally "astonish'd" at the lack of news on a matter of such great importance, but he was sure "the next Ship must certainly bring some."[31]

12

"Keeping Up the Flame"

The Penns and Politics
from 1774 to Lexington

John Penn must have received the two notes from his uncle's secretary just about the same time he received another letter from Lord Dartmouth. Dartmouth tersely declared that England had been insulted by Philadelphia's reception of the *Polly*. He wanted to know why John Penn had been unable to keep order in the province and why the *Polly* had returned without so much as an explanation from the governor. He closed his letter with the ominous phrase "I have too good an opinion to think you inattentive."[1]

John Penn failed to understand why this insignificant tea incident seemed so important and what, if anything, he had been expected to do. He wrote essentially the same message to Lord Dartmouth, Thomas Penn, Lady Juliana, and the family solicitor, Henry Wilmot, about his seeming inaction. He said he had heard that Parliament would not interfere on behalf of the East India Company—and, besides, he had had no instructions. He added that by the time he was aware that the *Polly* had arrived, he had also heard she was leaving. Neither the ship's captain, the tea agents, nor any customs officer had requested his help. There had been no riots and no major problems. Though he warned of dire consequences should Parliament try to enforce the Tea Act, he firmly contended that there was no trouble brewing in Pennsylvania.[2]

By March the commotion seemed to be over. Newspapers were quoting letters from London applauding Philadelphia's sedate conduct during the tea crisis. James Tilghman at the land office wrote Thomas Penn, "There is a perfect calm in politicks," though he added, "Nothing but some unhappy misunderstanding with the mother Country can hurt us."[3] Thomas welcomed this information almost as much as he welcomed the huge remittances he received that spring. He commented, "News from America was never more acceptable than at present."[4]

British authorities were not so pleased by the news they had heard about Boston's destruction of her own tea consignment. Boston would, of course, be punished. Philadelphians learned what Boston's fate would be on May 19, when Paul Revere rode into town and met with the leading merchants who had quickly assembled at the London Coffee House. According to Revere, a vessel had arrived in Boston on May 10 with a copy of the Boston Port Act, which closed the port of Boston to trade. This legislation was followed by other measures that later came to be collectively called the Coercive Acts or the Intolerable Acts. The various measures mandated that the king, not the Massachusetts assembly, would appoint the governor's council, that town meetings would be limited, that troops would be quartered in Boston, that government and customs houses would be removed from Boston, and that customs officers accused of committing crimes in the line of duty would be tried in England. These measures would be effective until Boston paid for the tea its radicals had destroyed.

Many Americans were shocked to learn that England would punish Boston so severely. Closing the city's port meant that thousands of innocent people would suffer. During the course of 1774, James Tilghman had numerous occasions to write Henry Wilmot about Pennsylvania's many boundary problems. His letters often touched on other news. About a month after Paul Revere came to Philadelphia, Tilghman revealed his own reaction to the Boston Port Act and the Coercive Acts: "The late measures have stagger'd me."[5]

Revere had come to Philadelphia hoping to capitalize on just such sentiments and asking that thousands of Pennsylvanians share Boston's suffering by once again instituting a nonimportation agreement. His suggestion was not popular among Philadelphia's wealthy Quaker and Anglican merchants, many of whom considered the Boston Tea Party a clumsy destruction of private property for which that city *should* be made to pay, though perhaps not quite so severely. The Penns in England would have agreed. Certainly they knew what had been going on in Parliament, but they had given their American contacts no advance warning about the Coercive Acts, indicating that they considered them no threat to Pennsylvania. On the opposite side of the issue were emerging radical leaders like Charles Thomson, Joseph Reed, and Thomas Mifflin, who were hoping to rally the city in Boston's support.

The day after Revere arrived in Philadelphia, Reed, Mifflin, and Thomson made plans to manipulate public opinion in Philadelphia. First they decided to enlist the help of popular moderate John Dickinson. They called on him at his home and carefully worked out a strategy for conducting a public meeting to be held that evening at the new City Tavern on Second Street. When their plans were made they parted company, having agreed to arrive separately at the tavern so they could not be accused of having formed a conspiracy.[6] They carried out their plans that evening in the second-story "long room" at the City Tavern, where more than two hundred men had gathered. Reed read the letter Revere had delivered and asked Philadelphia to unite with Boston in common cause. Mifflin and Thomson then vehemently denounced the closing of Boston's port and demanded immediate nonimportation. By this time it was so hot in the crowded room that Thomson fainted, adding to the atmosphere of general hysteria. Conservative merchants shouted their disapproval at an unexpected threat to business. It looked as if the meeting would dissolve in chaos until Reed managed to restore order and urged Dickinson to speak. Dickinson calmly suggested that the governor be petitioned to call the assembly to consider the matter. Compared with an immediate and sudden boycott, this sounded quite reasonable. The squabbling continued a while longer, but the moderates and conservatives were won over. Thomson recovered sufficiently to convince the crowd that a letter of support should be sent to Boston. The meeting also established a committee of correspondence of nineteen members. Most of these men were merchants, and both radical and conservative political viewpoints were represented.[7]

The petition for John Penn to call the assembly was not signed until June 8, but the governor knew what was coming well in advance. He promised Lady Juliana that he would treat the petition as it deserved, noting that sympathy for Boston was still not the prevailing sentiment in Philadelphia. He considered the petition a play for time. "I have however been informed that the movers of this extraordinary measure have no expectation of succeeding in it," he wrote. "Their real design is to gain time by it in order to see what part the other Colonies will take in so critical a Juncture." He added that he was trying to keep tempers cool in Philadelphia but warned, "At present a great number of people are very busy in all the Colonies in keeping up the flame & what will be the end of it, God knows."[8]

The radicals John Penn alluded to were not happy with the number of conservatives on the committee of nineteen. They also wanted to stir up the mechanics whose support had been so helpful in the past. On June 8 a broadside was circulated to the "Manufacturers and Mechanics of Philadelphia," warning in fiery language that "the enemies of liberty . . . have . . . drawn the sword of power against our common freedom" and urging them to attend a meeting to adopt measures to support Boston.[9] The resulting public meeting resolved that the Boston Port Act was oppressive, that a general congress of colonial representatives was needed to restore peace, that Speaker of the House Joseph Galloway should call the assembly, and that a "large and respectable Committee" should be formed to instruct its members. A second public meeting would be held on June 18 at the State House to vote for committee representatives.[10]

It was estimated that about eight thousand people attended the State House meeting, but Thomas Willing and John Dickinson presided, and compromise still prevailed. Like the mechanics' meeting a few days earlier, this meeting resolved that Boston suffered in the common interest and that a Continental Congress was necessary. Yet the committee of nineteen was also expanded to forty-three members, and it has been suggested that, through its expansion, radicals forced their way onto a committee originally organized by merchants. In any case, the new committee was no longer dominated by Philadelphia's merchant princes but generally consisted of younger members of more modest fortune, about one-third of whom were artisans and many of whom were Presbyterians, Baptists, and Lutherans.[11] These men would correspond with county committees and try to choose and instruct delegates to the Continental Congress.

By mid-July, John Penn found it necessary to call the assembly, not because of any committee's demands but because border problems in the west threatened yet another Indian war. He took this step "reluctantly," he reported, fearing the assembly might "enter into resolves that may be irritating & tend to make more uneasiness & widen the breach that is already made." On the other hand, the governor hoped the assembly would prove more moderate than the recent town meetings that might have been triggered by his previous refusal to convene the legislature and that he had been in no position to prevent.[12]

While the assembly sweated over frontier problems, the committee of forty-three held a provincial conference in July with representatives from county committees at Carpenters' Hall. No doubt both groups believed they represented the interests of Pennsylvania. Thomas Willing chaired the provincial conference, Thomson was clerk, but Dickinson guided its thinking. It resolved that Pennsylvania's delegates to the upcoming Continental Congress would advocate a petition but support a nonimportation agreement should the Congress generally desire one. It also resolved that Parliament could not tax Americans. At the nearby State House the assembly agreed to admit representatives from the provincial conference and listen to their resolves. While the assembly agreed that a Continental Congress was necessary, its conservative speaker, Joseph Galloway, ensured that the assembly would name its own committee to instruct Pennsylvania's congressional delegates.[13] Galloway undoubtedly hoped that the Congress would smooth things out with England and probably harbored a few fears about whether Dickinson and his friends posed a threat to his own political career.[14]

At the beginning of the summer, John Penn noted that the public temper was becoming "very warm." People were coming to accept that Boston was suffering for the liberty of all the colonies. By June everyone wanted a Continental Congress to state the colonists' rights and grievances to the throne. John Penn grimly predicted another nonimportation agreement,[15] but after the provincial conference and assembly met he became more confident that all would be well. Yes, there would be a Continental Congress, but Pennsylvania's delegates had been charged to avoid showing disrespect for the mother country. If all the delegates were as wise and cautious, the Congress would prove "moderate" and "cool."[16]

The British ministry had one more unpleasant surprise that summer. Parliament passed the Quebec Act establishing a huge new province stretching south and west to the Mississippi. Quebec would have a civil government with no representative assembly. There would also be special privileges for the Catholic church. Many Americans interpreted the Quebec Act as further punishment for the Boston Tea Party. Connecticut, Massachusetts, and Virginia all had charters naming the Pacific Ocean as their western boundary and stood to lose a great deal of land to Quebec. The establishment of Quebec would also deny British colonists already settled in the area their customary rights. To largely Protestant colonies, it meant a tyrannical government and a corrupt Catholic church on their western frontiers. One Philadelphia newspaper reported a rumor that England planned to raise 30,000 troops in Quebec to fight under Lord North's command. Lord North, it seemed, had sworn to "lay the Americans at his feet."[17] John Penn reported sadly that the radicals were touting the Quebec Act as additional evidence of an evil plot to enslave America.[18]

By then, the Penns in England were so wrapped up in border problems that they failed to anticipate or consider American reaction to the Quebec Act. The Penn family had already lobbied successfully against one of its provisions. Originally, Quebec was to extend to the Ohio River within the boundaries of Pennsylvania. Although the Penns had not yet definitely laid out Pennsylvania's western boundary, they were in a position to realize they could lose some of the land their charter entitled them to and quickly rallied to protest this potential threat to their rights. Parliament then agreed that land already granted would not be reassigned. Quebec's border would coincide with Pennsylvania's western extent.[19] The Penns hoped the Quebec Act would provide the impetus to get Pennsylvania's boundaries firmly established at last. Lady Juliana wrote that the legislation "will have shorten'd that business between Virginia and Pennsylvania and must be an agreeable consideration."[20]

By September 1774 many were anticipating the upcoming Continental Congress, each with his or her own thoughts on what it should accomplish. The American branch of the Penn organization generally favored the idea of a Congress, though some might have shared Lady Juliana's wish that the delegates were meeting in some city other than Philadelphia. The Penns had no fears that the crown or the ministry would blame them for this, but, according to Lady Juliana, "It cannot fail of occasioning noise & disturbances."[21] In England the prospective Congress was being viewed with suspicion. Back in July, Lord Dartmouth had informed John Penn that he hoped Pennsylvania would be an example to the other colonies, reminded him of his duty to uphold British authority, and instructed him to "Defeat any attempt to trample upon and insult the Authority of this Kingdom."[22] In September, Dartmouth added that if the Congress was simply going to state each colony's grievances, these complaints would be more welcome if they came from the colonies individually. He hoped the Congress would not cut off all hope of reconciliation with England.[23]

When delegates to the Continental Congress began arriving, members of the Penn organization became political outsiders, powerless and able to do nothing more than comment and speculate on their actions. John Penn wrote Lady Juliana and her son-in-law, "The ablest & wealthiest men in America are now met at Philadelphia." He found the Virginians to be the "richest" and "ablest" and the most determined to do whatever was necessary to escape being what they termed "slaves."[24] Although these men were John Penn's peers, the governor was careful to take no part in the extralegal Congress. He made sure that Penn solicitor Henry Wilmot knew he had "had no Connection or Intercourse whatever with the Delegates."[25] Richard Penn tried to befriend a number of the delegates. Delegate Caesar Rodney wrote that "Mr. R. Penn is a great friend to the cause of Liberty and has treated the Gentlemen delegates with the greatest Respect." One or another delegate from the Congress dined with him every day. Rodney added a curious sentence: "His brother [John Penn] wishes his station would admit of his acting the same part,"[26] a sentiment John Penn had expressed openly to no one. Yet even Richard Penn's friends did not supply the Penn family with any news about Congress proceedings, because the meetings were behind closed doors. James Tilghman's own brother had come as a delegate and was staying with Tilghman, but still would not reveal what was going on. These secret proceedings must have exasperated the Penns and their officers. Perhaps Tilghman spoke for them all when he wrote: "My Liberty, my Fortune and perhaps my Life may be involved in the matters now in Agitation."[27]

The Continental Congress also made an outsider out of the formidable Joseph Galloway. Galloway perceived two distinct parties among the delegates. The "wealthy" properly wanted to avoid "anarchy," while the "bankrupt" and "the Presbyterians" wanted "mob rule." But Galloway had reason to be bitter. He had planned to be one of the leaders in the Congress, but the Congress had rejected his offer to meet at the State House, choosing Carpenters' Hall instead. Radical Charles Thomson had been chosen clerk, and Galloway's conciliatory "Plan of Union" for a new relationship with England was tabled and ultimately defeated, signaling the start of Galloway's demise as a powerful political leader in Pennsylvania.[28]

Overall, the Continental Congress was disappointing to Pennsylvania's conservatives and moderates. It adopted the Suffolk Resolves, which Paul Revere brought to Philadelphia on September 16. The Suffolk Resolves declared that Parliament's legislation against Massachusetts was unconstitutional and proposed that it be not only ignored but also actively opposed through commercial measures. Although Dickinson's leadership did produce a petition and a declaration of rights, radicals convinced the body to approve the Continental Association, prohibiting imports from Great Britain, the West Indies, and the East India Company as of December 1, 1774, as well as exports from America to those same entities beginning September 1775 — provided the colonies' grievances were not redressed by then. The Continental Association was also a standardized agreement among all the colonies, which meant that Pennsylvania's Quaker and Anglican merchants could no longer frustrate attempts at another boycott of imported goods.

The Continental Association would be enforced by local committees of observation and inspection that now had a quasi-official status. In Philadelphia a new committee of sixty-six members was elected at another public meeting at the State House. Prominent citizens like Joseph Galloway and John Penn might have considered the committee members upstarts and nobodies—they were generally younger men, many of them holding more radical views. To enforce the Continental Association, they would be able to set prices, inspect vessels, and decide whether the merchandise they carried would be stored, auctioned, or shipped back where it came from. The committee of sixty-six began publishing the names of violators in the newspapers. The original idea may have been to let citizens choose not to do business with those who did not comply. But frequently these supposed violators became victims of mob violence, resulting in damage to their property. In general, the merchants complied. For some, business was crippled; others muddled along, still able to pay their debts as long as they could still export.[29]

It was a time of watching, waiting, and anxious speculation for the Penns and their appointees. While the Continental Congress met, Thomas Penn wrote: "America is the general Topic of conversation."[30] Lady Juliana earnestly requested "Intelligence that may be depended on," explaining that the newspapers each said something different.[31] She later added that the accounts she read were "some to their [the Congress's] advantage, and some the contrary. But I think more of the former."[32] At the end of September, Lady Juliana had interesting political news of her own: She informed John Penn that Parliament was being dissolved. John hoped the new Parliament that would replace it at the end of November would be more successful in dealing with the American crisis. He warned that England could no longer expect moderation from America. If Parliament tried to enforce its recent acts, "This Country must be involved in all the horrors of a civil war." The outcome he foresaw was injury for England and ruin for America.[33]

In January, John Penn got a message from Lord Dartmouth suggesting that each colony send its own petitions to the king—a British attempt to destroy what unity the Continental Congress had fostered. The governor recommended this move to the assembly. With practical language that made him sound much like his uncle, John Penn suggested that wisdom "dictates the Use of such Means as are most likely to attain the End proposed" and concluded that individual petitions were "the only proper and constitutional Mode of obtaining Redress."[34] Galloway favored the measure, but Galloway was no longer speaker of the house, nor was he quite so influential in the assembly. Many new delegates had been elected in the fall of 1774. The assembly was also feeling pressure from the members of a second provincial conference, which was meeting simultaneously to further coordinate nonimportation efforts and encourage home manufactures. Following a "debate of considerable length,"[35] the assembly postponed the issue and finally rejected the governor's suggestion, perhaps prompting Galloway's retirement from politics that spring.

In May 1775 John Penn recommended that the assembly consider a reconciliation gesture being proposed by Lord North and recommended by Lord Dartmouth. This measure would not rescind Parliament's assertion that it could extract revenue from the colonies, but it would allow them to make their own annual contributions to the British treasury, essentially taxing themselves. John Penn told the assembly Pennsylvania had been the first colony to receive the proposition and urged them to be wise and take measures that would avoid war. The assembly, now without its conservative leader, had just received a letter from its London agents with a different type of message. The letter implied that Parliament's attitude had not really changed, that it still demanded obedience, and that more regulations were on the way. The assemblymen respectfully rejected the governor's suggestion, telling him they could not desert their sister colonies.[36]

While John Penn struggled in vain to get the assembly to comply with the wishes of British authorities, he also found himself powerless to help local British customs officers who were by then being openly defied. In February 1775 Francis Welch, a tides surveyor, had boarded the schooner *Isabella* at Gloucester Point but found no captain aboard. The mate, John Ritchey, told him the peculiar story that the ship had nothing but ballast in the hold. Welch ordered a search, but the mate brandished a pistol. Both men retired to the cabin, and in this more private setting Ritchey confided that the ship was really full of illegal dry-goods from France. When the ship's captain returned that evening and ordered the anchor up, three unidentified men offered Welch a bribe not to pursue the ship. Welch did pursue, his own small vessel catching up with the *Isabella* around two o'clock in the morning. Welch ordered the pilot to take the vessel back to Philadelphia, but the captain pointed his pistol at the pilot's head and ordered him to continue taking the ship downstream. The *Isabella* had drifted as far as Chester, where Welch landed briefly and sought the help of Chester's justices and sheriff. They refused to get involved. Welch boarded the *Isabella* again as she drifted to New Castle, where he also failed to get help from local customs officers. The captain allowed Welch to remain on board until he was five miles out to sea.

Then he ordered Welch and his men into their own boat and abandoned them, forcing them to row to shore.

John Penn and his council considered Welch's deposition in the spring of 1775, but the governor issued no proclamations. As John Penn saw it, little could be done.[37]

In February 1775 Lady Juliana Penn wrote: "Pray God those in power may be blessed with wisdom and Prudence in their councils."[38] Her choice of words indicates that she, at least, no longer considered the Penn family among the powerful. Events were being shaped by new leaders whom neither the Penn family nor their appointees could influence or control. In one short year the American colonies had cooperated in creating a nonimportation agreement that allowed a new group of Pennsylvania radicals, former political outsiders, to adopt the merchants' old method of forming associations for collective opposition. In Pennsylvania, Anglican and Quaker merchants felt particularly threatened that many of these new leaders were Presbyterians. As self-proclaimed spokespersons for the public good, they were manipulating the province's economy, and their growing power seemed to menace Pennsylvania's long-standing religious freedom. Meanwhile, American leaders in the Continental Congress had boldly questioned the colonies' relationship with England and demanded a return to the relationship they had enjoyed with their mother country before 1763. Parliament might have liked to comply but seemed unable to figure out how to do so. Where would these new leaders take the proprietorship of Pennsylvania? "The times make it almost unsafe to think with moderation," James Tilghman commented.[39]

Like many Pennsylvanians, the Penn family sensed even more changes in the wind, and by early 1775 the Penns had much more to lose than ever before. The public meetings and furor in Philadelphia had not affected their cash flow in the least—in fact, they were suddenly collecting more money than they had in years. John Penn commented, "Amazing sums of money have been received."[40]

While they no doubt hoped their financial situation would not change, members of the Penn family realized that one more devastating personal crisis was about to occur in England. Throughout 1774, Thomas Penn had been anxiously urging all his officers to see that matters relating to his estate were in order. Lady Juliana Penn began writing more of the family letters and kept sending hints that Thomas's health could not be expected to improve. The death of the patriarch was imminent. The Penns would soon have to function without the leadership of Thomas Penn.

13

"Surrounded with Many Vexations"
The Penn Family and the Death of Thomas Penn

The year 1774 was one of illness and death for the Penn organization. Early in the year John Penn heard that Lady Juliana had been dangerously ill and remarked that her loss would have been distressing.[1] James Tilghman also expressed dismay and commended her value, stating, "The Loss of her would be a most unfortunate stroke to that family."[2] That same spring Thomas Penn reported he was as well as he had been in a long time, and by April he was pressuring auditor Richard Hockley for news and remittances with some of his old verve. Yet, by September, Thomas was again too ill to write. The chief proprietor's health received another blow when he heard from Receiver General Edmund Physick that his old friend and loyal auditor Richard Hockley had died on September 13.[3] An ailing Thomas Penn wept when he heard the news. He called his young son John to his side and made him promise to "love, and befriend any descendants of that good Man's."[4]

Lady Juliana observed the health and spirits of her husband and began dropping hints that his own end was near. Although few of the Penns or their officers expressed much emotion in their letters, Lady Juliana knew that many of the men Thomas Penn employed or dealt with in America were fond of him. In October she wrote the Rev. Richard Peters, "I cannot flatter myself that Mr. Penn's state of health is likely to admit of great Amendment."[5] To James Tilghman she explained that Thomas was not in pain, though "recovery from such a disorder, as his, is not to be expected."[6] She wrote John Penn that he grew weaker during the course of the winter,[7] and John took the hint. He assured her that Edmund Physick had the account books in order for whoever would look after the affairs of Thomas's underage son John.[8]

In the meantime, John Penn's dispute with his brother Richard over Richard's claim to the reserved Penn manors had been compounded by Richard's resentment over his loss of the governorship. While this family feud apparently went unnoticed by the general public, those closest to the Penns were well aware of it. John's friend and brother-in-law James Allen observed that Richard had absented himself from the crowd that had gathered to welcome the governor and his wife on their return to Pennsylvania. James Allen suspected that the change in governors would "lay the foundation of a lasting animosity between the brothers."[9] In the spring of 1774, John Penn reported to both his aunt and his uncle that he saw no prospect of ever being on good terms with his brother.[10] Thomas Penn was "exceeding sorry" to hear this news and blamed Richard for the strained relationship.[11]

John Penn took the initiative in trying to bring about a reconciliation. He sent Richard a message via Edmund Physick saying that he only wanted Richard to release the claim on the reserved manors in "mild & friendly Terms."[12] Surprisingly, Richard agreed and had an agent tell Physick he was ready to comply. Physick hurried to obtain a formal quitclaim. To get back on speaking terms, John Penn told Physick that Richard would be received if he should call, although he made it clear that this did not constitute an invitation.[13] At first, Richard refused to humble himself by calling on his brother, and he contended that John Penn was imposing terms he well knew that Richard would never agree to. John stood firm, insisting that he would meet with Richard nowhere but at his own house. John wrote Lady Juliana that Richard "was the first mover in this difference & has used me very ill by the grossest abuse in a very public manner."[14] Richard then avoided the problem by taking his family to the Jersey seaside for two months.

Shortly after he returned in September, Hockley died, and John Penn made another conciliatory gesture by offering his brother a lucrative naval office that Hockley had held. John and Richard then both let their wives test the waters of a new relationship. Edmund Physick reported that the Penn ladies had visited each other, an indication that a complete reconciliation could not be far away.[15] By October 1774 John Penn was able to write that Richard had finally called to thank the governor for the favor of preferment made possible by Hockley's death. The brothers had dined at each other's houses, and Richard now loyally swore that their relationship would never suffer such a breach again.[16]

Those connected with the Penns rejoiced. With Thomas Penn's health failing, and faithful old Penn officers like Hockley succumbing to age and death, they did not need factions in the organization. Even though John Penn had essentially used Hockley's office to buy his brother off, Lady Juliana commended him "for omitting no opportunity which offer'd to effect so desirable an end."[17] John Penn received the congratulations with a classic understatement. In the spring of 1775, after a turbulent fall and winter filled with border problems and Philadelphia politics, he wrote, "[I] am much obliged to you & my Uncle for your kind Congratulations on the reconciliation between me & my Brother, which as you observe was happily timed for I was then surrounded with many vexations, and I do not yet see an end to them."[18]

During Thomas Penn's lingering illness, Lady Juliana stepped in and managed his business affairs just as she had several years before, during his first strokes of palsy. "I have a good deal of Business fallen upon me," she wrote John Penn.[19] Like the typical eighteenth-century woman, Lady Juliana frequently apologized for her lack of ability in doing a man's job. "You will pardon all Blots & Blunders in Mr. Penn's present Secretary for he has nobody yet besides me," she explained to her nephew, adding that she and Thomas had dismissed their former secretary, Mr. Upsdell, after having discovered that he had embezzled several hundred pounds.[20] Despite these hardships, Lady Juliana was determined that her husband's health would not put a stop to proprietary business. She appears to have handled Penn affairs very capably, assuming a role reminiscent of that played by Thomas's mother Hannah during William Penn's long final illness and in the years after his death. Lady Juliana told Penn officers to send her all correspondence, including bills of exchange, assuring Physick that she would be able to draw drafts from Thomas Penn's banker. She also snapped her fingers at Physick, demanding that the quarterly accounts (then several quarters in arrears) be brought up to date. She realized Physick was busy, but she needed the clear statement of Penn finances the quarterly accounts would give her. This would be necessary for her son's guardian "when it shall please God to remove [Thomas Penn]."[21]

Although Lady Juliana was no more insistent or demanding than her husband had been in his better years, Physick may have resented having a woman in charge. He took offense when she seemed to imply that because he was behind in the quarterly accounts he was somehow being negligent and wrote back petulantly that he was working as hard as he could, not only "Morning till Night" but "many of those days that people in general hold sacred." Just because he had not completed the quarterly accounts, it didn't mean the Penn account books in America were not in order.[22] Lady Juliana immediately backed down and became conciliatory. She apologized to Physick for expressing herself so ill and assured him he was not suspected of negligence, that she simply needed complete financial information.[23] Lady Juliana appears to have had no difficulties with any other Penn appointee.

It was Lady Juliana Penn who sent the necessary letters bordered in black to the governor and his brother. On March 22 she informed her nephews that Thomas Penn was dead. After his steady decline over the previous several months, he had suffered his last stroke only two days before. "It pleased God to release him yesterday March 21st in the Evening," Lady Juliana wrote John.[24] Her notes were short and to the point. She had much to do, but she wanted John and Richard to hear the news from no one but herself. In a later letter to her friend Richard Peters she expressed much more sentiment: "By this Misfortune you will know that my children have lost an affectionate Father & I a kind Husband."[25]

News of Thomas Penn's death reached the Penns in America on May 10, 1775. A few days later the citizens of Pennsylvania were officially informed through notices in the press. An obituary in the moderate but consistently Whiggish *Pennsylvania Gazette* credited Thomas with William Penn's "virtues as well as abilities." It noted that Thomas had been principal director of Pennsylvania for half a century, a kind landlord who had encouraged public institutions, and a preserver of Pennsylvania's precious Charter of Privileges. Acknowledging the temper of the times, the obituary also called him a "friend to *universal liberty.*" In general, it commended him for having been a great and good man.[26]

Thomas Penn's death brought a new Penn family member into the spotlight. William Baker, Thomas Penn's son-in-law, had been named trustee for Thomas's personal estate and guardian to his underage children. Baker's wife, the daughter of Thomas and Lady Juliana, had tragically died only about a year after her wedding, but Baker had remained connected with the Penns through the daughter his late wife had borne him. Baker had also conceived a great affection for the Penn family, especially Lady Juliana. As a member of

Parliament, Baker had argued the Penn interests before Parliament in the debate on the Quebec Bill. He had been extremely frustrated on hearing that Parliament would be dissolved, because he would thereby lose his seat. He felt he could happily retire to private life, but he regretted having been cast out of a position in which he could make himself useful to the family. He warmly wrote Lady Juliana: "It is impossible for me to forget my Connection, or my obligations with and to your family, . . . it grieves, it mortifies, it almost distracts me to think I must be thus forcibly driven from the only station in which I could with any effect have it in my power to serve you & yours."[27]

Though Lady Juliana might have developed into an able chief executive for the Penn organization, custom demanded a man in charge, and Lady Juliana was glad for Baker's assistance, especially in the days immediately following Thomas's death. She wrote the Rev. Richard Peters: "It has pleased God to raise us up in England a most active and capable Friend in Mr. Baker, who is Guardian with me to the Children, and without whom I should not have known what to have done."[28] To John Penn she explained that Baker had been like a brother to Thomas's heir. He had also behaved, she wrote, "to myself as a son, ever since the loss of your poor Dear Uncle."[29] To the Rev. William Smith, she added: "We are indeed very happy to have such a Friend as He is. My poor abilities without such a help cd. do but little for my Family."[30]

Thomas Penn had written his will while John's brother Richard Penn Jr. was governor and had not revised it to reflect altered circumstances. The will appointed Richard Penn Jr. and the late Richard Hockley joint American executors. Although John and Richard Penn were finally reconciled, past experience may have made the Penns and their officers hesitant to have Richard involved with family wills. William Baker and Lady Juliana quickly assured Richard Penn that there was little for him to do since his brother was a Penn proprietor and was currently residing in America. Richard was simply instructed to consult with John to see that Thomas Penn's "good ends" were promoted. They made a point of adding that nothing was more important than "the preserving of peace and harmony in the Family."[31]

The Penns may have been relieved to hear Richard Penn was planning to return to England in the summer of 1775 with his wife, her sister, and his wealthy mother-in-law. Richard wrote Lady Juliana: "God be praised! . . . the Happy and advantageous Marriage I have contracted in this country enables me to live like a gentleman in England for which place I intend to Embark this Summer."[32] Perhaps the Penns felt they could keep better control over proud and volatile Richard in England. Lady Juliana wrote she would be very glad to see him.[33]

After Thomas Penn's death, Lady Juliana and William Baker had to accomplish a number of important tasks to ensure the continuation of the proprietorship and the Penn organization. They jointly wrote key officers urging them to continue their service to the family. They worried about an old law passed during Queen Anne's day implying that the crown could interfere in proprietary affairs after the death of a chief proprietor. They sounded out Lord Dartmouth, but concluded the ministry had no plans to create problems. They told John Penn there would be no difficulty recommissioning him as governor.[34] They also hurried to recommission the Penn officers involved in land sales. Until these commissions were finally received by Penn officers in America, the land office was officially closed. Every member of the Penn organization knew this was just a formality, but it was also an opportunity for certain citizens to withhold payments due. Lady Juliana and William Baker admonished the governor to let no one doubt that the same Penn officers would all be recommissioned and continue to do their jobs, particularly those involved in land sales.[35]

The capable leadership of William Baker and Lady Juliana made it seem that the Penns would soon be back to conducting business as usual, at least as far as land and related business issues were concerned. But before all the paperwork was completed, the Penns in England got disturbing news that the market for American land had suddenly become bleak. That autumn, Physick also noted that his current cash reserves would barely cover expenses. He blamed not only the closed doors at the land office but also "the times."[36]

The politics of 1774 and 1775 had finally caught up with the Penns' cash flow, and "the times" would soon affect more than their incomes. Even more devastating changes were to follow.

14

"A Difficult Card to Play"

The Penns, Independence,
and the Pennsylvania Constitution of 1776

In 1775, while the bereaved Penn family worked to maintain their income and make a smooth transition to a new generation of Penn proprietors, politicians on both sides of the Atlantic conspired to ensure that nothing would ever be the same. Just a few weeks after Thomas Penn died, Lady Juliana and William Baker wrote James Tilghman about the legislation they called "the Bill for restraining the Trade of the 5 middle Colonies."[1] This retaliatory action, now known as the Prohibitory Act, essentially stipulated that if the five middle colonies would not trade with England, England would not allow them to trade with anyone else.

Lady Juliana and William Baker anticipated economic repercussions in America and cautioned their appointees to work around it. Receiver General Edmund Physick was advised to remit what cash he had on hand immediately, in case remittances became difficult to send.[2] Tilghman was requested to concentrate collections of arrears in the lower counties (now Delaware). Because the bill would still allow these counties to export their produce and manufactures, settlers there were likely to have more cash.[3] During the summer of 1775, Physick began a litany of complaints that American economy was indeed distressed, making collections difficult. He hoped for better times but did not anticipate immediate changes.[4]

The same spring, the Penns in England heard that violence had erupted in America. The news was no less shocking because it came from far-off Massachusetts. On April 18, 1775, they heard that the British army had begun marching toward Concord, Massachusetts, to seize some gunpowder the colonists had stored there. They got only as far as Lexington when a previously alerted American militia began firing on them. After the British found nothing at Concord, other hastily gathered American militia companies turned their march back to Boston into a bloody retreat. The Penns later heard that on June 17, in an attempt to repress such American opposition, the British had seized a hill the Americans had fortified near Boston. It was said that the Americans had fought bravely at what was then called the Battle of Charlestown, the battle now known as the Battle of Bunker Hill.

The Penn letters exchanged that summer gave further evidence of the family's apprehension and feelings of helplessness. In June, Lady Juliana wrote Physick: "The New and distressful situation in America puts all those any way concerned about it, & in it, at their wits end to conjecture what is to be the end of it; and every Packet brings news more interesting than the last, and tho' we earnestly wish for Letters, we open them with fear."[5] In a letter written just three days later, she thanked Physick for news of Lexington, saying, "I am therefore greatly obliged to you for procuring the Intelligence and be it ever so unpleasant it is more desirable than suspense and Ignorance."[6] In April 1775 John Penn wrote his aunt: "Miserable I am that I can only wish for Peace & harmony without being able to do anything towards their reestablishment: however nothing in my power shall be wanting for this purpose."[7] William Baker could not understand why both sides could not make concessions. He wrote James Tilghman: "Truly I believe the boldest of our Ministers wish to see an End of the Contest, as the more moderate have long since been sick of it. . . . If our People on this Side of the water will abate a little of their dignity, not refusing any proposals which come from the Congress merely because they do not allow the legality of its Constitution, but weighing them such as they may be with a serious view towards Accommodation, and that body [the Congress] are not extravagant in their Demands, a happy end may yet be put to this melancholy scene."[8]

Historians have long defined Lexington and Concord as a kind of watershed after which American resistance became armed rebellion. Even in Pennsylvania, Americans began preparing for war. In Philadelphia, members of the Committee of Observation and Inspection, or the committee of sixty-six, organized to enforce the nonimportation agreement, became the leaders of the city's quickly organized thirty-one militia companies. By the end of April, John Penn informed Lady Juliana: "The people here are forming themselves into companies & are daily exercising in order to be prepared for the worst."[9]

John Penn's letters did not mention that these militia companies were trampling traditional proprietary rights on their parade grounds. The terms of the Penn proprietorship had made William Penn captain general of the province and had given him and his heirs the duty of defending his territory. In 1775 the militia companies spontaneously organized to fight British soldiers not only assumed this role but would also make it impossible for the governor to carry out his other duty: to defend crown authority in Pennsylvania. John Penn also failed to comment when the assembly approved the organization of Pennsylvania's militia companies and voted money for defense, something the Penns were well aware that the assembly had been traditionally reluctant to do.

Middle-class men, artisans, and wage earners joined Pennsylvania's militia companies. They elected their officers and would no longer automatically defer to the wealthy leaders of society. The militia associators, as they came to be called, also wanted to make military service universal and compulsory. At first the rules allowed men who were called into service to send substitutes or pay a small fee. Associators resented the ease with which rich Quakers sent servants as substitutes or willingly paid a fee they could easily afford. Associators pressured the assembly for harsher restrictions.[10] John Penn's brother-in-law James Allen joined a militia company. In his diary, Allen wrote that he would rather associate than be "suspect."[11]

The Committee of Observation and Inspection also increased its pressure on and control over the city's wealthy merchants. In August the committee was expanded to one hundred members, including its most radical members yet. Naturally, its restrictions primarily affected the merchants who made their living through importation. These merchants were expected to bear economic loss uncomplainingly without concessions and without thanks, while Pennsylvania craftsmen actually prospered by fulfilling the contracts the Congress issued to make preparations for war. By the fall of 1775 those who grumbled against nonimportation or the resistance movement were paraded around the city in carts, displayed at the Coffee House, and urged to recant the error of their ways publicly. Radical leaders proved effective in using such humiliation tactics to keep the disaffected quiet.[12]

Even the Penn family was not immune from the direct effects of non-importation. In the spring of 1775, Lady Juliana had had a limited number of prints made from Benjamin West's painting of Penn's Treaty, which had been owned by Thomas Penn, and also had a silver medal struck with the figure of William Penn. She wanted to send these items to important Penn appointees in memory of their service to her husband, but she could find no means to get them to America. Ships' captains bound for the colonies were not accepting parcels. The reason? "So very observant are they to the Non exportation [i.e., America's nonimportation] Agreement," she explained to John Penn.[13]

The colonies were happy, however, to receive Benjamin Franklin that spring after he left England in disgrace. Franklin had obtained and published some letters secretly written by Massachusetts Governor Thomas Hutchinson to a member of Parliament. In these letters, Hutchinson had lashed out at the Boston radicals and suggested they be forcibly restrained. Right after the Boston Tea Party, Solicitor General Alexander Wedderburn of the privy council had formally castigated Franklin as a thief and instigator of riots, and the next day Franklin received a letter relieving him of his job as postmaster general. In March 1775 Franklin returned to America, his political future uncertain. Yet Franklin need not have worried. Philadelphians welcomed him warmly, and the Second Continental Congress reappointed him postmaster general in the American colonies.[14]

When the Continental Congress met in 1775, it pursued what might have seemed like conflicting interests: It made preparations for war while promoting a last-ditch peace effort. Penn officers probably all shared the hope that its delegates would have a "sufficiency of parts" to preserve order. Instead, the Continental Congress established the Continental Army under the command of George Washington. John Penn warily reported that the army quickly attracted thousands of soldiers who were spoiling for a fight.[15] But the Congress also adopted John Dickinson's plan for a humble and dutiful petition to the king—a move that was quite popular in the middle colonies and especially in Pennsylvania, where congressional delegates were still being instructed by the assembly to work for peace and unity. Probably because of Richard Penn's friendships with many members of the Congress, and because he planned to return to England anyway, he was asked to deliver the petition. John Penn tried to second-guess Congress's next move. To William Baker he wrote: "I wish I could give you some Account of the temper of the Congress that could be depended upon. Many of them are very moderate & the Delegates from Boston are not held in so high estimation as they were at first but what they intend to do I cannot tell or whether Moderation or violence will influence the Majority. All thinking sensible people are anxious in the highest degree for peace & quietness."[16]

In a letter to Lady Juliana written the same day, John Penn began predicting the formal downfall of the Penn government. "Our form of government still continues, but I think it cannot last long unless a reconciliation should take place sooner than, how the present appearance of things, there seems reason to hope for. I am much obliged to you for your concern about my Situation which is at present a very disagreeable one, however I shall endeavor to do the best I can, & wish for that peace & happiness which might be again restored if people would suffer themselves to cool." John Penn clearly foresaw the complete loss or arrogation of his position as governor followed by certain war, which he thought could bring only misery to America.[17]

In January 1776 Thomas Paine contributed a new concept to the body of radical thinking with his pamphlet *Common Sense,* which proposed that the American colonies declare their independence from England. His suggestion split the radicals into factions: Those who ardently favored armed resistance could be either pro-independence or anti-independence. The wealthy, even those like James Allen, who had joined militia associations, generally did not favor independence. The Pennsylvania assembly did not favor independence either and continued to instruct its congressional delegates not to vote for it. This frustrated radicals both in Congress and on Philadelphia's Committee of Observation and Inspection, who demanded that a provincial conference, supposedly more representative of the people's will, be called to instruct the delegates.

In light of allegations that they did not truly represent the people, particularly the western settlers, assembly members responded by declaring they would hold a by-election on May 1, 1776, and admit seventeen new members. Both radicals and moderates nominated a ticket for the election. The democratic spirit of the radicals is evident in at least one example of their campaign literature: A sarcastic broadside suggested that the opposition print an "advertisement" signed "the King's judges, the King's Attorneys, and the King's Customs-House Officers." The broadside recommended that these members of society admit they had "grown rich from *nothing at all,* and *engrossed* every Thing to [themselves and] would now willingly *keep* every Thing to [them]selves." Elect the old regime, this broadside warned, and you only help them keep their places and perquisites.[18] Despite such campaigning, the moderate ticket headed by Andrew Allen and promoted by John Dickinson carried the day, making it look as if those who could vote in Pennsylvania would never oust the moderate leaders, who would continue to block independence indefinitely.

Then, on the afternoon of May 7, violence came to Philadelphia and put the issue of independence in a new light. Newspaper accounts reported that on May 7 the British ships *Roebuck,* a man-of-war, and *Liverpool,* a frigate, which had been on patrol at the mouth of the Delaware, began sailing up the river. According to the *Pennsylvania Gazette,* this was "either for the purpose of procuring a supply of fresh water, or [the ships were] on their way to the city." The *Pennsylvania Journal,* which referred to these British ships as "His Majesty's pirates," guessed that the British were sounding the channel in some sort of military preparations. The *Journal* also reported that on May 6 several British had landed in New Jersey and stolen some cattle. Those in charge of the defense of Philadelphia ordered out the city's row galleys, whaleboats armed to protect the city against possible attack. The following afternoon the galleys met and cannonaded the British ships, which returned their fire for about four hours. During the engagement, the *Roebuck* ran aground and the *Liverpool* anchored to cover her. That night, the *Roebuck* managed to float free, but an American schooner called the *Wasp,* which had been chased up Christina Creek by the British ships, escaped and retook a brig previously captured by the *Liverpool.* On May 9 the city galleys renewed their attack "with so much spirit and skill," according to the *Gazette,* that the British ships were forced back downriver to New Castle severely damaged; observers heard their ships' carpenters patching and mending for the following two days. The American galleys were damaged only lightly. The *Journal* commented that the *Roebuck* was one of England's finest warships and wondered what would be said in London when it was heard she had been bested by the provincials in their makeshift vessels.[19]

Philadelphia had panicked during the bombardment. In this city yet untouched by war, frightened citizens had heard the sounds of battle for the first time. Alarm guns warning of imminent attack had been fired in Philadelphia. There had been rumors that New Castle was in flames and that mercenaries were en route to Philadelphia. Those who could afford to do so had made hasty plans to leave town.[20] It suddenly became clear to Philadelphians that there would be war and that Pennsylvania, along with the other colonies, would be attacked by the British.

In the Congress, John Adams used the crisis to forward the cause of independence. He recommended that all colonies rethink any instructions they might have given their delegates preventing them from voting for independence. His motion was defeated, and Pennsylvania moderates continued to insist that their delegates could not be made to vote for independence while Pennsylvania's constitution, the 1701 Charter of Privileges, remained intact. On May 15 John Adams replied by proposing that all governments deriving their authority from the crown be replaced. It was obvious that he had Pennsylvania's government in mind.

In his diary James Allen, then also an assembly member, described how Pennsylvania's moderates had received John Adams's suggestion. Allen wrote that he had been present at the Coffee House when John Adams's proposal of May 15 was read. "In general," he noted, "it was ill received. We stared at each other. My own feelings of indignation were strong." But having already been involved in several heated Coffee House discussions, and feeling the pressure not to voice dissent, Allen found it "necessary to be mute." He also recorded how the assembly belatedly tried to stem the tide by changing their instructions to allow but not compel Pennsylvania's congressional delegates to vote for independence. When the assembly recessed in June, Allen, like other wealthy and formerly powerful men, retreated to his country house in an attempt to escape the disagreeable conflict.[21]

Meanwhile, Philadelphia's Committee of Observation and Inspection carefully orchestrated yet another public meeting in support of Adams's call for a new government in Pennsylvania. On May 20, 1776, between four and five thousand people heeded their call to gather at the State House. Major John Bayard, of the Committee of Observation and Inspection, informed them that the meeting had been called "at the request of a considerable number of respectable citizens." The meeting chairman, Daniel Roberdeau, moved that John Adams's May 15 proposal be read. The *Pennsylvania Gazette* reported, "The people, in testimony to their warmest approbation, gave *three cheers.*" Next, the assembly's former instructions to its congressional delegates were read, while radical leaders suggested that these instructions, which had previously prohibited the delegates from voting for independence, had had "a dangerous tendency to withdraw this province from that *happy union* with the other colonies, which we consider both as our *glory* and our *protection.*" Leaders questioned whether Pennsylvania's government was "competent to the exigencies of our affairs." According to the *Gazette,* the question was unanimously answered "No!" The meeting finally resolved that the committee of Observation and Inspection would organize a provincial conference together with members of provincial committees in the backcountry to determine how to elect delegates to a convention to rewrite Pennsylvania's constitution. It forestalled the obvious alternative of simply having the assembly modify the existing constitution by declaring that the assembly had not been elected for that purpose and could not take the liberty "without assuming *arbitrary power.*"22

The radicals staged the provincial conference as quickly as possible. Their actions may have been spurred by a "remonstrance" signed by some six thousand citizens and received by the assembly on May 29 demanding that the Charter of Privileges be retained.23 On June 18 Philadelphia's Committee of Observation and Inspection met with county committee representatives at Carpenters' Hall. They confirmed that Pennsylvania's government was not "competent" for such times of crisis and proposed a convention to draw up a new constitution for Pennsylvania. They extended suffrage to those who had not previously been able to vote due to restrictions requiring voters to own certain amounts of property. And they denied the vote to those who had been previously published as "enemies to the liberty of America." The net effect was that thousands of associators could vote for the first time but disaffected conservative merchants could not. The provincial conference ensured that the Pennsylvania constitutional convention would be controlled by the radicals.24

During June 1776 Penn officers managed to exchange a few letters for the first time in several months. They complained of having been unable to write because of the political situation, but their letters concentrated on land office problems and their own cash flow and touched little on the imminent demise of the Penn government. William Baker acknowledged that James Tilghman had the land office open again but that people were now paying in "Congress money"—paper money issued by the Continental Congress that would not be recognized as legal tender in England.25 John Penn and Edmund Physick both noted that recent rent collections had netted some money that might have been remitted had they been able to purchase bills of exchange, the Bank of England's more secure paper money, which had been their former vehicle for transferring cash.26 On the topic of politics, John Penn merely alluded to the "present unhappy state of affairs in this Country" and noted that Tilghman's son was leaving to seek his fortune in the East Indies.27

Between June and the opening of the constitutional convention another dramatic event took place in Philadelphia. On July 4 a majority of Pennsylvania's congressional delegates finally voted for independence, and on July 8 the *Pennsylvania Gazette* reported: "The DECLARATION of INDEPENDENCE was proclaimed at the State-House in this city, in the presence of many thousand spectators who testified their approbation by repeated acclamations." Several associators tore the king's coat-of-arms from the State House entrance and took it to the London Coffee House, where radicals burned them later that day.28

Philadelphia's radical leaders celebrated, but they also campaigned to ensure that their newly enfranchised voters would elect the right kind of people to the upcoming constitutional convention. They advised voters to choose no rich or learned people and promised that simple, honest citizens would create a simple, honest government. They probably also wanted to ensure that they had no competition for control of the convention. As a result, when the convention opened on July 15 its ninety-six delegates were mainly farmers and artisans, many with military titles. There were no Penn officers and no recognizable Quakers.

Laws would be made directly by the representatives of the people elected to a single legislative body, and the governor and his council would be replaced by an executive council elected by the assembly. Technically, Pennsylvania's government would not be structured that differently, but the constitution formalized popular rule and abolished the ancient proprietary right to make and execute laws. No public role whatsoever was planned for the Penn family. Under the new regime, suffrage would also be broadened and county officials would be elected at the local level, enabling many new people to enter politics and government.

During the two and a half months of its duration, the constitutional convention also drafted a bill of rights, increased fines for nonassociators, ousted congressional delegates who had not voted for independence, and changed the relatively moderate Committee of Safety into the Council of Safety with more radical members. Among its more controversial actions was the passing of a harsh treason bill declaring that all residents owed loyalty to the newly formed state of Pennsylvania: Citizens who did not take an oath to uphold and accept the new constitution would not be able to vote.[29]

In the privacy of his diary, James Allen expressed his opinion on the constitutional convention and the changes it had wrought. He resented that the convention had illegally assumed all governing powers until even the most radical Whigs protested, forcing them to write a constitution and be done with it. The loyalty oath, he said, had "split the Whigs to pieces" preventing many who did not like the new constitution from voting for new assembly members. As for the new assembly, he contended that few people had voted for its members. Allen remained a member of the old assembly, and in his opinion that now powerless body "finished the Year with some eclat." They met that fall and paid the governor and other officers before disbanding themselves like proper gentlemen.[30]

The Penn family correspondence barely mentioned the new constitution. By the time it was adopted war was clearly inevitable, but it was also logical to think that America's radical Whigs were not going to emerge the victors. Probably thinking that the old order, including the Penn government, would somehow be restored, the Penns concentrated on keeping their collective cash flow from the sale of land as healthy as possible. In September, Edmund Physick managed another letter to England. He sent a newspaper in which the new constitution had been published for public consideration before its hasty adoption on September 28, 1776. Physick did not editorialize on the merits of the constitution, but he did comment that the governor was well. He apologized for the few and insufficient bills of exchange he had been able to scrape together.[31]

In November 1776 Lady Juliana replied to Edmund Physick expressing concern about the untransferable remittances in his hands. "I have had no application from anyone here to supply their Friends in America for no one knows where their Friends may be," she wrote. She also failed to comment on the new constitution, but she did mention that her son John, Pennsylvania's new chief proprietor, was off to the university. She hoped that by the time he completed his education and attained his majority all would be well and peaceful again.[32]

John Penn's surviving letters to England never mention the new constitution, though as former governor he was one of Pennsylvania's most concerned parties. What was John Penn doing during the summer of 1776? A letter John Allen wrote Lady Juliana the following spring gives a clue. Allen wrote from British-occupied New York telling Lady Juliana that John Penn had asked him to relate the truth about his situation—something he himself dared not put on paper. "He has had a difficult card to play," Allen reported, "and has conducted himself hitherto with such prudence as I make no doubt will give entire satisfaction to all his friends." John Penn, the last royal governor in America, "supported the authority of the Crown, in most points, long after it had been lost in every other part of the Continent, and when the frenzy of the people became too high to be opposed, & they had thrown off all allegiance to his Majesty, he thought it proper to retire to his house over Schuylkill, where he has lived in the most private manner."[33]

15

"Very Alarming to the Inhabitants of Those Parts"

Pennsylvania's Border Problems from 1774 to 1776

In the years 1774 to 1776 a great deal of Penn attention was claimed by trouble on the province's frontiers. In the northeast, where the Yankees were already dug in, Connecticut formally sought land that the Penns considered part of their proprietorship, creating renewed bloodshed and confusion. These problems were complicated by new conflicts in the west, where Pennsylvania's border with Virginia had not yet been firmly established. When John Penn retired to Lansdowne, the country estate he had built on the Schuylkill River, he was also surrendering in a losing battle to exercise the Penn family's rights as proprietors and governors on Pennsylvania's frontiers.

The Penns and their appointees had long anticipated that there might be trouble in the west and had made repeated attempts to protect their interests there. In 1754 Pennsylvania had allowed Virginians to establish Fort Pitt, with the understanding that this would not compromise the Penn claim to the land on which it was built.[1] As people took up residence near Fort Pitt, Thomas Penn had observed that some seemed of "very loose character,"[2] and

James Tilghman had speculated that these settlers would prefer Pennsylvania's western boundary to remain unsurveyed indefinitely—that way there were no established counties and they remained out of all legal jurisdiction and could do as they pleased. For exactly the same reason, Tilghman urged that the Pennsylvania/Virginia border be established soon.[3]

In 1772 the Penns planned their petition to the British government to survey a Western boundary. William Penn's old charter had specified a border five degrees west of the Delaware. There had been mention of a line exactly parallel to the Delaware, but Tilghman pointed out the enormous expense of trying to survey every meander in the river. Instead, he suggested several straight lines roughly parallel to the river. Penn solicitor Henry Wilmot advised Thomas Penn that this was a good idea even if some land was lost by it.[4]

While Richard Penn had been serving as governor, Pennsylvania missed an excellent opportunity to strengthen its claims in the west. Lord Hillsborough had ordered General Gage to withdraw from Fort Pitt, which made local settlers fear they would be defenseless against potential Indian attacks. Several groups petitioned the Pennsylvania assembly to garrison the vacant fort with Pennsylvanians.[5] Richard championed the request, but the assembly was no help, questioning whether the western settlers were in any danger at all. They asked him whether "your Honour would acquaint us, whether from any hostile Transactions, or other Circumstances, Government had Reason to believe that there is a Disposition in the Indians to violate the solemn Treaties which have been repeatedly made and ratified between them and His Majesty's colonies?"[6] When Richard was unable to do this, they refused the petitions on the advice of crown Indian agent George Croghan, who convinced them that manning Fort Pitt might provoke exactly the sort of attack it was supposed to prevent.[7]

In 1773 the Pennsylvania proprietors had filed their western boundary petition with the Privy Council and began making actual surveys. In the spring of 1773 Tilghman arranged to survey a line from the Maryland border to the Ohio, and another line running north from Philadelphia that would be the first of the straight lines the planned western boundary would parallel. His work revealed that Fort Pitt would definitely fall within Pennsylvania, but only by a narrow six miles.[8]

Before much work could be completed, the governor of Virginia decided to exploit his own claim to the area. In January 1774 James Tilghman wrote Thomas Penn that Lord Dunmore, then governor of Virginia, "hath taken it into his head, that Pittsburgh is not within Pennsylvania and consequently within the Government of Virginia."[9] To promote his province's interests, Dunmore selected John Connolly, a relative of George Croghan, whom he sent to the western frontier, apparently to make trouble.

Connolly's actions brought violence and confusion to the area around Fort Pitt throughout 1774. John Connolly told the local settlers that what Pennsylvania had named Westmoreland County was really in Virginia and would be renamed Augusta County, and that Fort Pitt would become Fort Dunmore. Connolly declared that he himself would be appointing new magistrates and would act as captain of a local militia.[10] Settlers who had come from Virginia immediately began using Connolly's information as an excuse to stop paying Pennsylvania taxes.[11] But perhaps more disturbing was the news that regularly reached Philadelphia from two local officials, Prothonotary Arthur St. Clair and Justice of the Peace Aneas McKay (sometimes spelled Makay, Mackay, or McKee). These two men told how Connolly had encouraged the Virginia settlers to rise up against the Pennsylvanians. "Our village is become the scene of anarchy and Confusion," McKay wrote John Penn in April.[12]

Throughout 1774 John Penn's council received frequent reports citing specific acts of violence committed or incited by John Connolly. In April a letter from Westmoreland County reported that Connolly had formed a sort of army, a party of "Men without Character and without Fortune."[13] Another report told how this gang of outlaws had gone to the house of Joseph Spear, Esq., where they had found only his servant, a man named William Amberson, busy tying up skins. Connolly insisted that Amberson come with him, and Amberson was willing to go quietly, asking only sufficient time to lock up his master's storeroom. But Connolly seized him violently by the breast and shouted, "Let the Skins and Store go to the Devil, if your Master was here I would serve him in the same manner." Amberson was then marched to Fort Pitt and summarily confined there.[14] A member of Connolly's gang was jailed by a Pennsylvania official for insulting McKay. Connolly's followers retaliated by marching on McKay's house, where they committed "violent outrages" during which Mrs. McKay was wounded on the arm by the thrust of a cutlass.[15] Connolly's men also arrested and jailed various Pennsylvania justices of the peace, intending to transport them to Virginia. Because this would take them away from the area for the entire summer, Justice McKay lamented "the distressing situation of [his] Wife and Children, left here exposed to the Insults and Tyranny of a lawless Mob, whose aim is to subvert Government and enrich themselves with the spoils of their Neighbors."[16]

Extracts of letters from the west were occasionally published in Philadel-

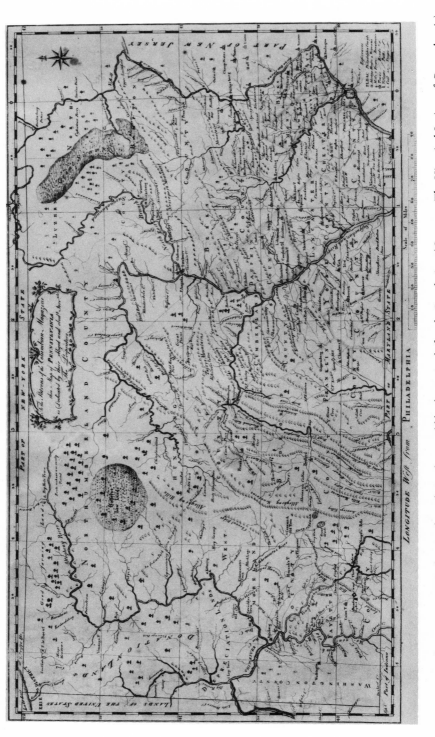

Map 3. Pennsylvania, circa 1787, showing boundaries that would be determined after the Revolution. (Courtesy, The Historical Society of Pennsylvania)

phia newspapers. The *Pennsylvania Gazette* stated that Westmoreland County residents were being "harassed in a manner that cannot be borne." They were daily insulted and abused, their property wantonly seized and they themselves left without recourse. "Do [the Virginians] want provisions?" one writer rhetorically asked. "It is only ordering out a party, to shoot down the first they meet with of any kind. It is true, if an owner appears, they are appraised, and he gets a certificate; — but what is he the better? He must take a journey of 250 miles to *Staunton* [in Virginia], to get it allowed by the Court, and he must take another of the same distance to get his money, and all this to a poor man for perhaps the only cow he has in the world, and on the milk of which an infant family is depending."[17]

In the spring and early summer of 1774, reports from the west also warned of impending troubles among the Indians, with whom the Penn government wanted so much to keep peace. At the end of April it was reported that eleven Delawares and Shawnees were murdered about ninety miles below Pittsburgh by two parties of white men thought to be Virginians.[18] The Shawnees were particularly alarmed to observe Connolly's armed followers and to see Virginians openly building forts on the Ohio in Indian country. The Shawnees had never really been satisfied with the peace of 1764 and seemed eager to meet the apparent challenge offered by Connolly and his followers.[19] In the spring of 1774 there were reports of a skirmish between the Indians and the Virginians, with fatalities on both sides.[20] The *Pennsylvania Journal* warned of the threat this situation posed to all settlers, saying, "We may depend, as soon as [the Indians] strike Virginia they will also fall on us."[21]

However, the Indians did not blame Pennsylvania for their injuries and carefully exempted Pennsylvanians from their hostilities in what has been called Lord Dunmore's War. In fact, Pennsylvania traders whose business took them through the backcountry were often escorted by friendly Indian guides. A newspaper account told how one group of Shawnees escorted some Pennsylvania Indian traders from "the Shawanese towns" to Fort Pitt. Upon their arrival, one of the traders innocently asked Connolly for protection for their Indian guides. Connolly refused it and sent an armed party after the Indians. The Pennsylvania traders helped the Shawnees cross the Allegheny safely. The report concluded: "Connolly's party returned this evening, and both he and they are much enraged at being disappointed in the execution of their murderous purpose."[22]

John Penn concluded that Dunmore actually wanted to provoke an Indian war. He confided to Lady Juliana that Dunmore was "said to be deeply concerned in grants of Land near and I suppose at Fort Pitt."[23] In July, Pennsylvania newspapers reported that a Virginian had received a letter of thanks from Lord Dunmore after starting a quarrel by murdering some Indians.[24] The *Gazette* suggested that Dunmore wanted both Indians and Pennsylvanians to desert the area and stated: "From hence it appears that a scheming party in Virginia are making a tool of their Governor, to execute the plans formed by them for their private emolument, who, being mostly land jobbers, would wish to have those lands."[25] A full-scale Indian war would also justify Virginia's military presence in the area should it be questioned by British authorities.

By the end of 1774 Lord Dunmore's War ended. Newspapers reported a battle between the Virginians and the Indians at a river called the Great Kanhawa, where Virginians had been building forts. One hundred and fifty Virginians were killed or injured, while only nineteen Indians fell.[26] Less than a month later Virginia made peace with the Shawnees. A deposition received from the west in February 1775 stated that western settlers no longer feared Indian war.[27] John Penn received this news cautiously and wondered how the Six Nations would react, because the Shawnee treaty had given Dunmore certain lands without their approval.[28]

John Penn made many attempts to deal reasonably with Lord Dunmore. In January 1774 he wrote Dunmore that Connolly's actions were "a great Surprise to me, as well as very alarming to the Inhabitants of those Parts" and informed him that Fort Pitt was indeed within Pennsylvania. If Dunmore disagreed, he should join Pennsylvania in establishing a temporary line of jurisdiction until the King in Council granted commissions to run Pennsylvania's western boundary.[29] Dunmore justified all his and Connolly's actions by reminding him that Virginia had erected and manned Fort Pitt to defend the area against the French. Back then the Pennsylvania assembly had refused to help because its members had not been sure whether the area would fall within Pennsylvania. "I will take the Liberty of endeavoring to set you right in some matters which you do not seem to be fully informed of," John Penn wrote back. He told Dunmore how Thomas Penn had obtained written assurances from Virginia's former governor that Fort Pitt would in no way prejudice Pennsylvania's claim to the area.[30] John Penn also protested when Dunmore established an office to sell western land, again imploring him to let the matter be settled by higher authorities in England and in the meantime to calm rather than incite His Majesty's frontier subjects.[31] John Penn also pleaded with Dunmore not to allow Connolly to provoke the Indians.[32]

Dunmore refused to listen or cooperate with the Penn government. His attitude is evident in the way he received James Tilghman and Andrew Allen when they visited Williamsburg in 1774. The ultimate objective of these Penn government emissaries was to keep peace on the frontier for as long as it took the crown to grant commissions to survey the Pennsylvania-Virginia border. Their more immediate objective was to get Dunmore to understand both the surveys Tilghman had already administered and his proposed western boundary consisting of lines parallel to the Delaware. Tilghman and Allen also hoped to get Dunmore to join Pennsylvania in establishing a temporary line of jurisdiction, but despite their best efforts Dunmore continued claiming that Virginia had first exercised jurisdiction in the west. He would agree to nothing unless Pennsylvania gave up all claim to Fort Pitt, and he himself would not relinquish Fort Pitt without His Majesty's express order. And while Dunmore would be happy to apply for commissions to run border lines, he refused to bear any part of the expenses. Tilghman and Allen gave up and returned to Philadelphia.[33]

Historians conjecture that when John Penn called the assembly into special session during the summer of 1774 his justification of Indian trouble was just an excuse. They contend that the governor was actually worried about political events and the impending Continental Congress. Yet during the summer of 1774 the threat of Indian war in the west was very real. John Penn was extremely concerned about John Connolly and his gang of followers, whom he later described as "the Greatest Rascals that could be mustered on the Frontiers."[34] Pennsylvania's western settlers had petitioned the governor for protection from potential Indian attacks, and John Penn needed the assembly to approve funds. As he wrote to Lady Juliana, "I have it not in my power to do without the assistance of the Assembly as I cannot dispose of sixpence of the publick money. I had refused to call the Assembly upon an application from the Inhabitants in consequence of the Act of Parliament for shutting up the Port of Boston, but find upon this occasion I cannot avoid it; indeed I could not answer it to my own conscience, if the Indians should fall upon the back settlers, as may probably be the case."[35]

When the assembly met, the governor explained that Westmoreland County citizens had raised a party of rangers to keep the peace. He had already supplied these rangers with arms and ammunition, certain the assembly would approve this expense.[36] The assembly agreed that the situation was critical and voted to finance two hundred rangers until September if needed. The assembly minutes noted: "The House with Horror look upon the frequent Murders that have been of late committed on some of the Western Indians."[37] It also voted money for public buildings, specifically frontier courthouses and jails.[38]

In addition to provisioning rangers and calling the assembly, John Penn did everything else in his power to quiet the western frontier. He issued proclamations contradicting Dunmore's claim to the area, but these were ignored. Many people assumed that Dunmore was acting with the support of the British government—surely no one could be so brazen without official sanction.[39] Penn also sent messages to the Indians. As he explained to the assembly in 1774, he had already assured the Indians that "these Outrages had been committed by wicked People without the Knowledge or Countenance of any of the English governments."[40] Perhaps the governor's most effective action was to establish a town on the proprietary manor at Kittanning to accommodate Indian traders, an action that also helped assure the Shawnees that Pennsylvania wanted to maintain friendly relations. Arthur St. Clair thanked the governor for his efforts.[41]

Ironically, events leading up to the American Revolution finally calmed the unrest in the west. By April 1775 John Penn gave Lady Juliana the good news that the Virginians were becoming less troublesome. Westmoreland County court sessions had actually been held in peace.[42] It seems that Dunmore had been accused of trying to incite a slave uprising against the Virginia Patriots and was forced to abandon Williamsburg and take refuge on a British ship. Later that year, Connolly, on his way to join the British army, was captured in Maryland and spent the next five years of his life in colonial prisons. The revolutionary government of Virginia then dropped the issue of jurisdiction around Fort Pitt during the fall of 1775 in order to promote a spirit of unity among the colonial representatives to the Continental Congress.[43]

The Penns were lucky that the west settled down in 1775 because, that same year, the situation in Shamokin and the Wyoming Valley exploded into renewed violence. When John Penn returned to America in 1773, there had been relative peace and order in northeastern Pennsylvania. As he mentioned to Lady Juliana, "When I arrived here it was expected they [the Connecticut settlers] would give up their claim every day."[44] All that changed in 1774, when Governor Jonathan Trumbull of Connecticut notified John Penn that Connecticut had incorporated land on the Delaware and on the eastern branch of the Susquehanna into something they called Litchfield Township, which was annexed to a Connecticut county also named Westmoreland. Connecticut gave this new township power to appoint its own officers. Connecticut settlers Zebulon Butler and Nathan Dennison set themselves up as justices of the peace. By April, John Penn reported that this official Connecticut claim "has given great Spirits to the Settlers, the number of whom by the last accounts were more than a thousand & they are daily encreasing, & if a speedy Determination is not got of this affair . . . they will overrun a great part of the Province."[45] Penn officers soon reported that Connecticut intruders were once again dispossessing Pennsylvania settlers and creating numerous other disturbances.

By the fall, it seemed that more bloodshed was imminent. In September 1775 there was a message that three hundred armed Connecticut settlers commanded by Zebulon Butler had gone to reinforce a Connecticut settlement on the west branch of the Susquehanna at a place called Friedland's Mill, about twelve or thirteen miles from Sunbury, the town that had been established in the forks of the Susquehanna River.[46] These Connecticut settlers wrote to local official Colonel William Plunket explaining their intent to settle on vacant land and to be governed by the laws of Connecticut.[47] They claimed they intended no hostilities, but Colonel Plunket organized a militia and took some of them prisoner.[48] In November the speaker of the Pennsylvania assembly received word that two magistrates and a sheriff had arranged a meeting with Butler and other leaders to ask them to submit to Pennsylvania law. Butler and his cohorts angrily replied that they "despised the Laws of that Province, and would never submit to them, unless compelled by Force."[49]

John Penn was convinced that only Massachusetts was siding with Connecticut in their unlikely claim and hoped that the Continental Congress might have a solution. In the fall of 1775 the Congress appointed a committee to hear both sides of the story. At the outset the committee declared: "It was not the Intention of the Congress to take upon them the Decision of any Matters touching the Merits of the Controversy" but to "devise some Way by which the Recommendation and Authority of the Congress may be reasonably interposed for keeping the Peace till a Decision of this Matter."[50] The Connecticut delegates proposed a temporary line of jurisdiction to unify the colonies in their resistance efforts, but this was one offer the Pennsylvania delegates refused even to consider.

When the Pennsylvania assembly considered the stalemated outcome of the Congress hearings, it also rejected the idea of a temporary line that would give Connecticut jurisdiction in a place where Yankee squatters so clearly had no right to be. The assembly advocated a final decision by the King in Council but would allow the Yankees "to enjoy their present Settlement till a Determination of this Controversy by the King in Council; provided Assurance be given that they will abide by that Determination." If such an agreement could not be concluded, the assembly agreed to "concur with the

Governor in every reasonable Measure for protecting and supporting the Inhabitants of the Said Counties."[51]

Accordingly, in November 1775, John Penn authorized the Penn government's final attempt to dislodge the Yankees. He instructed Colonel William Plunket and other Northumberland County justices of the peace to use "utmost diligence and Activity, in putting the laws of this Province in Execution, throughout the county of Northumberland," assuring them that the house would cover their expenses.[52]

Upon receiving his orders, Plunket organized what has been called Plunket's Expedition. He mustered between five and seven hundred men at Fort Augusta near Sunbury. They marched on December 15, their progress reported to Zebulon Butler by Yankee scouts. Bad weather resulted in their taking five days to reach Nescopeck Creek. Butler had prepared to meet them in the vicinity of Harvey's Creek, where he deployed some four hundred men on one side of the creek, erecting log and stone breastworks at a place of natural defense called Rampart Rocks. Butler ordered his Pennsylvania ally, the infamous Lazarus Stewart, to the other side of the river, where he might have a chance to ambush Plunket as he advanced. Plunket advanced on Butler's defenses but was driven back, taking several casualties. Unable to dislodge Butler, Plunket decided to cross the river secretly at night and march on the town of Wilkes-Barre, but as his men tried to cross the river in detachments thick ice slowed them down and alerted Lazarus Stewart. Stewart fired on Plunket's men, inflicting casualties and forcing their boats into a channel, where they were sucked into rapids. After one more unsuccessful attempt to storm Rampart Rocks on Christmas Day, Plunket gave up and retreated, contenting himself with looting a number of Yankee homes on his way.[53]

On December 27 Butler wrote a friend in Connecticut: "We have lately had a visitation by a body of Tories."[54] During the summer of 1775, Connecticut delegates to the Continental Congress had written Yankee leaders to make peace with Pennsylvania in order to unite against England. The Connecticut settlers had agreed to make "accommodations" and to ask Pennsylvanians to help them defend the area in case of British attack. A Yankee Committee of Correspondence and Inspection was formed, and Yankees tried to force Pennsylvanians to associate in militia companies under Connecticut articles, implying that they were Tories if they refused. After Plunket's Expedition the main objective of the Yankee militia became defending Connecticut settlers against additional "Tory raids." Connecticut settlers later used America's treason laws to further harass Pennsylvania settlers. During the American Revolution the conflict in the northeast remained the same, but both parties acquired new names to call one another.[55]

For two years the Penn government had failed to protect the proprietorship against increasingly bold incursions on Pennsylvania's frontiers. Pennsylvania settlers had been helpless in the west against Connolly's outrages, while only discrimination on the part of the Indians saved Pennsylvania lives during Lord Dunmore's War. In the northeast the best efforts of Penn appointees had been insufficient to drive off the Connecticut invaders. While Pennsylvania's new constitution had deprived the Penns of their right to govern Pennsylvania, officials and settlers from other American provinces were nibbling away at proprietary land.

Pennsylvania's border problems did make the newspapers in 1774 and 1775, but they never received as thorough an analysis as other contemporary political issues. Philadelphians were either not interested or too ill-informed to care much about these matters. It is also possible that Whig leaders in the city purposely suppressed news of such frontier events as Plunket's Expedition, which might have raised the question of whether the colonies could effectively cooperate without the higher authority of the British government.

Throughout these difficult years, the Penns continued to look confidently to England for an ultimate solution to their border problems, but England failed them on both frontiers. The Board of Trade discussed the Penn petition to survey a western boundary in the spring of 1775, but their meeting dissolved into arguments about whether Fort Pitt was really in Pennsylvania. In the interests of peace, the Penns had offered to adhere to a temporary line of jurisdiction, but they worried that once such a line was established Dunmore would never consent to fix the true boundary.[56] William Baker explained to John Penn why some board members argued against Penn interests. No one in England was siding with Lord Dunmore, but many important people in authority were suspicious of proprietorships in general. Others had "a notion that the colonies [were] less likely to resist the mother Country in proportion as they [were] more embroiled with one another."[57]

John Penn called Lord Dunmore "the strangest man in the world"[58] and urged a personal complaint against him with the crown. Lady Juliana declined, replying, "This Family have at present a sufficiency of business upon their hands."[59] However, John did manage to get Lord Dartmouth to reprimand Dunmore—a political setback for which Dunmore never forgave Penn.[60]

In the case of the Yankee settlers, the Penns fully expected that England's ultimate decision would favor them, but such a decision was delayed again and again. In September 1774 Lady Juliana reported that their petition against Connecticut was before the privy council. Unfortunately, she also noted that because the boards were all near adjournment no immediate action could be expected.[61] In July 1775 solicitor Henry Wilmot reported to Baker that he had been to the Board of Trade regarding their petition. At that time he believed it would be winter before the board reached a decision, commenting, "And in what Situation America will be at that Time, God only knows."[62] In November, Wilmot reported that the Board of Trade had been reorganized and was not sitting. It would soon have a new head, and the Penns would have to begin all their arguments again. He could no longer guess when the board would review the Pennsylvania-Connecticut situation.[63] In January 1776 Wilmot reported that the board had pigeonholed their case for at least another three months and would probably wait until the larger question of the contest between England and America was resolved. He added ominously, "If the Event of the Dispute is, that America is to be Independent of this Country, it never will be Decided here at all."[64]

During the same trying years, the Penns attempted to end yet another controversy regarding Pennsylvania's southern border with Maryland. This particular boundary had been a problem since the days of Thomas Penn's youth. Compared with the enormous problems the Penns faced elsewhere, by the years immediately preceding the Revolution it was no more than a minor annoyance. However, the Penn comments about it are particularly revealing of their opinions regarding England's handling of colonial affairs in general.

Back in 1732 Lord Baltimore had signed an agreement recognizing Pennsylvania's southern border as a line fifteen miles south of Philadelphia, but a subsequent visit to America quickly convinced him he had given up too much. At his direction, commissioners appointed by Maryland to survey this border had obstructed the work while Lord Baltimore returned to London to demand that the king transfer control of Pennsylvania's lower counties (now the state of Delaware) to Maryland. Although the Duke of York had long since awarded these counties to William Penn to give Pennsylvania access to the sea, Lord Baltimore claimed that the land belonged by rights in his own proprietorship. The Privy Council had merely suggested that either party might begin a suit in Chancery to determine the exact location of the Maryland-Pennsylvania border. On June 21, 1735, the Penns had filed such a suit, initiating another legal battle that had dragged on for fifteen years until a weary Lord Baltimore had finally agreed to appoint new commissioners to run a definite boundary.[65]

Surveyors Charles Mason and Jeremiah Dixon had been commissioned to survey the boundary in 1760. Thomas Penn had communicated with them frequently, sending them the latest equipment from Europe and emphasizing that he wanted the line run with "great exactness."[66] He had elaborate marking stones made in England. Some were marked with an "M" on one side and a "P" on the other, while fancier ones had the Penn coat-of-arms on one side and Lord Baltimore's arms on the reverse. Despite Thomas's repeated urging, the surveyor's work had crawled along for nine years, occasionally halting completely when Mason and Dixon discovered that the Indians would not let them work in certain areas. Surveying the boundary had also been extremely expensive. At one point Thomas Penn testily demanded that Receiver General Richard Hockley check Mason and Dixon's accounts, saying, "I want much to know, what they can lay out so much money for."[67] It had been summer 1769 before the crown confirmed the Pennsylvania-Maryland boundary and Council President James Hamilton could congratulate Thomas Penn that the "troublesome and expensive controversy" was finally over.[68]

Before the land could be settled with law-abiding citizens, the governors of Maryland and Pennsylvania had to agree on their respective jurisdictions. John Penn had already tried and failed to get the governor of Maryland to cooperate. In 1774, after Pennsylvania settlers near the Mason-Dixon line petitioned John Penn to extend Pennsylvania's jurisdiction to the line itself, John had simply issued a proclamation to that effect.

John Penn was then instructed by Lord Dartmouth *not* to do exactly what he had just done. It seemed that the heirs of the late Lord Baltimore had not yet ratified the Mason-Dixon line. John was forced to rescind his proclamation, but he also protested to Lord Dartmouth that the Mason-Dixon line had finally resolved a dispute of ninety years duration and that reopening such a controversy would benefit no one. He also mentioned that he had issued his proclamation at the request of local settlers solely in the interest of keeping peace.[69] To Henry Wilmot, John Penn voiced his suspicion that Maryland's Governor Eden had not supplied Lord Dartmouth with full and correct information.[70]

William Baker wrote James Tilghman that he agreed with John Penn, noting that this was just one more example showing "on how weak a foundation all the measures of Government are Built." It had been Baker's experience that British officials frequently based important decisions deeply affecting the colonies on "the very trifling application of interested persons." Such decisions were often the wrong ones. "They think they are doing business," Baker wrote, "by thus getting rid of it. But it returns upon them, as might reasonably be expected, in an Accumulated degree, marking their counsels with instability, and the Authors of them with shame."[71]

16

"Calm Spectator of the Civil War"

Pennsylvania as a Commonwealth,
John Penn as Private Citizen

There is little documentary evidence on how John Penn spent his first year of retirement at Lansdowne. Until he wrote his private account of his arrest and exile during the summer of 1777, he put little in writing that survives. Yet his thoughts immediately following publication of the Declaration of Independence and the new constitution of Pennsylvania are suggested by the diary kept by his brother-in-law, James Allen, another formerly wealthy and influential man. Like John Penn, James Allen also retired to his country house in 1776, a place he called Trout Hall (now in Allentown), where he proposed to wait out the struggle like a gentleman. "During October & November I remained at Trout-hall a calm spectator of the civil War," Allen wrote.[1]

Late 1776 and early 1777 were anything but calm for the revolutionary government of Pennsylvania. The fall elections in 1776 clearly showed that support for the new constitution was not universal. Even though the new regime had decreed that annual elections would be held in November, conservative citizens in Bucks and Chester counties held their regular assembly elections in October as though nothing had changed.[2] James Allen reported that voting was light.[3] Nevertheless, the election held on November 5 brought new people to power; the new assembly was dominated by Presbyterians, and Quakers were in the minority. The assembly did, however, elect John Jacobs, one of its few remaining Quakers, as speaker.[4]

A political faction formed, united by its opposition to Pennsylvania's new constitution. Its members were largely prosperous conservative and moderate merchants. Their major complaint was that the new constitution had not created a legislative upper house to counteract measures that the new assembly might take. Also, those who wanted to vote were required to take an oath promising to uphold the constitution. This precluded all change, which was especially disturbing because the new constitution had never been ratified by the general public.[5]

Anticonstitutionalists quickly organized committees and public meetings to protest. One public meeting was held on October 17, 1776, and a second one, held on October 21, was so long it had to be continued the following day. Anticonstitutionalists used such meetings to urge the people to elect representatives who would revise the constitution despite the oath.[6] In the new legislature, anticonstitutionalists formed a minority but used their strength to block quorums and thereby make the assembly useless for many months. As James Allen wrote, "The minority who disliked the Frame threatened to leave the rest if they proceeded to business."[7]

When many justices and lawyers who were members of the old elite refused to support the new government, Pennsylvania's judicial branch of government ceased to function too. Allen reported that, since the summer of 1776, "we have ever since continued without Justice, in a State of nature."[8] Thomas McKean was sworn in as chief justice in September 1776, but the courts did not open until the following spring. In the meantime, radical patriots held their own trials at the Indian Queen Tavern, and those who did not support independence were hauled in on charges of having performed such acts of disloyalty as raising a toast to the king.[9]

In January 1777 Allen wrote: "This Province is now Governed by the Council of Safety."[10] Pennsylvania's Council of Safety was led by the relatively moderate Thomas Wharton, a prosperous merchant associated with the Anglican community. In July 1776 the Council of Safety had succeeded the province's Committee of Safety originally organized in 1775 under the presidency of Benjamin Franklin to coordinate defense efforts and act as an administrative agency for Pennsylvania's militiamen. The council would continue to function until the end of 1777.[11]

The commonwealth's government was in such confusion that the Congress threatened to step in and take over. Perhaps this prompted the squabbling factions in the assembly to come to an agreement. Anticonstitutionalists agreed to attend sessions if the assembly would later vote for a new constitution. Constitutionalists later reneged on this agreement, causing anticonstitutionalists to withdraw once again from government—but not before the assembly had organized its Supreme Executive Council, which would form the executive branch of government. Thomas Wharton was elected president of the council, George Bryan was elected vice-president, Timothy Matlack was elected secretary, and David Rittenhouse was chosen treasurer. All four officers were constitutionalists except for Wharton, who had accepted the position for the practical purpose of getting some sort of government moving.[12] Anticonstitutionalists noted that, once the new government began to function, the new people in power were quick to take advantage of the patronage positions they could give away to reward supporters all over the state, just as the Penns used to do. One anticonstitutionalist wrote: "The clamors of the red-hot patriots have subsided into easy places and offices of profit."[13]

Although it took from September until March to get the new government off the ground, it might have been even longer had Pennsylvania not faced the threat of British invasion. Late in the summer of 1776, General Howe began chasing George Washington and his Continental Army across New Jersey, making it obvious that Philadelphia was his eventual target. In November and December 1776 the Council of Safety issued proclamations urging men to join Washington's forces. To ensure that people understood the alarming situation, such publications often depicted scenes of horror being perpetrated in Jersey by British and Hessian soldiers. The council published a letter, supposedly from an American officer, that described what was happening to that state's innocent citizens. "One man had the cruel mortification to have his wife and only daughter (a child of ten years of age) ravished," it read. Another girl of thirteen was "taken from her father's house, carried to a barn about a mile, there ravished, and afterwards made use of by five more of these brutes." The letter also warned of property being looted, saying, "Wanton mischief was seen in every part of the country; every thing portable they plunder and carry off, neither age nor sex, Whig or Tory is spared."[14] Another letter noted that a lawyer in Hopewell had been robbed of virtually all his worldly goods, "injuring him to the value of £2000 in less than three hours."[15] On Christmas Eve 1776 the assembly sent a letter to the counties warning of "the rapacious and plundering Soldiery" who were now looking toward Philadelphia "to glut their inordinate Lust of Rapine and Desolation in the Plunder of that rich and prosperous City."[16]

Not everyone was buying the bleak picture the Council of Safety was trying to paint. When James Allen's brother John wrote Lady Juliana Penn in April 1777, he was looking forward to a British invasion of Philadelphia, hoping it would restore society to its former order: "From the contemptible Persons in point of character, abilities & fortune chosen to fill the first offices in Pennsylvania, I flatter myself that Mr. Penn will be able to congratulate you, before the end of summer, upon the re-establishment of regal Authority & the rights of the family throughout the province."[17] That same month John Penn wrote his receiver general Edmund Physick: "It will be necessary to consider how you are to get to Town when General Howe gets possession."[18]

Such attitudes among society's former leaders might have been occasioned by what appeared to be a new impertinence among the lower classes. In the winter of 1776–77 James Allen wrote that radicals were actively persecuting "Tories." Nor was it difficult for any single individual to be stamped as a Tory: "under which name, is included everyone disinclined to Independence tho' ever so warm a friend to constitutional liberty and the old cause."[19] Allen was particularly incensed by an incident involving his wife, his daughter, and one of their friends that occurred while these ladies had gone visiting in the Allen carriage. Along the way, they met several militiamen on foot heading in the other direction. The ladies' driver tried to force these lower-class citizens to make way, but instead of yielding the road the men beat the driver with their muskets. The driver defended himself with his whip, causing the men to attack the carriage with bayonets and attempt to overturn it with the ladies inside. Only the intervention of a friendly American officer saved the Allen ladies from certain injury. "This accident has disturbed my peace," James Allen wrote, "as I for some time expected the violence of the people, inflamed by some Zealots would lead them to insult my person or attack my house." For the old gentry of the proprietorship, society had changed indeed. Allen deeply resented that the "insignificant" could now lord it over the "respectable" with such impunity.[20]

Formerly wealthy landowners must also have resented their rapidly deteriorating financial situation in 1777. The conflict had created enormous economic changes. Paper money steadily declined in value, while prices rose, greatly undermining the incomes of those invested heavily in land. In his diary James Allen lamented that his tenants were using worthless continental money to pay arrears in rent. Thanks to orders from the Continental Congress, he dared not refuse to accept it.[21] The Penns were also feeling the pinch. In the spring of 1777 John Penn had urgently requested that Physick find him some spending money. "I have parted with three servants since you were here," he wrote. "If some relief does not come soon, I suppose I shall be obliged to turn off all the rest & become bankrupt."[22] In August 1777 Tilghman and Physick offered to go on half salary, and John Penn gratefully accepted.[23]

As 1777 wore on, a British invasion began to look more and more inevitable, and the commonwealth's radical leaders attempted to identify the disaffected and get them out of Philadelphia so they would be in no position to help the invading army. The assembly passed a "test act," requiring everyone to swear allegiance or lose many of their civil rights, including one that would have been quite important to the Penn family: the right to buy and sell land. When Howe's troop ships were sighted leaving New York, plans were made to exile certain persons. Congress came up with a list of names, and the Supreme Executive Council added a few more. The names of prominent Quakers, former leaders, and crown officers were included, as well as the former governor and his council and most of the Allen family.[24] James Allen called it "the mark of the most wanton Tyranny ever exercised in any Country" toward people who had given no real offense to the usurpers of their positions.[25]

On August 25, 1777, John Penn, then in Philadelphia, wrote a hasty note to Edmund Physick, informing the receiver general that he was in hourly expectation of being obliged to leave his residence for some remote part of Pennsylvania or some other state. Penn told Physick that Washington's army had marched through town the day before and that there were rumors the British had already landed and were on their way to Philadelphia. "I shall be obliged to leave all my affairs in a very confused situation. What to do with papers & valuable affects I know not," John Penn explained. Physick replied on the same sheet, saying he would be with the former governor "tomorrow at Breakfast time."[26] The two men apparently devised a way to protect their property from being plundered during the inevitable strife of invasion: Anne Penn would remain in the Penn townhouse, possibly to follow John into exile later, while Edmund Physick would move into Lansdowne with his own wife and daughter.

Of all the former Penn officers asked to sign paroles, John Penn and his friend Benjamin Chew, Pennsylvania's former chief justice, were particularly reluctant and nearly suffered a more distant exile because of it. The minutes of Pennsylvania's Supreme Executive Council for August 12, 1777, noted that Penn and Chew were under house arrest "agreeable to the recommendation of Congress." The next day, the Continental Board of War asked the council to appoint an officer and several gentlemen to escort Penn and Chew to Fredericksburg, Virginia, where a number of prominent Quakers were also being sent.[27] That same day, the *Pennsylvania Gazette* reported that "diverse persons, who have late been in office under the late hereditary Government of Pennsylvania or otherwise in the service of the King of Great Britain," had become prisoners of war. "These gentlemen," the report continued, "are to be considered as servants and subjects of the Enemy, at least they had not renounced him, nor given any pledge of assurance of their fidelity to the State. . . . We hear that John Penn, Esquire . . . and Benjamin Chew . . . having declined signing paroles, are to be secured at Fredericksburgh in Virginia."[28] Apparently their belated decision to swallow their pride and sign paroles gained Penn and Chew the reward of a more pleasant exile at the New Jersey farm the Allen family called "the Union."

Former Governor James Hamilton also swallowed his pride when he petitioned the council in September 1777. He acknowledged that he was a prisoner, and he begged to be allowed to remain in his home, explaining that he had committed no crimes against the American cause, that he was old and ill, and that his property was likely to be plundered in his absence. If forced to depart, he asked, he would like to name his own place of exile and to be allowed to have a family member remain in his house while he was away. His letter concluded that he could not believe the president of the Executive Council "intended so great an injury to his private fortune as the refusal of this request must amount to."[29] James Hamilton was allowed to join James Allen at Trout Hall.

The exile of these key Penn government officers shows just how drastically the position of the proprietors in Pennsylvania society had changed. Once endowed with the right to create government, make laws, and enforce them through their appointees, the Penns and their officers were reduced to petitioning the new government to retain their personal freedom and private property. According to James Allen, "It was hard to forget we were once freemen who lived under the happiest & freest Government on earth."[30]

While the Penn officers had been packing to leave Philadelphia, the long-expected General Howe was finally on his way. Howe might have occupied Philadelphia much sooner, but after landing at the Elk River he came to Philadelphia by the most circuitous route. Howe's forces met George Washington's forces in several engagements along the way, including the Battle of Brandywine on September 11, 1777, and the Paoli Massacre on September 20—both British victories but neither decisive. Howe's troops marched into the city on September 26, the light horse first, the foot soldiers following, all looking appropriately grave and most unlike the rampaging, conquering army Philadelphians had been warned about. Howe guaranteed the security of persons and property, and some Philadelphians even commented that the occupation had improved order in the city.

The former speaker of the assembly, Loyalist Joseph Galloway, reentered Philadelphia with the British army. Galloway had left his home for a British camp in December 1776, and Howe had appointed him superintendent general in charge of police and matters relating to imports and exports. Galloway was empowered to issue business-related proclamations and was given three magistrates to help carry out his orders.[31] Years later, after John Penn's death, his wife confessed that, although politics had always been the favorite topic of conversation in her husband's household, she herself took little interest and rarely listened much. However, Anne Penn was still in the city, and she took time to warn Lady Juliana about Galloway. Galloway had been given "very uncommon powers," she wrote, "which I am afraid may affect the Proprietary Interest, as he has always been a great enemy to it." Even Anne, with no interest in politics, remembered Franklin's and Galloway's movement for royal government. Anne believed that Galloway still had designs on the Penn proprietorship: "He has given his opinion as a Lawyer that all the estates in America are forfeited by the present Rebellion, & has declared that all Proprietary Governments were inadequate to support the Interests of the Crown. These opinions which are the effects of his prejudices & resentments may perhaps render him a dangerous person to fill so important a Station." Anne asked Juliana whether she might "exert [her] interest at home to counteract any designs he may have with regard to the Proprietary affairs as soon as possible."[32] With such sentiments abroad, it's interesting to speculate whether the proprietorship would have been fully restored even if England had won the war.

After a skirmish at Whitemarsh and victory at the Battle of Germantown, the British soldiers stationed in Philadelphia found they had little to do during the winter of 1777–78. To pass the time, they attended cockfights and horse races, organized plays and concerts, and held regular balls at the City Tavern. Social events culminated the following spring with the Meschianza, an elegant and expensive masquerade, pageant, and ball presided over by General Howe and his paramour, Mrs. Loring.[33] There is no documentary evidence whether Anne Penn joined in any of these social activities.

The occupation also created many hardships for both the populace and the soldiery. Soldiers and officers needed housing and sometimes insisted on lodgings in Philadelphia homes. Some Philadelphians complained of stolen property—particularly firewood—but General Howe proclaimed against

Map 4.   Philadelphia and vicinity at the time of the British occupation in 1778.
(Courtesy, The Historical Society of Pennsylvania)

plundering and tried to keep this practice under control. The women of Philadelphia were not taken advantage of, though British soldiers did pursue servant girls, and officers wooed the daughters of the gentry. A number of British-American marriages were recorded.[34]

Once Howe had opened the Delaware to commerce, business picked up. New artisans and merchants emigrated to Philadelphia, setting up shop on premises that more radical artisans had just vacated. Everyone catered to the British soldiers, who could pay for goods and services in specie rather than the worthless paper money the Continental Congress had issued. Radicals outside Philadelphia railed impotently against the self-serving Pennsylvania farmers who regularly crossed enemy lines to sell their produce in the city.[35]

John Penn's account of his exile does not indicate that it was particularly trying, but that account appears to be incomplete. The one unpleasant incident he describes occurred at the outset of his stay in New Jersey, when a colonel in the Jersey militia arrived with orders that he be moved to somewhere in New England. John Penn discovered that New Jersey's Governor Livingston had issued the orders and wrote: "It seems his dignity was not a little hurt that the Congress should send me into Jersey without his permission." Fortunately, John Penn still had "some friends amongst the prevailing party & with their Interest & by a letter to Governor Livingston, I got my removal delayed 'till I had time to make an application to Congress then in York in Pennsylvania to remain where I was." American General John Armstrong also interceded in Penn's behalf, petitioning Thomas Wharton to let John Penn be moved south instead of north if he had to leave Jersey. Wharton replied that Penn was going nowhere without orders from the Board of War. More confusion might have resulted, but Governor Livingston consented to the request from Congress that John Penn's letter had spurred.[36] Nor was the former governor completely cut off from his friends and family. In February, James Allen and Anne Penn traveled to Jersey for a visit. Allen's diary implies that Anne later joined her husband, returning with him from his exile in July.[37] Lady Juliana also thanked Edmund Physick for also having visited her nephew.[38]

By March it began to look as if the British would soon evacuate Philadelphia, prompting revolutionary leaders to discuss the fate of the exiled Penn officers. Congress appointed another committee to examine this issue. This committee gave the noncommittal answer that John Penn and the other exiles might be returned to their homes if this could be done safely. The committee cautioned that, once back in Philadelphia, the officers might be used by the enemy even without their consent. Yet, if they remained in exile "it might occasion discontent and caballing." Pennsylvania's Supreme Executive Council informed the committee that the assembly was discussing a bill on the same issue and had resolved that the officers' arrest had been proper in that they might later create a party against the radicals. Such bills, committees, resolves, and red tape kept John Penn, Benjamin Chew, and James Hamilton in exile until British plans to evacuate Philadelphia were definite.[39]

In the spring of 1778, England sent peace commissioners to treat with revolutionary leaders. The Penns in England took advantage of this development to send a few messages to America. William Baker assured Edmund Physick that the letter he sent with the peace commissioners was secure—no one would dare search the commissioners' belongings. Physick, acting business head of the Penn organization, was advised not to expect too much. According to Baker, "Our Ignorance of the true Situation of Affairs and, in some Instances our willful Blindness to evident & confessed Truths, have already in so many Instances betrayed us into Misfortune & Disgrace, that, while we continue under the Guidance of the same wreched Ministers, we have little better to hope for." Baker mentioned that he was aware the Penns had been ousted from government by a new constitution, and he expressed his confidence that Physick was managing business affairs as well as could be expected. He realized that property values must be low and that, given the inflated state of the currency, Baker was just as happy that more money was not being received. Physick was requested to write about the province and proprietary affairs when it was safe to do so, and to provide information on Pennsylvania's current temper toward its proprietors.[40] To James Hamilton, Baker expressed his sympathy for what the governor and his councillors had been through. He said it must be a condition of any peace treaty that those who had been restrained could go free. Baker hinted that any oaths they had taken or paroles they had signed were justifiable, adding, "It will not be for the Interest of such Persons to decline acknowledging the Independence of America when Great Britain herself has perhaps been obliged to subscribe to it."[41]

Edmund Physick used the occupation to send word to England about what he had been doing to preserve Penn wealth. He purchased a distressed estate for Lady Juliana's son with the continental money he had on hand, fortunately completing this transaction before it was necessary to take the loyalty oath to purchase real estate.[42] He also hoarded specie and old paper money, even after Congress had ordered it all exchanged for continental bills. He made sure that Lady Juliana appreciated the attendant risk. "Places of Safety are difficult to be found," he wrote.[43] Physick even managed to purchase a few bills of exchange during the occupation, for which Lady

Juliana sincerely thanked him, assuring him that she and Baker were grateful for his services. "Everyone must have their portion of loss in property and comfort," she commented philosophically.[44]

The peace commission that had brought news from the Penns in England failed to end the American Revolution. As it turned out, the peace commissioners had little negotiating power because their mission had not been properly coordinated with plans made by those in charge of the war. The peace commissioners might have offered the Americans Philadelphia back, but by the time they arrived evacuation plans were already under way. The British evacuated Philadelphia only ten days after the peace commissioners got there.

After the evacuation brought Philadelphia's radical Patriots back into town, John Penn was freed, but he hesitated to communicate much in writing. Apparently he went back into quiet retirement. In July 1778 he briefly wrote Lady Juliana that he was well, but he told her to expect little more news or information: "I returned from my Exile the first of this month & have had no opportunity of writing to you before, & now as I am obliged to send my letter open, I do not think it prudent to say any thing respecting the public or our own private affairs. I am infinitely obliged to you for the anxiety you express on my Account, indeed my time has been spent in a very disagreeable manner for a long while past, and I still ardently wish an end to our present troubles, when I may have an opportunity again of writing to you without restraint."[45] After this letter, the Penns in England were again cut off from their friends and relations in America. As the war dragged on, the two branches of the Penn organization were prevented from freely communicating literally for years.

In 1778 the face of Pennsylvania's government changed. The relatively moderate Thomas Wharton died and was replaced as president of the Executive Council by George Bryan and then by Joseph Reed, who was reelected to the same position in 1779 and 1780. Scots-Irish Presbyterians then dominated both the council and the assembly, and they actively tried to convert the commonwealth's pacifists and disaffected, demanding that everyone take an oath of loyalty to the state of Pennsylvania by December 1779.[46]

In 1779 Pennsylvania's key problem became its steadily worsening economy. The value of currency continued to drop, and prices continued to rise. The Supreme Executive Council tried to fix the prices of certain items, alienating merchants who wanted a free market. At mass meetings, radicals denounced those they called "forestallers and engrossers"—merchants the populace suspected were manipulating prices and getting rich.

Pennsylvania's economic problems probably led to the formation of the Republican Society in March 1779. Its founders were primarily wealthy Anglican and Quaker merchants and their associates who favored free trade, generally including Pennsylvania's anticonstitutionalists, who still opposed the constitution because it lacked safeguards against the will of the majority. Prominent members included Robert Morris, James Wilson, George Clymer, John Nixon, and Samuel Meredith.[47] Late in March, those opposed to the Republicans formed the Constitutionalist Society, whose members were primarily Scots-Irish Presbyterians.[48] The Penns and their associates generally avoided joining either group.

The high-water mark of conflict between these groups was probably the peculiar incident known as "the attack on Fort Wilson." This occurred in October 1779, shortly after a radical committee surrendered its attempts to fix prices. More than a political or ethnic clash, it manifested some aspects of a class struggle.[49] That afternoon a crowd of militiamen were marching through the streets of Philadelphia intent on picking up disaffected gentlemen and parading them about town. They rounded up four captives and led them down Arch Street, their drums beating the Rogue's March. James Wilson was in the vicinity of the City Tavern with some other gentlemen, and these men, believing themselves to be the next victims of the militia, armed themselves and entered Wilson's house at the southwest corner of Third and Walnut streets. The crowd had passed the house when suddenly shots rang out. No one knew who had fired first, but that afternoon six or seven people were killed, and seventeen to nineteen were injured. The city troop of cavalry led by Joseph Reed finally broke up the melee.[50]

Civil problems in the city were matched by continuing unrest on Pennsylvania's frontiers. Connecticut Yankees retaliated for Plunket's Expedition by harassing the Pennsylvania settlers in northeastern Pennsylvania. When a real opportunity came for the Pennsylvania "Tories" to ally themselves with the British, many jumped at the chance. After the British had evacuated Philadelphia, British Colonel John Butler organized companies of Indians, rangers, and Pennsylvania "Tories" to drive out the Connecticut settlers. On July 3, 1778, the Yankees' Forty-Second Regiment marched out to meet the British and were quickly mopped up by vastly superior forces. Then the Indians and Pennsylvania Tories burned and plundered many Yankee houses, driving the survivors away. The battle came to be called the Wyoming Massacre. Throughout the rest of the war, Indians and Pennsylvania settlers attacked remaining and returning Connecticut Yankees, prolonging the animosity between these two groups.[51]

The new government of Pennsylvania had more success than the old Penn government in ending the long-standing conflict over whether the area around Fort Pitt was part of Pennsylvania or Virginia. Since the fall of 1776, the British farther west had purposely incited Indians against American frontier settlements. In 1777, Pennsylvania newspapers reported murders and scalpings near Fort Pitt. Settlers around Fort Pitt became convinced that supporting the Revolution would exacerbate such depredations in their area, so they became "Tory" too. Revolutionary leaders realized something had to be done to hold the frontiers. In 1777 Thomas Wharton proposed to Virginia leaders that the two commonwealths confer on their border problems. By August 1779, commissioners from Virginia and Pennsylvania met in Baltimore and agreed to run the Mason-Dixon line five degrees west of the Delaware, and then run a line due north to serve as Pennsylvania's western border.[52] This new line definitely put Fort Pitt in Pennsylvania.

In other circumstances, the Penn organization might have been delighted to hear that Virginia had finally agreed Pittsburgh was in Pennsylvania; Penn lands in this area were sure to sell at good prices after the war. By 1779, however, there were ominous rumors about whether the revolutionary government of Pennsylvania would allow the Penns to keep any of their proprietary lands.

17

"Unjustly Deprived of Their Property"

The Divestment Act of 1779

When John Allen wrote Lady Juliana in April 1777 to inform her of John Penn's retirement from politics, he also suggested that radicals in Pennsylvania were after more than just the Penn government: "As the Proprietary Estate is not the less the object, of the wretches who have got into power, than the Government, they have been watching with impatience for any act of [John Penn's] that would enable them to irritate the people against him, but fortunately he has hitherto baffled them. A motion was indeed made in their [constitutional] convention, to seize upon the Quitrents and vacant lands, and to apply them to the support of their new Government, but the Injustice was too glaring to pass even there. I make no doubt however than an intercepted letter would be sufficient ground to renew it, & with more success now."[1]

Allen was clearly predicting that attempts would be made to divest the Penn proprietors of their real estate. Despite the venom in his words, the motive was probably not malice but necessity. From the first, Pennsylvania's new leaders must have known they were taking on the expense of two additional branches of government without the asset—the sale of Penn lands—that had always financed them. But if John Penn had to be careful of his words and actions, so did the new leaders, particularly when it came to confiscations of private property.

The Penns were not alone in fearing and facing confiscations. James Allen's diary first mentions talk of confiscations during the summer of 1776, but at that time the war's outcome was still uncertain, so attempted confiscations might have meant harsher retaliations against the radicals if they lost the war.[2] In September 1777 a committee of assembly members drafted a bill stipulating that the estates of those who joined the enemy would be confiscated. The bill was not passed, but in October the Council of Safety proclaimed that the personal property of those who aided the enemy would be seized.[3] That same month James Allen observed a change in Pennsylvania's attitude toward property in general. Property rights had always been sacred to the British, but Allen found that "the prevailing idea now is, that no man has any property in what the publick has use for." In Allen's eyes this was just more evidence of radical tyranny.[4]

Earlier in 1777 the Penns began experiencing a few subtle violations of their own property rights. In January, James Tilghman learned that wood was being cut for the use of American soldiers on the ungranted common areas in Philadelphia. He informed the Council of Safety that the proprietors had "claimed a Right to the ungranted Woods on the Common" ever since Philadelphia had been founded. "They have disposed of the wood from time to time as they saw proper." John Penn had lately ordered that two hundred cords of wood be distributed to the city's needy. Tilghman asked for an explanation. If the council was assuming the right to dispose of this wood, his letter formed a written record of objection so it could not be claimed that the proprietors had silently acquiesced.[5]

In March 1778, when it began to look as if the British would evacuate Philadelphia, the assembly passed a bill requiring certain persons attainted for treason to report for trial. Failure to show up meant the individual was automatically deemed guilty and forfeited all real and personal property. Once the British evacuated Philadelphia, returning radicals were incensed to find that their homes and shops had been used, and in some cases damaged or plundered, during the occupation. Many of the wealthy who opposed independence further angered Pennsylvania's new leaders by leaving Pennsylvania with the British. This put much real and personal property in the hands of an absentee opposition. Week after week, Pennsylvania's newspapers listed the names of absent traitors.[6]

The loyalty oath requirement passed by the Pennsylvania assembly in 1778 stated that the penalty for not repudiating the king and swearing loyalty to the commonwealth of Pennsylvania was confiscation of both real and personal property. This has been interpreted as a Scots-Irish Presbyterian attack on Quakers and pacifists,[7] but it also put a great deal of Penn property at risk. John Penn recognized the danger to his family and took the oath. According to James Allen, John Penn did this with the knowledge and approval of the rest of the Penn family. Allen wrote that the former governor had been "under the cruel necessity of abjuring the King & swearing allegiance to the mob-government of Pennsylvania & the united states to prevent the confiscation of his whole property. This step was taken by the advice of his friends & in consequence of a letter from Mr. Baker in England, advising him to become an American."[8]

For Joseph Reed, who became president of the Supreme Executive Council in 1779, the Penn proprietorship was one of two remnants of an old order that had no place in Pennsylvania's new regime. Reed also wanted to wrest control of the College of Philadelphia from the former leaders of society. Under his direction, the assembly replaced the College of Philadelphia (formerly headed by a Penn family friend and supporter, the Anglican Rev. William Smith) with the new University of Pennsylvania under Presbyterian minister John Ewing.[9]

In February 1779 Reed turned his attention to the Penn proprietorship. He addressed the assembly, and his speech was reprinted in Pennsylvania newspapers. Reed asked the assembly to examine "the nature and extent of the claims or estates of the late Proprietaries, and their consistency with the interests and happiness of the people under the late revolution. To reconcile the rights and demands of society with those of private justice and equity in this case will be worthy of your most serious attention; nor ought the magnitude of the object, or the splendor and influence heretofore annexed to the power derived from that source, deter you from the enquiry, or dazzle you in the pursuit. The just regard due to the suspended rights of many individuals of this State, and the common interests of all, do not admit that it should any longer be kept out of sight; though war, with its calamities and confusion, has hitherto excluded it from the notice of a government founded on the authority of the people only."[10]

Accordingly, the assembly debated the case in March 1779. The Supreme Executive Council attended sessions of the assembly at which John Penn's counsel argued with those "employed by the State." Former Penn appointees Benjamin Chew and James Tilghman appeared to argue for the Penn interests, contending that Penn holdings were private property. The radicals tried to justify confiscation by arguing that the proprietors were merely trustees who had held crown land in trust for actual settlers. They also argued that too much land in the hands of any individual or family was inimical to liberty. A report was drawn up so the legal opinion of Chief Justice Thomas McKean could be solicited.[11]

A hiatus of six months followed, but by September attempts were made to speed the process of divesting the Penns of proprietary lands. The assembly may have felt it was responding to the will of the people, thanks to petitions like the one from Lancaster County asking that "the claim of the late proprietaries of Pennsylvania to the soil of the same and to quit-rents, not be admitted."[12] Another petition, from "several districts of the County of York," noted that "the estate of the late proprietaries of Pennsylvania must prove dangerous to the liberties and happiness of this commonwealth, if possessed as extensively by them as formerly."[13] President Reed addressed the assembly again, urging it to proceed quickly, since "neither the Peace, Liberty, nor Safety of Pennsylvania can be deemed secure while this powerful interest attached in all its branches to the powers we have abjured and abandoned, is permitted to retain its full force and influence among us." Were the issue allowed to rest, he warned, it might become an obstacle to favorable peace negotiations between America and England.[14] By the end of September the assembly incorporated all its arguments and deliberations in one bill, which it ordered printed for public consideration on September 23, 1779. Subsequent debate resulted in additional transcriptions and two additional publications in November and December.

The bill, called "An ACT for vesting the estates of the late Proprietaries of Pennsylvania in this Commonwealth," had been drafted by George Bryan and Jonathan D. Sergeant. The language of the bill justified its action in legal, moral, and patriotic terms. The December version of the bill stated:

> Whereas the claims heretofore made by the late Proprietaries to the whole of the soil contained within the bounds of the said charter, and in consequence thereof the reservations of quit-rents and purchase-money upon all the grants of lands within the said limits, cannot longer consist with the safety, liberty and happiness of the good people of this Commonwealth, who, at the expence of much blood and treasure, have bravely rescued themselves and their possessions from the tyranny of Great Britain, and are now defending themselves from the inroads of the savages. . . . Be it therefore enacted . . .

that all and every estate, right, title, interest, property, claim and demand of the heirs and devisees, grantees, or others claiming as Proprietaries of Pennsylvania . . . are hereby vested in the Common-wealth of Pennsylvania.[15]

Of the approximately twenty-nine million acres that Charles II had granted William Penn, the Divestment Act of 1779 deprived the Penns of approximately twenty-four million acres of unsold land. Quitrents were abolished, and arrears of purchase money would be payable to the commonwealth.

Yet the Divestment Act did not strip the Penns of all their personal wealth. It allowed them to keep the private estates and proprietary manors that had been surveyed before July 4, 1776, plus the associated quitrents and rent arrears. The Penns would also receive a cash settlement of £130,000 "in remembrance of the enterprizing spirit which distinguished the founder of Pennsylvania, and mindful of the expectations and dependence of his descend-ants on the propriety thereof."[16] This money would be paid in installments to the devisees and legatees of the late Richard and Thomas Penn after the war.

There may be several explanations for this relative liberality toward the Penns. One was probably the steadfast neutrality of John Penn. Another might have been the conservative legal opinion of Chief Justice McKean, whose deliberations upheld the legality of the grant to William Penn, as well as its absolute and hereditary nature.[17] A contributing factor might have been the hard work of Edmund Physick, whose careful figures clearly showed that the Penns had hardly been getting rich from the land they had been granted. Having anticipated confiscation, Physick had prepared what he called the "Cash Accounts," a summary of all records showing what revenues the Penns had received. From 1701 to 1778, the Penns had grossed only £688,486 and were still owed £118,569. His records showed that £130,000 would amount to a mere fraction of what the Penn lands were worth.[18]

The assembly minutes for Wednesday, November 24, 1779, read: "A letter from John Penn, esquire, objecting against the bill now depending, intituled 'An act for vesting the estate of the late proprietaries of Pennsylvania, in this commonwealth' was read, and ordered to lie on the table. The house resumed the consideration of the aforesaid bill."[19] The minutes do not record the contents of John's letter, but there remains a multipage document in his hand that appears to be several drafts of his letter to the assembly. He wrote: "I observe in the News Papers that a Bill for vesting the proprietary estate in the Commonwealth of Pennsylvania is printed for public consideration. Though I am so much interested in this Matter, no other Notice of the Bill has been given me by the house of Assembly." (This much cannot be true. The speaker of the house had written John Penn in March enclosing the assembly's resolves to examine proprietary claims,[20] while Tilghman and Chew had already argued the claims of the Penn proprietors on the floor of the legislature.) Penn's tone was incensed and outraged. Now that he had nothing more to lose, his language finally became what he would have termed "warm." The proposed divestment, he suggested, was an attempt to deny the proprietors "their just & legal rights to the lands & Quit-rents of Pennsylvania, with very few Exceptions." He continued, "I have always understood it to be a Maxim founded in Reason and Justice that no Persons Property can be taken from him without his consent.... I have no power from the other Proprietor, who is still a Minor to give his Consent to a transaction that would divest him of the principal Part of his Estate, so neither Can I give my Consent to any Measure that will deprive me of my own. The house, I hope will not proceed to pass a Law, so repugnant in my opinion, to the principles of Right."[21] John Penn's letter changed no one's mind. After debating the bill paragraph by paragraph, the assembly overwhelmingly voted to engross the bill and make it law.

On that day in November there were only seven votes against the bill; forty assembly members voted for it. The seven who voted nay offered several reasons for their dissent. They disagreed with the retrospective nature of the bill, "which kind of laws, have been cautiously barred by the bills of rights of several states in the union, and we think ought to be carefully guarded against by the legislatures of every free state, as we conceive, in that case, principally consist, the security a man has, or ought to have, for his life, liberty, or rightful estate and property." The second paragraph of the dissenters' opinion elaborated on the first objection, noting that citizens who had lawfully purchased land from the Penns since 1776 might have to forfeit it. The dissenters also objected that the bill distinguished between proprietary land titles and the titles of all other Pennsylvania citizens, "whereby, we humbly conceive, the equal rights of all men, in point of property, are not duly observed." Finally, they believed the Penns should be granted the arrears of purchase money lest these funds be collected by the state and used to pay the Penns their compensation. This would make it seem that the Penns had been compensated with money that had technically been owed them all along. They wrote: "Nor can we think we do our constituents an acceptable service, in any act, of the justice of which they have the smallest doubts."[22]

Physick did what he could to preserve the Penn account books and documents. In February 1780 Reed wrote him: "It becomes my Duty to demand of you as Receiver General under the late Proprietors, the Books, Certificates, Orders & other Documents, Instruments, Records, Writings, and Seals belonging to said [Physick's] Office."[23] Physick protested that all he had were personal records belonging to the Penn family. His office, he explained, had never been held at public expense. Such excuses created enough delay for Physick to make another complete copy of the cash accounts, which might in the future be of some interest or use to the Penns.[24]

The dissenting opinion written by seven assembly members and John Penn's drafted letter form the few records of protest against the Divestment Act of 1779. Surviving correspondence would tend to indicate that the Penns themselves expressed very little rancor over the legislation that deprived them of Pennsylvania's vast unsold lands and reduced them to private landowners, eliminating their special place in Pennsylvania society. Perhaps they were still being cautious, lest they fail to collect the fortune the commonwealth had admitted it owed them, for surely the family and their appointees must have agreed with the sentiments expressed in John Penn's draft of his letter to the assembly, in which he wrote, "I shall consider the Proprietaries as unjustly deprived of their property."[25]

18

"Without Repining What Is Out of Our Power"

The Penns in the Wake of the American Revolution

The long war dragged on, its theater of battle moving south while life in Pennsylvania settled into new routines. After John and Anne Penn returned from exile in July 1778, they apparently continued their retirement from public life. A few brief notes to a Doctor Parke in 1780 and 1781 indicate that they were again residing at Lansdowne and hint at their domestic life. In August 1780 John and Anne both suffered sore throats, and the doctor was asked to ride out and send a dose of salts.[1] Later, Anne reported to Dr. Parke that her husband felt feverish. Should he continue taking medicine? Could he eat grapes and melon?[2] Early in 1781, presumably when the Penns were better, Dr. Parke received two invitations to dine with them.[3]

Later in 1781, with considerable help from America's foreign allies, George Washington isolated the British General Lord Charles Cornwallis at Yorktown and on October 19, 1781, accepted his surrender. Most of the fighting was over, but officially the war continued until September 1783, when a final peace agreement was signed in Paris. In April 1783 the *Pennsylvania Journal* reported that a cessation of hostilities had been proclaimed by the city magistrates at the State House. The commonwealth's flag was hoisted at the Market Street wharf, and joyful citizens once again rang the city's church bells.[4] In Paris, John's brother Richard had apparently been making his own peace with an old family enemy. Richard wrote two cordial notes to Benjamin Franklin, then involved as an American diplomat in the peace negotiations. In one note, Richard mentioned that his wife and family joined him in expressing "sincere wish's for [Franklin's] Health & happiness."[5]

As hostilities neared an end and peace negotiations were under way, the Penn family slowly resumed their transatlantic correspondence. In September 1781 William Baker wrote James Hamilton of Lady Juliana's return from the continent, where she had resided for two years. Baker and his new wife had also been in France together with Richard Penn and his family. Lady Juliana's son John, sometimes called John of Stoke, had completed his education at Cambridge and traveled in Europe for a while. Baker lamented the disastrous times in which they all lived, when "Friendships seem Dead, & the best Feelings of Humanity almost annihilated." He mentioned that he and the other English Penns were grateful for such steadfast loyalty of American friends and appointees as Hamilton, who "from the Wreck of their affairs had collected something for their present relief, under Difficulties of which [he was] not longsighted enough to see the End."[6] Edmund Physick's first letter to the man who would have been Pennsylvania's new chief proprietor, the son of Lady Juliana and Thomas Penn, had the same tone of grief and loss. Physick assured the younger John Penn that he had consistently promoted the family's interests in time of war: "I have always endeavored to act for the best in all your affairs, but the Times have puzzled many, and Injured many."[7]

Pennsylvania's former governor stoically accepted the injuries he and the family had suffered. In 1781 Pennsylvania established a new land office, its officers chosen by the assembly, although the sale of vacant land to the general public would not begin until after the war. The following year, in a letter to Benjamin Chew, John Penn mentioned the orders the Supreme Executive Council had issued to surrender the old Indian deeds in his possession. John felt it would be vain to defy the request, "not being inclined to run the risk of suffering the penalties of the law, which I suppose some people would be glad to see inflicted upon me."[8]

The commonwealth also assumed the vexatious, long-standing conflicts with Virginia and Connecticut. The legislatures of both Pennsylvania and Virginia ratified the line that would separate their commonwealths in 1780. A brief movement to establish a new western state called Transylvania flared up in 1782, and there were still local hostilities as late as 1784, but Pennsylvania's then president of the Supreme Executive Council did not consider them serious enough to warrant sending in the militia.[9] In 1780 Pennsylvania initiated negotiations with Connecticut, and the two states finally agreed that the Wyoming Valley and Shamokin were part of Pennsylvania. This settled the matter between the states but failed to reconcile the settlers. In 1782 a federal court also declared that the disputed territory was in Pennsylvania, but it stipulated that Yankees settled there could keep their land. Ignoring this second part of the decree, Pennsylvania sent in its militia, leading to more conflict and another brief separatist movement. In 1786 Connecticut and Pennsylvania agreed that Connecticut would acquire additional land beyond the western boundary of Pennsylvania called the Western Reserve. Pennsylvania then created Luzerne County to provide a local government for the Yankees still firmly planted in the northeast. In 1787 a Confirming Act secured the titles of genuine Yankee claimants.[10]

In the final years of the war there had been confusion in England over whether the proprietorship might be reestablished or continue to exist in some form or other. At the end of 1782 Lady Juliana received a letter asking whether the proprietors intended to remit their own traditional quitrent to the king. Samuel West wrote to her, "desiring to know if the two Beaver Skins would be wanted as heretofore to present at Windsor on New Years Day." If so, they could be had at the same price as the previous year.[11] The same year, the Penns in Europe heard that Pennsylvania's Republicans had secured a majority in the house, electing the moderate John Dickinson as president of the Supreme Executive Council. Pennsylvania's radicals had gone down to defeat amid the commonwealth's inflation, frightening property seizures, and futile attempts at price control. Until the fall election in 1784, the Republicans remained in power, urging many changes. William Baker wrote James Hamilton that even in Europe there was news of "the Assembly being composed of Different Persons from those who have been elected of late years." The Penn family had "the most sanguine Expectations" that these new men might reconsider "the Proceedings by which the Property of the Family has been so deeply affected."[12]

Such a move would require the presence of the new chief proprietor in America. In her first postwar letter to Edmund Physick, Lady Juliana confided that she had asked the men negotiating the Treaty of Paris where and when her son's situation would be considered. She had been told that each new American state would settle its own affairs.[13] Accordingly, the younger John Penn was packed off to London to embark for America to reopen the issue of the Penn proprietorship, as William Baker put it, in such a way "as shall neither give offense to the New Government and yet produce a satisfactory Settlement of the Matter."[14]

Thomas Penn's son arrived in the fall of 1783, and by March of the following year he had prepared a memorial jointly with the former governor and Tench Francis, the agent and attorney for Richard Penn. This memorial stated that the Penns did not intend to "question the Merits of the late Revolution in America, nor the Forms of Government, which the People may have established in their Wisdom, or supported by their Valor." Yet it reminded the assembly that the Penns had suffered "the Overthrow of their Government, the Sequestration of their Estates, and almost total Wreck of their better Fortunes." While they were willing to give up their government for the public good, their real property was a different matter. They asked for revisions to the legislation respecting their property and hoped they would not become the only people in America for whom independence was no blessing. The assembly was also asked to reconsider whether their compensation was adequate and whether its payment in "distant and uncertain Installments" would provide them sufficient funds. Finally, they asked whether they might keep proprietary manors for which warrants had been duly issued but which had not been surveyed prior to July 4, 1776, due to the laxity of land office surveyors.[15]

In the summer of 1785, at the request of the Supreme Executive Council, the two John Penns submitted information on "the state of their respective claims to the Province of Pennsylvania of which they were sies'd on the 27th day of November, 1779." The younger John Penn claimed three-quarters of the land described in the royal grant of Charles II to William Penn, which he would have inherited from Thomas Penn. The former governor claimed the remaining one-quarter. Lady Juliana claimed a sum of £500 a year, which had been promised at the time of her marriage for her use after the death of her husband. The Supreme Executive Council ordered the consideration of their claims by a committee, which examined the wills and documents supporting these claims and concluded: "The vouchers support the said claims as stated."[16] Essentially, the committee verified that the two John Penns were indeed joint proprietors under the old system. But this did not restore their land.

One month later, Edmund Physick reported to Lady Juliana how all the attempts to regain the Penn lands were being received. Back in 1783, he wrote, there were "many worthy, sensible Persons of all Sects" who believed the Penns should have been compensated more handsomely for their estates. Physick implied that he had drawn up the first Penn memorial but that some of the former governor's friends had advised against submitting it so soon.

The petition had been shuffled around and revised by the two John Penns working together with Tench Francis. It had not been submitted until just before the 1784 election.[17] Unfortunately, since 1781, the constitutionalists had been accusing the Republicans of plotting to restore confiscated Tory estates and reestablish the proprietorship. The chief proprietor's arrival in Pennsylvania seemed to confirm this. The specter of restoration of the old system with its inconvenient quitrents proved extremely unpopular. Although Republicans denied the charges, they lost control of the house in 1784, and the Penns lost the chance even to increase their compensation.[18]

The Penns did, however, receive their promised money and worked to make the most of their situation. In 1784 the assembly stipulated that land in the northern liberties be sold to create a fund from which the Penns' cash settlement of £130,000 would be paid. From 1786 through 1789, compensation money was indeed paid in installments. The John Penns continued petitioning the assembly for confirmation of certain private estates and manors of which their ownership was in question because surveys had not been made before the July 4, 1776, deadline, although warrants had been issued. Their tone was always respectful. One petition asked for a settlement "as may do honour to the feelings and councils of a great and generous people" who did not forget Pennsylvania's founder William Penn.[19] A letter from Benjamin Chew to the former governor advised that it would be difficult if not impossible to collect quitrents even on confirmed proprietary manors where the commonwealth had given the Penns the right to do so. The problem was that the Penns had been stripped of "the Powers and Influence [they] were once possessed of." Chew suggested that John Penn sell the rents to tenants who wanted to "purchase the encumbrance off."[20]

The governor's cousin John commented on the spirit of the new republic. While remaining in America, he traveled extensively and recorded his observations in a "commonplace book," a personal record of observations. In England, John Penn was considered a nobleman by virtue of his mother's birth. In his commonplace book he described meeting a genial old man at a tavern who addressed him as "Honorable Proprietor" yet failed to rise in his presence, provoking John to observe "how qualified respect is in this democratical country." While traveling in Reading, John made a point to stay at the one tavern whose proprietor "had not lately petitioned against the confirmation of the proprietary estate." John was uncertain whether he would remain in America. He built himself a fashionable country house on the west bank of the Schuylkill that he named "Solitude." In 1784 he admitted in his commonplace book that he sometimes felt "a republican enthusiasm, which attached me to America, & almost tempted me to stay." Yet he continued, "I may date my becoming wholly an Englishman from the breaking up of that Assembly, & publication of its minutes relative to the treatment of our testimonial; from the abuse of one party, by which, tho robb'd, we were almost branded as thieves, & the other's apparent desertion, in their answers." John Penn concluded that America had liberty but no justice and that he would one day return home.[21]

The younger John Penn was in America during the time when nationalists attempted to overhaul the Articles of Confederation and create a new U.S. Constitution. Many Americans who came to be known as Federalists believed the nation was drifting and foundering while its ineffective Congress proved unable to regulate commerce, pay debts, maintain civil order, and generate respect abroad. In 1786 the Virginia assembly recommended a convention to amend the Articles. This meeting, held in Annapolis, was presided over by Pennsylvania's John Dickinson. Its delegates advised Congress to hold a second meeting in Philadelphia. Pennsylvania's delegation to this constitutional convention was a large one. Its secret proceedings were made public in Philadelphia on September 18, 1787, when the new constitution was read to the Pennsylvania assembly. Pennsylvania's Federalists advocated an immediate convention to ratify the new constitution, but opposers absented themselves from the house, trying to rob it of a quorum and prevent it from doing business. Thanks to the legislature's sergeant-at-arms and a mob of angry citizens, two dissenting assemblymen were physically hauled into the legislature, which promptly voted for a ratifying convention. Despite a nasty war of words in the press, Pennsylvania ratified the Federal Constitution on December 12, becoming the second state after Delaware to ratify. Pennsylvania's old governor, John Penn, then in London, wrote his friend Dr. Parke of his hopes that the new constitution would be successful. The government, he observed, had certainly needed a few changes when he had left America.[22]

The former governor had left for England in the spring of 1788 at about the same time his cousin did so. The two John Penns had heard that commissioners were being appointed in London to examine the losses of American Loyalists and evaluate them for compensation from the British government. The Penns wanted to ensure that their own family, which had lost perhaps the largest estate in America, was given due consideration. In a letter to Richard Penn, attorney Tench Francis wrote that the John Penns expected great things from the British government, but he speculated that success in England would prevent them from making further claims on Pennsylvania.[23] The younger John Penn had been so anxious to get to

England that the last travel entry in his commonplace book ends in mid-sentence. He left Edmund Physick, with whom he had become friendly, in charge of finding a tenant for his townhouse and selling his furniture and plate.[24] The former governor and Anne Penn hurriedly leased John Penn's beloved Lansdowne to the wealthy William Bingham and arranged to sell their own furniture at vendue.[25]

Once in England, the younger John Penn almost immediately wrote Physick for more information, including a copy of the Divestment Act with the great seal, records of what compensation moneys the Penns had already received, and a tally of their unpurchased acres in 1779.[26] In September 1788 the Penns presented a memorial to the British commissioners that was subsequently presented to the House of Commons. The two John Penns jointly claimed losses of £944,817. Parliament awarded them £4,000 a year payable in perpetuity to the Penn heirs.[27] The younger John Penn wrote Edmund Physick: "I like what appears of this arrangement. From part of it the Americans will see that they have not the same rights of enmity over the family, as over the British loyalists & we shall hope regard us accordingly."[28]

John and Anne Penn stayed in Europe for several more years, returning to America around the middle of September 1792. By then, Pennsylvania had a new state constitution incorporating many reforms. Several old Penn officers went back into politics, but John and Anne merely settled once again into private domestic life. They lived quietly until 1795. That February, Chief Justice Thomas McKean received a brief note asking him to serve as pall-bearer in John Penn's funeral procession, which would leave his townhouse in Pine Street on Thursday at 9:00 A.M.[29] John Penn was buried in Christ Church near the altar rail, where he still lies, now the only proprietor buried in Pennsylvania.

After John Penn's death, Richard Penn plagued his widow with a lengthy lawsuit. In the year 1787, John had agreed to pay his brother one-third of what he received from the Penn settlements and from the land he inherited from their father and sold after 1779.[30] Very soon after John Penn died, Richard claimed a share of all money still due John on all sales made during John Penn's lifetime but not collected by a certain date after his decease.[31] His suit was probably inspired by his own financial problems. In a 1797 letter to Edmund Physick, Richard wrote: "For God's sake my dear Friend, exert yourself or I am lost. If I do not very soon receive a large sum from you, I shall not be able to keep my head above Water."[32] Richard's case against Anne was finally decided in her favor, but not until the year 1800, after it had caused Anne Penn considerable anxiety. She wrote John F. Mifflin, executor of her husband's will, that she had always wanted to be a friend to Richard but was not much pleased with this attack on her property. She suspected the suit had been instigated by Edmund Physick, who had never liked her. She only hoped that Physick was not prejudicing her late husband's cousin against her as well.[33]

The younger John Penn clung to the old lifestyle of a privileged British gentleman. Most of the Penn compensation money went to him, enabling John to take up the gentrified pursuits of politics, literature, and architecture. He served in Parliament and became governor of the Island of Portland, where he built a residence he named "Pennsylvania Castle." He also built a townhouse in London and made improvements to his inherited estate at Stoke. He considered himself a writer and produced plays and poetry, but he charmed neither the critics nor the public. Anne Penn wrote of him: "I believe he is an honest man, though an odd one."[34]

Anne herself returned to England, where she found life surprisingly expensive. In 1801, unable to maintain both a town and a country residence, she wrote that she had "commenced country gentlewoman" and was living in a small house on three and a half acres, where she hoped to maintain two cows and tend a kitchen garden, perhaps keeping a carriage if she could afford one. She had started life as the daughter of a wealthy American merchant and had been the wife of a provincial governor. As it had for the Penn proprietorship, the Revolution had brought great changes for Anne. She accepted her new life patiently, writing, "We should be thankful for the good we enjoy, without repining what is out of our power."[35]

Epilogue

In the biographical note appended to his *History of Proprietary Government in Pennsylvania* (1896), William R. Shepherd wrote of his research among the bound and unbound Penn family correspondence that had been acquired by the Historical Society of Pennsylvania in 1870: "While . . . it is an absorbingly interesting, it is also a very tedious and arduous piece of work to wade through this mass of material, by far the larger portion of which has hitherto been wholly unexplored." He added his hopes that the papers would soon form the basis for a comprehensive work on colonial Pennsylvania to complement his own history of proprietary government.

In the almost one hundred years since Shepherd completed his history, the Penn papers have been used by probably hundreds of students and scholars. There have been many books and articles on colonial and revolutionary Pennsylvania, yet rare is the work with much to say about the Penn family. Perhaps the Penns' consistently conservative actions and their steadfastly neutral position during the war make them seem colorless. However, as John Franklin Jameson pointed out in his book *The American Revolution Considered as a Social Movement,* theirs was the largest estate confiscated during the American Revolution. Their experience and their changing role has much to say about the times.

In John Penn's first five years as governor, Penn authority was challenged by Pennsylvania's assembly. Since William Penn's own day, Pennsylvania's largely Quaker and elected representatives had been steadily assuming powers and prerogatives granted to the proprietors in the charter issued by Charles II. In the 1750s, Thomas Penn had made moves to halt what he considered a dangerous trend toward democracy and to strengthen his family's influence in Pennsylvania politics. This created a backlash for John Penn to deal with when the assembly mounted their movement for royal government under the leadership of Benjamin Franklin. To forward their plans, the assembly capitalized on every recent misfortune, whether or not blame could be properly attributed to the Penn family. The Conestoga Massacre, the march of the Paxton Boys, and the Frederick Stump affair were all exploited for this purpose. An irate John Penn sometimes used strong language against the assemblymen, but Thomas Penn in England was able to shrug off this threat. Thomas had a good grasp of how things worked in the mother country and knew that the crown had no intention of dismantling what legally belonged to the Penns. Between 1766 and 1768, the assembly and the Penn family moved toward rapprochement. After that, although the assembly often failed to help with issues high on the Penn agenda, its members posed little threat to the proprietorship.

As citizens challenged British authority elsewhere in America, the Penns were slow to perceive a threat to themselves. Both John Penn and Thomas Penn spoke of a gathering storm when Whigs protested the Townshend duties, but neither speculated about what a potential war might mean to themselves. Apparently they could not conceive of Americans winning such a war and creating a nation with no room for their proprietorship. Throughout most of the revolutionary period, the Penns believed it was more important to protect their government from blame in the eyes of the mother country. John and Thomas both urged legal, conservative means of protest. Pennsylvania did not embarrass the Penns in contesting the Stamp Act or the Tea Act, but eventually the Penn government was unable to contain or direct the protest. While the Penns lost touch with the Whigs and became helpless outsiders, extralegal organizations emerged and assumed their governing role. When a new constitution finally formalized popular rule, the Penns accepted this state of affairs and retired to preserve their personal fortunes and their land.

Land issues had consistently preoccupied the Penn family in the period leading up to the American Revolution. The family had long been dealing with squatters and trying to exact the fees and quitrents due them. The end of the French and Indian War brought the first serious Indian trouble in Pennsylvania's history. Penn authority on the frontier was then challenged by the Stump affair and the claims of Virginia and Connecticut. Because the Penns were running a minimalist government, they were unable to assert their authority. Instead, they looked to England for solutions—but England failed them, its officials almost gloating over intercolonial squabbles. It is also interesting to note that virtually all the rifts among Penn family members and their appointed officers arose out of some issue concerning land.

To preserve their land, the Penns were willing to take steps they might otherwise have avoided. John Penn called the assembly into special session to deal with problems around Fort Pitt, after having refused to do so at the request of Philadelphia's Whigs. He was also willing to take an oath of loyalty to the revolutionary government of Pennsylvania in an effort to save the Penn lands, and he did that with the approval of the Penn family in England. Unfortunately, land ownership was an important component of the Penn proprietorship, and in the end the Penn lands too fell victim to the Revolution.

The demise of the Penn proprietorship cannot be attributed to any one cause. Its existence had always depended on a spirit of deference, which evaporated in America during the revolutionary period. Its feudal characteristics and hereditary nature were not consistent with the new American society emerging at the time. That the family received compensation both from America and from England is a tribute to the family's political skill. Although the money the Penns collected for their losses was only a fraction of what they thought they should receive, it was a generous fortune for the times. For many Americans, the Revolution created new opportunities and new beginnings. For the Penns, it terminated their political presence, capped their financial expectations, and ushered them into historical obscurity.

Condensed Penn Family Tree and Interests in the Proprietorship

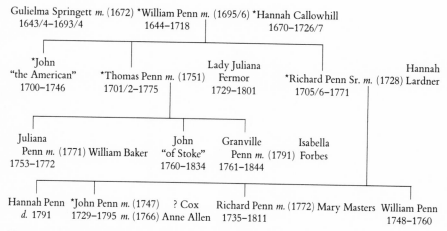

Gulielma Springett *m.* (1672) *William Penn *m.* (1695/6) *Hannah Callowhill
    1643/4–1693/4   1644–1718   1670–1726/7

*John "the American" 1700–1746 *Thomas Penn *m.* (1751) 1701/2–1775   Lady Juliana Fermor 1729–1801   *Richard Penn Sr. *m.* (1728) 1705/6–1771   Hannah Lardner

Juliana Penn *m.* (1771) William Baker 1753–1772   John "of Stoke" 1760–1834   Granville Penn *m.* (1791) Forbes 1761–1844   Isabella

Hannah Penn *d.* 1791   *John Penn *m.* (1747) 1729–1795 *m.* (1766) Anne Allen   ? Cox   Richard Penn *m.* (1772) Mary Masters 1735–1811   William Penn 1748–1760

NOTES: Asterisk (*) indicates served as one of the proprietors of Pennsylvania. Penn family members who served as governors include John Penn (1763–71, 1773–76) and Richard Penn (1771–73).

Summary of Interests in the Proprietorship

1. After William Penn's first illness in 1712, his wife Hannah began acting as proprietor. After much dispute, the proprietorship was confirmed to William Penn's sons by Hannah Penn in the following proportions:

    | John "the American" | Chief proprietor, ½ interest |
    | Thomas Penn | ¼ interest |
    | Richard Penn Sr. | ¼ interest |

2. Upon the death of John "the American" in 1746:

    | Thomas Penn | Chief proprietor, ¾ interest |
    | Richard Penn Sr. | ¼ interest |

3. Upon the death of Richard Penn Sr. in 1771:

    | Thomas Penn | Chief proprietor, ¾ interest |
    | John Penn | ¼ interest |

4. Upon the death of Thomas Penn in 1775:

    | John "of Stoke" (Thomas's son) | Chief proprietor, ¾ interest |
    | John Penn | ¼ interest |

1680	William Penn petitions Charles II for a colony in America
1681	William Penn receives charter for Pennsylvania
1682	William Penn receives deeds to the lower counties (Delaware) from the Duke of York
	William Penn arrives in Pennsylvania for the first time
1684	William Penn returns to England
1688	The "Glorious Revolution" deposes James II and brings William and Mary to the throne of England
1693/94	Death of Gulielma Penn, first wife of William Penn
1695/96	Marriage of William Penn to Hannah Callowhill
1699	William Penn arrives in America for the second time
1699/1700	Birth of John, son of William Penn
1701	William Penn completes a new frame of government for Pennsylvania known as the "Charter of Privileges" or "Charter of Liberties"
	William Penn returns to England
1701/2	Birth of Thomas Penn, son of William Penn
1702	Queen Anne ascends the throne of England
1705/6	Birth of Richard Penn, son of William Penn
1712	William Penn is disabled by a stroke

1714   George I ascends the throne of England

1718   Death of William Penn

1726/27 Death of Hannah Penn

1727   Formal resolution of dispute over William Penn's will confirms Pennsylvania proprietorship to the sons of William Penn by Hannah

         George II ascends throne of England

1729   Birth of John Penn, son of Richard Penn Sr.

1732   Thomas Penn, son of William Penn, arrives in Pennsylvania

1734   John Penn, son of William Penn, arrives in Pennsylvania

1735   John Penn, son of William Penn, returns to England

         Birth of Richard Penn Jr., son of Richard Penn Sr.

1741   Thomas Penn, son of William Penn, returns to England

1746   Death of John Penn (son of William Penn), whose one-half interest in the Pennsylvania proprietorship is inherited by Thomas Penn

1747   First marriage of John Penn, son of Richard Penn Sr.

1751   Marriage of Thomas Penn to Lady Juliana Fermor

1752   John Penn, son of Richard Penn Sr., arrives in Pennsylvania

1753   Birth of Juliana Penn, daughter of Thomas Penn

1754   Pennsylvania and Virginia cooperate to establish Fort Pitt on the western frontier

1755   John Penn, son of Richard Penn Sr., returns to England

         Braddock defeated by the French and Indians on western frontier

1756   French and Indian War (Seven Years' War) formally declared

1760   George III ascends throne of England

Surveyors Mason and Dixon are commissioned to survey Pennsylvania/Maryland border

Birth of John Penn, son of Thomas Penn

1763   French and Indian War ends when Peace of Paris is signed

John Penn, son of Richard Penn Sr., appointed governor of Pennsylvania

Pontiac's Uprising on western frontier

Governor John Penn and Richard Penn Jr., son of Richard Penn Sr., arrive in Pennsylvania

Colonel Henry Bouquet victorious at Bushy Run

Conestoga Massacre

1764   March of the Paxton Boys on Philadelphia

Ben Franklin touches off the movement for royal government

Publication of pamphlet *Cool Thoughts* by Ben Franklin

Ben Franklin and Joseph Galloway are temporarily ousted from Pennsylvania assembly

Parliament passes the Sugar Act

1765   Parliament passes the Stamp Act

Parliament passes the Quartering Act

1766   Marriage of Governor John Penn to Anne Allen

Ben Franklin's "Examination" by Parliament, instrumental in bringing about Stamp Act repeal

Parliament repeals the Stamp Act

Parliament passes the Declaratory Act

1767   Parliament passes the Townshend Acts

1768   Massachusetts sends its circular letter urging united action against the Townshend duties

Pennsylvania's "Incident at Middle Creek"

Penn family buys much Indian land with treaty made at Fort Stanwix

Lord Hillsborough advises Ben Franklin to give up the movement for royal government

1769   British crown confirms Pennsylvania/Maryland border

Philadelphia merchants agree to organized boycotts to protest Townshend duties

Richard Penn Jr., son of Richard Penn Sr., returns to England

1770   Parliament repeals Townshend Acts except for a tax on tea

1771   Death of Richard Penn Sr.

Governor John Penn returns to England

Richard Penn Jr., son of late Richard Penn Sr., appointed governor of Pennsylvania and returns to Pennsylvania

1771   Marriage of Juliana Penn to William Baker

1772   Marriage of Governor Richard Penn Jr. to Mary Masters

1773   Connecticut officially claims land within what the Penns claim are borders of Pennsylvania

John Penn, son of Richard Penn Sr., reappointed governor of Pennsylvania and returns to Pennsylvania

Parliament passes the Tea Act

Boston Tea Party and various tea parties in other colonies including Pennsylvania

1774   Parliament passes the Quebec Act

Parliament passes the Coercive Acts

America's first Continental Congress suggests boycotts to protest Coercive Acts

Lord Dunmore of Virginia claims that Fort Pitt lies in Virginia and attempts to exert authority there

Lord Dunmore's War

Governor John Penn calls special session of Pennsylvania assembly to consider threat of Indian war in the west

1775   Death of Thomas Penn, son of William Penn

Parliament passes the Prohibitory Act

Patriots take a stand at Lexington and Concord

Battle of Bunker Hill

Second Continental Congress convenes

Richard Penn Jr., son of Richard Penn Sr., returns to England bearing the "Olive Branch Petition"

Plunket's Expedition against the Connecticut settlers

1776   British warships *Roebuck* and *Liverpool* appear to sail on Philadelphia; the city defends itself

Second Continental Congress votes for American independence

Pennsylvania Constitution rewritten, divesting the Penn family of governing powers in Pennsylvania

1777   Occupation of Philadelphia by British General Howe

1777   Former Governor John Penn forced into exile in New Jersey

1778   British General Howe evacuates Philadelphia

Former Governor John Penn is allowed to return to Pennsylvania

Former Governor John Penn takes loyalty oath to new government of Pennsylvania

Wyoming Massacre

1779   "Attack on Fort Wilson," high-water mark of conflict in Pennsylvania over the 1776 state constitution

Pennsylvania passes the Divestment Act, divesting the Penn family of unsold land in Pennsylvania for compensation of £130,000

1780   Pennsylvania and Virginia governments ratify a line officially separating Pennsylvania and Virginia

Pennsylvania and Connecticut governments agree that Wyoming Valley and Shamokin lie within the borders of Pennsylvania

1781   George Washington forces surrender of Cornwallis at Yorktown

1783   Peace treaty signed marking end of the American Revolution

John Penn, son of Thomas Penn, arrives in Pennsylvania

1784   Pennsylvania government creates a fund from which to pay the Penn family for confiscated lands

1787   U.S. Constitutional Convention convenes in Philadelphia

1788   Former Governor John Penn and John Penn, son of Thomas Penn, return to England seeking to lobby Parliament for additional compensation for confiscated lands

Parliament votes a yearly pension paid to Penn family

1792   Former Governor John Penn and Anne Allen Penn arrive in Pennsylvania

1795   Death of former Governor John Penn

1801   Death of Lady Juliana Penn

Notes

The following abbreviations are used throughout the Notes:

HSP   Historical Society of Pennsylvania, Philadelphia, Pennsylvania

PAML   Penn Papers, Additional Miscellaneous Letters, at the Historical Society of Pennsylvania

PLB   Penn Letter Books, at the Historical Society of Pennsylvania

POC   Penn Papers, Official Correspondence, at the Historical Society of Pennsylvania

PPC   Penn Papers, Personal Correspondence, Historical Society of Pennsylvania

Introduction

1. John Penn, "After May 1778," Dreer Collection in Boxes, Historical Society of Pennsylvania, Philadelphia. Hereafter, the Historical Society of Pennsylvania is cited as HSP.

2. Ibid.

3. John Penn to Edmund Physick, April 16, 1777, Penn Papers from Friends, HSP.

4. Anne M. Ousterhout, "Controlling the Opposition in Pennsylvania During the American Revolution," *Pennsylvania Magazine of History and Biography* 105 (January 1981), 4–6.

5. Ibid., 9–11, 13.

6. Anne Penn to Lady Juliana Penn, October 26, 1777, Society Miscellaneous Collection, HSP.

7. John Penn, "After May 1778."

8. Ibid.

9. Ibid.

10. Ibid.

11. Ibid.

12. Ibid.

13. Ibid.

14. Ibid.

15. Ibid.

16. Anne Penn to Lady Juliana Penn, October 26, 1777, and December 14, 1777, Society Miscellaneous Collection, HSP.

17. Anne Penn to Lady Juliana Penn, October 26, 1777, Society Miscellaneous Collection, HSP.

Chapter 1

1. *Pennsylvania Gazette,* August 7–14, 1732.

2. Ibid.

3. Ibid.

4. William R. Shepherd, *The History of Proprietary Government in Pennsylvania* (New York: Columbia University Press, 1896), 5, 13–14, 15–17, 172, 179.

5. Ibid., 6, 14–15, 173.

6. Joseph J. Kelley Jr., *Pennsylvania: The Colonial Years, 1681–1776* (Garden City, N.Y.: Doubleday, 1980), 22.

7. Shepherd, *History of Proprietary Government,* 226, 234–35.

8. Ibid., 198.

9. Ibid., 199–200.

10. Ibid., 202.

11. "The Family of William Penn, A Collated Record," *Pennsylvania Genealogical Magazine* 25, no. 2 (1967), 84.

12. Shepherd, *History of Proprietary Government,* 17, 47–48.

13. Ibid., 31–32.

14. Ibid., 72.

15. Ibid., 13.

16. Ibid., 50–51.

17. Ibid., 37.

18. Alan Tully, *William Penn's Legacy: Politics and Social Structure in Provincial Pennsylvania, 1726–1755* (Baltimore: Johns Hopkins University Press, 1977), 6.

19. John, Thomas, and Richard Penn to James Steel, May 6, 1730, Penn Manuscripts, Unbound, HSP.

20. Thomas Penn to James Steel, May 6, 1730, Penn Manuscripts, Unbound, HSP.

21. Thomas Penn to James Steel, October 1, 1730, Penn Manuscripts, Unbound, HSP.

22. James Steel to Thomas Penn, "3rd Month" 6, 1731. James Steel's Letter Book, HSP.

23. "Family of William Penn, Collated Record," 85.

24. Nicholas B. Wainwright, "The Penn Collection," *Pennsylvania Magazine of History and Biography* 87 (October 1963), 393–94.

25. Thomas Penn to Samuel Blunston, April 3, 1734, Penn Manuscripts, Unbound, HSP.

26. Tully, *William Penn's Legacy,* 14.

27. Thomas Penn to "Dear Brother," January 14, 1733/4, Penn Manuscripts, Unbound, HSP.

28. Tully, *William Penn's Legacy,* 15.

29. Thomas Penn to John Penn, September 17, 1735, Pennsylvania Miscellaneous Papers, Penn and Baltimore, 1725–39, HSP.

30. Shepherd, *History of Proprietary Government,* 219–20.

31. Thomas Penn to Samuel Blunston, May 1, 1735, Penn Manuscripts, Unbound, HSP.

32. Tully, *William Penn's Legacy,* 11.

33. Thomas Penn to James Steel, March 2, 1741, Penn Manuscripts, Unbound, HSP.

Chapter 2

1. I can find no reference to Miss Cox's Christian name in the Penn correspondence, but a 1976 article summarizing known genealogical information on the Penn family identifies her as Grace Cox, daughter of James Cox. See "Family of William Penn, Collated Record," 89.

2. Thomas Penn to James Hamilton, March 9, 1752, Penn Papers, Official Correspondence, V, HSP (hereafter cited as POC).

3. Lawrence Stone, *The Family, Sex, and Marriage in England, 1500–1800* (New York: Harper & Row, 1977), 35–36.

4. John Penn to Thomas Penn, November 9, 1748, Penn Papers, Personal Correspondence, III, HSP (hereafter cited as PPC).

5. Copy of a letter John Penn received from the Cox family as transcribed in his letter to Thomas Penn, March 10, 1752, PPC, IV.

6. Thomas Penn to James Hamilton, March 9, 1752, POC, V.

7. Thomas Penn to John Penn, August 15, 1754, POC, VI.

8. Richard Penn to Thomas Penn, July 5, 1752, PPC, IV.

9. Thomas Penn to Richard Hockley, December 1, 1773, Penn Letter Books, HSP (hereafter cited as PLB).

10. Thomas Penn to John Penn, March 29, 1752, PPC, IV.

11. Thomas Penn's agreement with Robert Dunant, August 6, 1747, PPC, III.

12. John Penn to Thomas Penn, August 5, 1752, PPC, IV.

13. John Penn to Thomas Penn, December 1, 1747, PPC, III.

14. John Penn to Thomas Penn, January 29, 1747, PPC, III.

15. John Penn to Thomas Penn, March 10, 1752, PPC, IV.

16. John Penn to Thomas Penn, February 17, 1749, PPC, III.

17. John Penn to Thomas Penn, October 20, 1747, PPC, III.

18. John Penn to Thomas Penn, April 3, 1749, PPC, III.

19. John Penn to Thomas Penn, October 20, 1747, PPC, III.

20. John Penn to Thomas Penn, December 1, 1747, PPC, III.

21. John Penn to Thomas Penn, May 7, 1748, PPC, III.

22. John Penn to Thomas Penn, August 9, 1748, PPC, III.

23. John Penn to Thomas Penn, September 20, 1748, PPC, III.

24. Thomas Penn to John Penn, January 5, 1752 (letter continued January 9, 1752), PPC, IV.

25. John Penn to Thomas Penn, March 18, 1752, PPC, IV.

26. Copy of a letter John Penn received from the Cox family as transcribed in his letter to Thomas Penn, March 10, 1752, PPC, IV.

27. John Penn to Thomas Penn, December 11, 1751, PPC, III.

28. "Family of William Penn, Collated Record," 86.

29. William White to Elizabeth Graham, January 28, 1771, P. E. Bishops Collection, HSP.

30. Earl of Granville to Lady Juliana Penn, December 28, 1749, Society Collection, HSP.

31. Lady Juliana Penn to Richard Peters, December 24, 1764, Penn Papers, Saunders Collection, HSP.

32. John Penn to Thomas Penn, February 7, 1752, PPC, IV.

33. John Penn to Thomas Penn, March 18, 1752, PPC, IV.

34. Thomas Penn to John Penn, March 29, 1752, PPC, IV.

35. Richard Penn to Thomas Penn, April 24, 1752, PPC, IV.

36. John Penn to Thomas Penn, August 5, 1752, PPC, IV.

37. Thomas Penn to Richard Peters, March 9, 1752, PLB, III.

38. Tully, *William Penn's Legacy,* 42.

39. Thomas Penn to James Hamilton, March 9, 1752, POC, V.

40. Thomas M. Doerflinger, *A Vigorous Spirit of Enterprise: Merchants and Economic Development in Revolutionary Philadelphia* (Chapel Hill: University of North Carolina Press, 1986), 15.

41. John Penn to Thomas Penn, February 13, 1753, POC, VI.

42. Thomas Penn to John Penn, January 19, 1753, PLB, III.

43. John Penn to Thomas Penn, April 18, 1753, POC, VI.

44. Tully, *William Penn's Legacy,* 24–29.

45. Ibid., 37–40.

46. John Penn to Thomas Penn, December 16, 1752, PPC, IV.

47. James H. Hutson, "The Campaign to Make Pennsylvania a Royal Province," *Pennsylvania Magazine of History and Biography* 94 and 95 (October 1970 and January 1971), 428–29; James H. Hutson, *Pennsylvania Politics, 1746–1770: The Movement for Royal Government and Its Consequences* (Princeton: Princeton University Press, 1972), 13–15.

48. Kelley Jr., *Pennsylvania: The Colonial Years,* 307–8.

49. Hutson, "Campaign," 428–29; Hutson, *Pennsylvania Politics,* 17–20.

50. Stephen Brobeck, "Revolutionary Change in Colonial Philadelphia: The Brief Life of the Proprietary Gentry," *William and Mary Quarterly,* 3rd ser., 33 (July 1976), 419.

51. Ibid., 416.

52. Ibid., 426.

53. Thomas Penn to John Penn, January 30, 1753, PLB, III.

54. Document signed at council meeting, February 6, 1753, Pennsylvania Miscellaneous Collection, Pennsylvania and Baltimore, 1740–56, HSP.

55. John Penn to Thomas Penn, February 13, 1753, POC, VI.

56. Thomas Penn to John Penn, June 29, 1753, PLB, III.

57. John Penn to Thomas Penn, December 16, 1752, PPC, IV.

58. Thomas Penn to John Penn, January 30, 1753, PLB, III.

59. Richard Hockley to Richard Penn Sr., August 3, 1754, Penn Papers, Penn Family, 1732–67, HSP.

60. Thomas Penn to Richard Peters, August 15, 1754, POC, VI.

61. Richard Hockley to Thomas Penn, October 5, 1755, Penn Papers, Penn Family, 1732–67, HSP.

62. Thomas Penn to Richard Peters, July 3, 1755, Gratz Collection, Governors of Pennsylvania, Case 2, Box 33a, HSP.

63. John Penn to Thomas Penn, August 29, 1755, PPC, IV.

64. Thomas Penn to John Penn, June 4, 1755, Penn Papers, Saunders-Coates Collection, HSP.

65. Richard Penn Sr. to Richard Peters, February 24, 1755, Penn Papers, Saunders-Coates Collection, HSP.

66. John Penn to Thomas Penn, August 29, 1755, PPC, IV.

67. Richard Penn to Thomas Penn, October 20, 1755, PPC, IV.

68. Richard Penn to Thomas Penn, November 30, 1756, PPC, IV.

69. John Penn to Thomas Penn, August 10, 1760, PPC, V.

70. Thomas Penn to Richard Peters and John Penn, August 15, 1754, POC, VI.

71. Richard Penn Jr. to Thomas Penn, October 23, 1752, PPC, IV.

72. Richard Penn Jr. to Thomas Penn, June 12, 1761, POC, VI.

73. Richard Penn Jr. to Thomas Penn, July 11, 1761, POC, VI.

74. Thomas Penn to Richard Penn Jr., August 19, 1761, POC, IX.

75. Thomas Penn and Richard Penn Sr. to James Hamilton, January 7, 1763, Penn-Hamilton Correspondence, HSP.

76. Thomas Penn to James Hamilton, June 17, 1763, PLB, VII.

77. Undated document by John Pemberton, Penn Papers, Indian Walk, p. 4, HSP.

78. Thomas Penn to Richard Peters, June 3, 1763, PLB, VII.

79. Thomas Penn to Richard Peters, August 10, 1763, PLB, VII.

80. Thomas Penn to William Peters, July 9, 1763, PLB, VII.

81. John Penn to Thomas Penn, December 18, 1763, POC, IX.

82. Howard M. Jenkins, *The Family of William Penn, Founder of Pennsylvania: Ancestry and Descendents* (Philadelphia: Author, 1899), 187.

83. *Pennsylvania Gazette* and *Pennsylvania Journal,* November 24, 1763.

84. *Minutes of the Provincial Council of Pennsylvania,* vol. 9 of *Pennsylvania Archives, Colonial Records* (Harrisburg, Pa.: Theo Fenn & Co., 1852), 9:97–98.

85. John Penn to Thomas Penn, November 15, 1763, POC, IX.

Chapter 3

1. *Pennsylvania Gazette,* June 30, 1763.

2. *Pennsylvania Gazette,* July 21, 1763.

3. *Pennsylvania Journal,* September 15, 1763.

4. Ibid.; *Minutes, Provincial Council,* 9:43.

5. *Minutes, Provincial Council,* 9:15.

6. Ibid., 37–38.

7. Theodore Thayer, *Pennsylvania Politics and the Growth of Democracy, 1740–1776* (Harrisburg, Pa.: Pennsylvania Historical and Museum Commission, 1953), 80–81.

8. "Minutes of Conferences Held at Lancaster in August, 1762," in *Early American Imprints, 1639–1800,* ed. Clifford K. Shipton (Worcester, Mass.: American Antiquarian Society, 1967–74), no. 9412.

9. *Pennsylvania Gazette,* June 9, 1763.

10. *Pennsylvania Gazette,* June 16, 1763.

11. *Pennsylvania Journal,* June 16, 1763.

12. *Pennsylvania Gazette,* June 30, 1763.

13. *Pennsylvania Gazette,* July 7, 1763.

14. *Pennsylvania Gazette,* August 4, 1763.

15. Charles F. Hoban ed., *Votes of Assembly,* vol. 6, Pennsylvania Archives, 8th ser. (1935), 5431.

16. Thomas Penn to James Hamilton, November 11, 1763, PLB, VIII.

17. Thomas Penn to John Penn, February 10, 1764, PLB, VIII.

18. *Pennsylvania Gazette,* October 27, 1763.

19. Samuel Hazard, ed., *Original Documents of the Secretary of the Commonwealth,* vol. 4, Pennsylvania Archives, 1st ser. (Philadelphia: Joseph Severns & Co., 1853), 120; Hoban, *Votes of Assembly,* 6:5437–38.

20. Thomas Penn to James Hamilton, December 10, 1763, PLB, VIII.

21. Don Daudelin, "Numbers and Tactics at Bushy Run," *Western Pennsylvania Historical Magazine* 68 (April 1985), 162–68.

22. John Penn to Thomas Penn, November 15, 1763, POC, IX.

23. John Penn to Thomas Penn, December 18, 1763, POC, IX.

24. *Minutes, Provincial Council,* 9:102.

25. Ibid., 88.

26. Ibid., 93–94.

27. Hoban, *Votes of Assembly,* 6:5495.

28. *Minutes, Provincial Council,* 9:100.

29. Ibid., 103.

30. *Pennsylvania Gazette,* July 21, 1763.

31. Frank J. Cavaioli, "A Profile of the Paxton Boys: Murderers of the Conestoga Indians," *Journal of the Lancaster County Historical Society* 87, no. 3 (1983), 85.

32. George Edward Reed, ed., *Papers of the Governors,* vol. 3, Pennsylvania Archives, 4th ser. (Harrisburg, Pa.: William Stanley Ray, 1900), 258.

33. *Minutes, Provincial Council,* 9:101.

34. Hazard, *Original Documents,* 9:152.

35. John Penn to Thomas Penn, June 16, 1764, POC, IX.

36. *Minutes, Provincial Council,* 9:128.

37. John Penn to Thomas Penn, November 15, 1763, POC, IX.

38. *Minutes, Provincial Council,* 9:104–5; Reed, *Papers of the Governors,* 3:256–58.

39. Reed, *Papers of the Governors,* 3:254.

40. *Minutes, Provincial Council,* 9:110.

41. Brook Hindle, "The March of the Paxton Boys," *William and Mary Quarterly* 3 (October 1946), 472–73.

42. *Minutes, Provincial Council,* 9:124–25.

43. Ibid., 125–26.

44. Ibid., 9:132; Hoban, *Votes of Assembly,* 7:5537.

45. *Minutes, Provincial Council,* 9:118, 127.

46. Ibid., 109.

47. *Minutes, Provincial Council,* 9:132; Kelley, *Pennsylvania: The Colonial Years,* 495.

48. David Sloan, "A Time of Sifting and Winnowing: The Paxton Riots and Quaker Non-Violence in Pennsylvania," *Quaker History* 66 (Spring 1977), 5.

49. "A Battle! A Battle," in *Early American Imprints,* no. 9595.

50. Hindle, "March of the Paxton Boys," 478.

51. Kelley, *Pennsylvania: The Colonial Years,* 496–97.

52. Hindle, "March of the Paxton Boys," 479.

53. Kelley, *Pennsylvania: The Colonial Years,* 498.

54. John Penn to Thomas Penn, March 17, 1764, POC, IX.

55. Hindle, "March of the Paxton Boys," 480–81.

56. James E. Crowley, "The Paxton Disturbances and Ideas of Order in Pennsylvania Politics," *Pennsylvania History* 37 (October 1970), 319–21. The five frontier counties held only ten assembly seats, while the eastern counties held twenty-six.

57. Hoban, *Votes of Assembly,* 7:5553–54.

58. Ibid., 5554–56.

59. John Penn to Thomas Penn, June 16, 1764, POC, IX.

60. John Penn to Thomas Penn, March 17, 1764, POC, IX.

61. Thomas Penn to John Penn, April 13, 1764, PLB, VIII.

62. Thomas Penn to John Penn, July 13, 1764, PLB, VIII.

63. "A Narrative of the Late Massacres in Lancaster County," in *Early American Imprints,* no. 9667.

64. Thomas Penn to Richard Peters, April 13, 1764, Penn Papers, Saunders-Coates Collection, HSP.

65. "The Conduct of the Paxton Men Impartially Represented," in *Early American Imprints,* no. 9594.

66. "The Quaker Unmask'd; or, Plain Truth," in *Early American Imprints,* no. 9646.

67. "A Looking Glass for Presbyterians," in *Early American Imprints,* no. 9702.

68. Works consulted for this study that use this argument include Melvin H. Buxbaum, *Benjamin Franklin and the Zealous Presbyterians* (University Park: The Pennsylvania State University Press, 1974), 193; Cecil B. Currey, *The Road to Revolution: Benjamin Franklin in England, 1765–1775* (Garden City, N.Y.: Anchor Books, Doubleday, 1968), 45–46; Hindle, "March of the Paxton Boys," 475; Hutson, *Pennsylvania Politics,* 92–93; James H. Hutson, "An Investigation of the Inarticulate: Philadelphia's White Oaks," *William and Mary Quarterly,* 3rd ser., 28 (January 1971), 11; Joseph E. Illick, *Colonial Pennsylvania: A History* (New York: Charles Scribner's Sons, 1976), 238; Kelley, *Pennsylvania,* 496; Charles H. Lincoln, *The Revolutionary Movement in Pennsylvania, 1760–1776* (Philadelphia: University of Pennsylvania, 1901), 112; Benjamin H. Newcomb, *Franklin and Galloway: A Political Partnership* (New Haven: Yale University Press, 1972), 75; Carl Van Doren, *Benjamin Franklin* (New York: Viking Press, 1938), 310–11.

69. "The Paxton Boys: A Farce," in *Early American Imprints,* no. 9776.

70. John Penn to Thomas Penn, June 16, 1764, POC, IX.

71. *Pennsylvania Gazette,* March 8, 1764.

72. *Pennsylvania Gazette,* June 28, 1764.

73. *Pennsylvania Gazette,* August 9, 1764.

74. Ibid.; *Pennsylvania Journal,* August 8, 1764.

75. John Penn to Sir William Johnson, June 9, 1764, Gratz Collection, Case 1, Box 1, HSP.

76. *Pennsylvania Journal,* July 12, 1764.

77. John Penn to Thomas Penn, June 16, 1764, POC, IX.

78. *Pennsylvania Gazette,* October 25, 1764, and November 1, 1764. "Light horse" are light armed cavalry.

79. *Pennsylvania Gazette,* September 13, 1764.

80. *Pennsylvania Gazette,* December 6, 1764.

81. John Penn to Thomas Penn, December 5, 1764, POC, IX.

82. Hoban, *Votes of Assembly,* 7:5743, 5772.

83. Hoban, *Votes of Assembly,* 7:5749, 5753.

84. Thomas Penn to Edmund Physick, July 14, 1764, PLB, VIII.

85. Thomas Penn to Richard Hockley, August 4, 1764, PLB, VIII.

86. Thomas Penn to Sir William Johnson, September 7, 1764, PLB, VIII.

87. Thomas Penn to Richard Peters, August 31, 1763, PLB, VII.

88. John Penn to Thomas Penn, March 16, 1765, POC, X.

89. John Penn to Sir William Johnson, March 21, 1765, Gratz Collection, Case 1, Box 1, HSP.

90. Thomas Penn to John Penn, June 8, 1765, PLB, VIII.

91. *Minutes, Provincial Council,* 9:266.

92. Ibid., 267.

93. Hazard, *Original Documents,* 4:260.

94. Thomas Penn to John Penn, September 28, 1765, PLB, VIII.

95. *Minutes, Provincial Council,* 9:321.

Chapter 4

1. John Penn to Thomas Penn, March 17, 1764, POC, IX.

2. James H. Hutson, "Benjamin Franklin and Pennsylvania Politics, 1751–1755: A Reappraisal," *Pennsylvania Magazine of History and Biography* 93 (July 1969), 307.

3. Currey, *Road to Revolution,* 29.

4. Ibid., 31–32.

5. Hutson, "Franklin and Politics," 349, 352, 364; William S. Hanna, *Benjamin Franklin and Pennsylvania Politics* (Stanford, Calif.: Stanford University Press, 1964), 84–85.

6. Jack D. Marietta, *The Reformation of American Quakerism, 1748–1783* (Philadelphia: University of Pennsylvania Press, 1984), 150–51, 156, 158, 165.

7. Richard Peters to Thomas Penn, September 4, 1756, POC, VIII.

8. Hutson, "Franklin and Politics," 318, 326.

9. Shepherd, *History of Proprietary Government,* 488, 491.

10. Hutson, *Pennsylvania Politics,* 42–44.

11. Ibid., 44–47.

12. Hutson, "Campaign," 430–31, and *Pennsylvania Politics,* 58.

13. Newcomb, *Franklin and Galloway,* 64–65.

14. Shepherd, *History of Proprietary Government,* 463, 521.

15. Hutson, "Campaign," 431; Hutson, *Pennsylvania Politics,* 59–62.

16. Thomas Penn to John Penn, October 28, 1763, PLB, VIII.

17. Thomas Penn to Richard Peters, February 11, 1764, Gratz Collection, Governors of Pennsylvania, Case 2, Box 33, HSP.

18. Hoban, *Votes of Assembly,* 7:5578.

19. Ibid., 5567–68.

20. Ibid., 5576.

21. Ibid., 5585.

22. Ibid., 5587–91.

23. Ibid., 5599–5603.

24. Ibid., 5605–17, 5619–23.

25. Henry Wilmot to Thomas Penn, May 30, 1764, Penn-Physick Correspondence, V, HSP.

26. Richard Penn Sr. and Thomas Penn to John Penn, June 1, 1764, PLB, VIII.

27. Thomas Penn to James Hamilton, June 13, 1764, PLB, VIII.

28. John Penn to Thomas Penn, September 1, 1764, Penn Papers, Additional Miscellaneous Letters, I, HSP (hereafter cited as PAML).

29. "Cool Thoughts on the Situation of Public Affairs," in *Early American Imprints,* no. 9663.

30. William Allen to Thomas Penn, March 11, 1765, POC, X.

31. Thomas Penn to James Hamilton, June 13, 1764, PLB, VIII.

32. John Penn to Thomas Penn, March 17, 1764, POC, IX.

33. Hutson, "Campaign," 439–40; Hutson, *Pennsylvania Politics,* 127–28, 133.

34. "To the King's Most Excellent Majesty in Council . . . ," in *Early American Imprints,* no. 9786.

35. Thomas Penn to Benjamin Chew, January 11, 1765, PLB, VIII.

36. *Pennsylvania Gazette,* July 26, 1764.

37. Thomas Penn to Richard Hockley, August 4, 1764, PLB, VIII.

38. John Penn to Thomas Penn, October 19, 1764, POC, IX.

39. Hutson, "Campaign," 452; Hutson, *Pennsylvania Politics,* 150–52.

40. Hutson, *Pennsylvania Politics,* 165–67.

41. John Penn to Thomas Penn, September 22, 1764, POC, IX.

42. Thomas Penn to William Smith, March 8, 1765, PLB, VIII.

43. Thomas Penn to Richard Peters, November 18, 1764, Penn Papers, Saunders-Coates Collection, HSP.

44. "The Plot By Way of a Berlesk to Turn F out of the Assembly," in *Early American Imprints,* no. 9799.

45. Hutson, "Campaign," 452; Hutson, *Pennsylvania Politics,* 164–65.

46. "The Scribler," in *Early American Imprints,* no. 9831.

47. "To the Freeholders and Electors for the City and County of Philadelphia," in *Early American Imprints,* no. 9854.

48. John Penn to Thomas Penn, October 19, 1764, POC, IX.

49. William Allen to Thomas Penn, October 21, 1764, POC, IX.

50. John Penn to Thomas Penn, September 22, 1764, POC, IX.

51. William Allen to Thomas Penn, September 25, 1764, POC, IX.

52. William Allen to Thomas Penn, October 21, 1764, POC, IX.

53. Hutson, "Campaign," 442–43; Hutson, *Pennsylvania Politics,* 133–34, 246.

54. John Penn to Thomas Penn, October 19, 1764, POC, IX; Benjamin Chew to Thomas Penn, November 5, 1764, POC, IX.

55. Hoban, *Votes of Assembly,* 7:5687.

56. *Pennsylvania Journal,* November 1, 1764; Hoban, *Votes of Assembly,* 7:5688–89.

57. "Remarks on a Late Protest Against the Appointment of Mr. Franklin an Agent for This Province," in *Early American Imprints,* no. 9669; Hoban, *Votes of Assembly,* 7:5688–89.

58. *Pennsylvania Gazette,* November 8, 1764.

59. John Penn to Thomas Penn, October 19, 1764, POC, IX.

60. John Penn to Thomas Penn, March 16, 1765, POC, X.

61. Thomas Penn to John Penn, December 7, 1764, PLB, VIII.

62. Thomas Penn to Benjamin Chew, June 8, 1764, PLB, VIII.

63. Thomas Penn to William Peters, June 8, 1764, PLB, VIII.

64. Thomas Penn to Richard Hockley, June 9, 1764, PLB, VIII.

65. Thomas Penn to John Penn, July 13, 1764, PLB, VIII.

66. Thomas Penn to Benjamin Chew, December 7, 1764, PLB, VIII.

67. William Allen to Thomas Penn, March 11, 1765, POC, X.

68. Hutson, "Campaign," 459–61; Hutson, *Pennsylvania Politics,* 183–89.

69. Thomas Penn to William Allen, July 13, 1765, PLB, VIII.

70. William Allen to Thomas Penn, December 19, 1764, POC, IX.

71. Thomas Penn to William Allen, February 15, 1765, PLB, VIII.

72. Thomas Penn to John Penn, June 8, 1764, PLB, VIII.

73. Thomas Penn to John Penn, July 13, 1764, PLB, VIII.

74. John Penn to Thomas Penn, September 1, 1764, PAML, I.

75. John Penn to Thomas Penn, September 22, 1764, POC, IX.

76. Thomas Penn to William Allen, July 13, 1765, PLB, VIII.

77. Thomas Penn to Benjamin Chew, July 20, 1765, PLB, VIII.

78. Thomas Penn to John Penn, November 30, 1765, PLB, VIII.

79. *Pennsylvania Journal,* February 27, 1766.

80. Thomas Penn to William Peters, March 10, 1764, PLB, VIII.

81. Shepherd, *History of Proprietary Government,* 31, 72–73.

Chapter 5

1. Hoban, *Votes of Assembly,* 7:5688–89.

2. Thomas Penn to John Penn, February 10, 1764, PLB, VIII.

3. Hoban, *Votes of Assembly,* 7:5628, 5635.

4. Thomas Penn to John Penn, November 11, 1763, PLB, VIII.

5. Thomas Penn to John Penn, March 9, 1764, PLB, VIII.

6. Thomas Penn to John Penn, February 10, 1764, PLB, VIII.

7. Thomas Penn to Benjamin Chew, February 9, 1765, PLB, VIII.

8. Thomas Penn to John Penn, February 8, 1765, PLB, VIII.

9. Thomas Penn to William Allen, February 15, 1765, PLB, VIII.

10. *Pennsylvania Gazette,* May 10, 1764.

11. *Pennsylvania Gazette,* June 7, 1764.

12. William Allen to Thomas Penn, May 19, 1765, POC, X.

13. Stephen E. Lucas, *Portents of Rebellion: Rhetoric and Revolution in Philadelphia, 1765–1776* (Philadelphia: Temple University Press, 1976), 66–67.

14. Ibid., 48–49.

15. "The Late Regulations Respecting the British Colonies on the Continent of America Considered," in *Early American Imprints,* no. 9950.

16. Lucas, *Portents of Rebellion,* 34; Benjamin Newcomb, "Effects of the Stamp Act on Colonial Pennsylvania Politics," *William and Mary Quarterly,* 3rd ser., 23 (April 1966), 262; Newcomb, *Franklin and Galloway,* 116–17.

17. Thomas Penn to William Allen, July 13, 1765, PLB, VIII.

18. Hanna, *Benjamin Franklin and Pennsylvania Politics,* 174–77; Newcomb, *Franklin and Galloway,* 109–13, 136.

19. Thomas Penn to John Penn, April 13, 1765, PLB, VIII.

20. Thomas Penn to Mr. Young, September 28, 1765, PLB, VIII.

21. Thomas Penn to Richard Hockley, September 22, 1765, PLB, VIII.

22. *Pennsylvania Journal,* September 19, 1765.

23. Hutson, "Investigation of the Inarticulate," 18–21.

24. *Pennsylvania Journal,* October 3, 1765.

25. *Pennsylvania Gazette,* October 10, 1765; *Pennsylvania Journal,* October 10, 1765.

26. Edmund S. Morgan and Helen M. Morgan, *The Stamp Act Crisis: Prologue to Revolution* (Chapel Hill: University of North Carolina Press, 1953), 249–51.

27. Hutson, *Pennsylvania Politics,* 195–96.

28. Thomas Penn to Richard Peters, April 5, 1766, PLB, IX.

29. Morgan and Morgan, *Stamp Act Crisis,* 249–51.

30. Hoban, *Votes of Assembly,* 7:5765–67, 5769, 5779–80.

31. Thomas Penn to John Penn, December 15, 1765, POC, X.

32. Hutson, *Pennsylvania Politics,* 197–99; Hutson, "Investigation of the Inarticulate," 19–20, 21.

33. *Pennsylvania Journal,* December 19, 1765.

34. *Pennsylvania Gazette,* December 19, 1765.

35. *Pennsylvania Gazette,* May 22, 1766; *Pennsylvania Journal,* May 22, 1766.

36. Henry Conway to John Penn, March 31, 1766, Dreer Collection, HSP.

37. Thomas Penn to John Penn, March 18, 1766, PLB, VIII.

38. Thomas Penn to William Allen, March 17, 1766, PLB, VIII.

39. Hoban, *Votes of Assembly,* 7:5884–85.

40. *Pennsylvania Gazette,* June 5, 1766.

41. *Pennsylvania Gazette,* June 12, 1766.

42. Thomas Penn to Dr. Smith, February 9, 1765, PLB, VIII.

43. Thomas Penn to William Allen, February 15, 1765, PLB, VIII.

44. *Pennsylvania Journal,* May 8, 1766.

45. *Pennsylvania Gazette,* February 27, 1766.

46. "The Examination of Doctor Franklin," in *Early American Imprints,* no. 10300.

47. John Penn to Thomas Penn, September 12, 1766, POC, X.

48. Thomas Penn to John Penn, November 8, 1766, PLB, IX.

49. Newcomb, *Franklin and Galloway,* 139.

50. Thomas Penn to John Penn, November 8, 1766, PLB, IX.

51. Henry Conway to John Penn, October 24, 1765, Society Collection, HSP.

52. Thomas Penn to John Penn, November 9, 1765, PLB, VIII.

53. John Penn to Thomas Penn, December 15, 1765, POC, X.

54. John Penn to William Smith and John Reynolds, December 18, 1765, Lancaster County Collection, 1724–73, HSP.

55. *Minutes, Provincial Council,* 9:299–300.

56. John Penn to Thomas Penn, March 21, 1766, POC, X.

57. Hoban, *Votes of Assembly,* 7:5877, 5881.

58. Hutson, *Pennsylvania Politics,* 216; Hutson, "Campaign," 37–38.

59. John Penn to Thomas Penn, September 12, 1766, POC, X.

60. Thomas Penn to John Penn, December 14, 1765, PLB, VIII; Thomas Penn to John Penn, May 10, 1766, PLB, IX.

61. Thomas Penn to Benjamin Chew, January 11, 1766, PLB, VIII.

62. John Penn to Thomas Penn, March 21, 1766, POC, X.

63. Thomas Penn to John Penn, March 18, 1766, PLB, VIII.

Chapter 6

1. Thomas Penn to Colonel Armstrong, June 16, 1764, PLB, VIII.

2. John Penn to Thomas Penn, March 17, 1764, POC, IX.

3. Richard Penn Jr. to Thomas Penn, June 15, 1764, POC, IX.

4. John Penn to Thomas Penn, June 16, 1764, POC, IX.

5. John Penn to Thomas Penn, November 8, 1766, PLB, IX.

6. John Penn to Thomas Penn, September 1, 1764, PAML, I.

7. Thomas Penn to Richard Penn Jr., February 10, 1764, PLB, VIII.

8. John Penn to Thomas Penn, October 19, 1764, POC, IX.

9. Thomas Penn to Mr. Shippen, July 16, 1766, PLB, IX.

10. Thomas Penn to William Allen, July 13, 1765, PLB, VIII.

11. Thomas Penn to Richard Penn Jr., June 8, 1764, PLB, VIII.

12. Thomas Penn to Richard Peters, April 5, 1766, PLB, IX.

13. Thomas Penn to John Penn, January 11, 1765, PLB, VIII.

14. *Pennsylvania Gazette,* February 7, 1765.

15. John Penn to Thomas Penn, February 15, 1765, PPC, V.

16. Thomas Penn to James Hamilton, June 18, 1763, PLB, VII.

17. Thomas Penn to Richard Peters, August 10, 1763, PLB, VII.

18. Thomas Penn to John Allen, March 23, 1764, PLB, VIII.

19. Thomas Penn to James Hamilton, June 13, 1764, PLB, VIII.

20. Thomas Penn to John Penn, April 12, 1765, PPC, V.

21. John Penn to Thomas Penn, May 20, 1765, POC, IX.

22. John Penn to Thomas Penn, October 13, 1765, PPC, V; John Penn to Thomas Penn, October 14, 1765, POC, X.

23. John Penn to Thomas Penn, October 13, 1765, PPC, V.

24. John Penn to Thomas Penn, March 1, 1766, POC, X.

25. Thomas Penn to John Penn, May 16, 1766, POC, X.

26. Richard Penn to Richard Peters, October 17, 1766, Gratz Collection, Governors of Pennsylvania, Case 2, Box 33, HSP.

27. *Pennsylvania Gazette,* June 5, 1766.

28. Hoban, *Votes of Assembly,* 7:5881.

29. Thomas Penn to John Penn, July 18, 1766, PLB, IX.

30. Thomas Penn to Richard Peters, August 6, 1766, PLB, IX.

31. *Pennsylvania Gazette,* December 18, 1766.

32. Thomas Penn to Richard Hockley, November 8, 1766, PLB, IX.

33. Thomas Penn to John Penn, August 16, 1766, PLB, IX.

34. *Pennsylvania Gazette,* December 4, 1766.

35. William Allen to Thomas Penn, November 12, 1766, POC, X.

36. *Pennsylvania Gazette,* December 18, 1766.

Chapter 7

1. Primary source information on the incident at Middle Creek comes from depositions incorporated in *Minutes, Provincial Council,* 9:414, 487–88; and Hoban, *Votes of Assembly,* 7:6108–9. Two recent articles covering the incident include Linda A. Ries, "The Rage of Opposing Government: The Stump Affair of 1768," *Cumberland County History* 1 (Summer 1984), and G. S. Rowe, "The Frederick Stump Affair, 1768, and Its Challenge to Legal Historians of Early Pennsylvania," *Pennsylvania History* 49 (October 1982). My summary of events draws on all four sources.

2. Ibid.

3. Ibid.

4. *Minutes, Provincial Council,* 9:349, 351–53.

5. Ibid., 402–3.

6. Ibid., 405–6.

7. John Penn to Thomas Penn, January 21, 1768, POC, X.

8. *Minutes, Provincial Council,* 9:415–17.

9. Ibid., 424–25.

10. Ibid., 428–29.

11. *Pennsylvania Gazette,* February 11, 1768, and March 3, 1768.

12. Primary source information on this portion of the incident comes from *Pennsylvania Gazette,* March 3, 1768, and April 7, 1768; *Minutes, Provincial Council,* 9:512; Reed, *Papers of the Governors,* 3:374.

13. *Pennsylvania Gazette,* February 11, 1768.

14. *Minutes, Provincial Council,* 9:446.

15. Ibid., 441.

16. William Allen to Thomas Penn, February 25, 1768, POC, X.

17. Hoban, *Votes of Assembly,* 7:6131–33.

18. *Pennsylvania Gazette,* March 3, 1768.

19. *Pennsylvania Gazette,* February 11, 1768.

20. Ibid.

21. Ibid.

22. Ibid.

23. *Pennsylvania Gazette,* February 25, 1768.

24. John Penn to Thomas Penn, February 8, 1768, POC, X.

25. James Hamilton to Thomas Penn, May 23, 1768, POC, X.

26. Thomas Penn to John Penn, May 7, 1768, PLB.

27. Thomas Penn to John Penn, March 12, 1768, PLB, IX.

28. Nicholas B. Wainwright, *George Croghan: Wilderness Diplomat* (Chapel Hill: University of North Carolina Press, 1959), 249, 251–53.

29. Ibid.

30. "Minutes of Conference held at Fort-Pitt in April and May of 1768," in *Early American Imprints,* no. 11301.

31. Ibid.

32. Ibid.

33. John Penn to Thomas Penn, March 30, 1768, POC, X.

34. William Allen to Thomas Penn, October 12, 1768, POC, X.

Chapter 8

1. John Penn to Thomas Penn, July 31, 1768, POC, X.
2. Ibid.
3. Newcomb, *Franklin and Galloway,* 182–83.
4. "The Following Address was read at a Meeting of the Merchants at the Lodge in Philadelphia on Monday the 25th of April 1768," in *Early American Imprints,* no. 10896.
5. William Allen to Thomas Penn, October 8, 1767, POC, X.
6. Thomas Penn to William Allen, April 16, 1768, PLB, IX.
7. Thomas Penn to John Penn, April 20, 1768, PLB, IX.
8. John Penn to Thomas Penn, June 15, 1768, POC, X.
9. John Penn to Thomas Penn, July 31, 1768, POC, X.
10. Hoban, *Votes of Assembly,* 7:6187–88.
11. Ibid., 6243–44.
12. William Allen to Thomas Penn, September 23, 1768, POC, X.
13. William Allen to Thomas Penn, October 12, 1768, POC, X.
14. William Allen to Thomas Penn, December 4, 1768, POC, X.
15. Thomas Penn to John Penn, October 3, 1768, PLB, IX.
16. Thomas Penn to William Johnson, November 2, 1768, PLB, IX.
17. Thomas Penn to John Penn, October 3, 1768, PLB, IX.
18. Thomas Penn to John Penn, December 6, 1768, PLB, IX.
19. Thomas Penn to John Penn, October 3, 1768, PLB, IX.
20. Thomas Penn to James Hamilton, February 4, 1769, PLB, IX.
21. Hazard, *Original Documents,* 4:311.
22. "The Merchants of the City are Earnestly Requested to Meet at the Coffee House . . . ," in *Early American Imprints,* no. 11337.
23. Robert L. Brunhouse, "Effects of the Townshend Acts in Pennsylvania," *Pennsylvania Magazine of History and Biography* 54, no. 4 (1930), 366.
24. Richard Alan Ryerson, *The Revolution Is Now Begun: Radical Committees of Philadelphia, 1765–1776* (Philadelphia: University of Pennsylvania Press, 1977), 28–29.
25. Arthur M. Schlesinger, *The Colonial Merchants and the American Revolution* (New York: Atheneum, 1968), 192–93.
26. Hutson, "Campaign," 47–48, and *Pennsylvania Politics,* 227–30.
27. Schlesinger, *Colonial Merchants,* 191.
28. Brunhouse, "Effects of the Townshend Acts," 369–71.
29. Ibid., 366–68.
30. Thomas Penn to John Penn, May 9, 1769, PLB, IX.
31. Thomas Penn to the Philadelphia Merchants Committee, July 4, 1769, POC, X.
32. Thomas Penn to James Hamilton, March 5, 1770, PLB, IX.
33. Thomas M. Doerflinger, "Philadelphia Merchants and the Logic of Moderation, 1760–1775," *William and Mary Quarterly,* 3rd ser., 40 (April 1983), 219–21; Doerflinger, *Vigorous Spirit of Enterprise,* 192; Lucas, *Portents of Rebellion,* 41; Ryerson, *The Revolution Is Now Begun,* 30–32.
34. "The Subscribers to the Non-Importation Agreement are Desired to Meet at Davenport's Tavern . . . ," in *Early American Imprints,* no. 11878.
35. Doerflinger, *Vigorous Spirit of Enterprise,* 192–93.
36. Hutson, "Campaign," 48–49; Hutson, "Investigation of the Inarticulate," 23.

Chapter 9

1. *Pennsylvania Gazette,* July 18, 1771.

2. Oscar Jewell Harvey, *A History of Wilkes-Barre* (Wilkes-Barre, Pa.: Raeder Press, 1909), 256, 300, 391–92.

3. Deposition of Daniel Brodhead, Penn Papers, Wyoming Controversy, V, HSP.

4. Harvey, *History of Wilkes-Barre,* 423, 430–31.

5. Thomas Penn to Richard Peters, February 11, 1764, Gratz Collection, Governors of Pennsylvania, Case 2, Box 33a, HSP.

6. Thomas Penn to John Penn, December 12, 1767, PLB, IX.

7. Thomas Penn to William Johnson, January 7, 1768, PLB, IX; Thomas Penn to John Penn, January 7, 1768, PLB, IX.

8. John Penn to Thomas Penn, June 15, 1768, POC, X.

9. Thomas Penn to Richard Peters, November 2, 1768, PLB, IX.

10. William Allen to Thomas Penn, October 12, 1768, POC, X.

11. Benjamin Chew to Thomas Penn, November 13, 1768, POC, X.

12. Thomas Penn to Richard Hockley, July 23, 1768, PLB, IX.

13. Thomas Penn to John Penn, February 13, 1768, PLB, IX.

14. John Penn to Thomas Penn, November 6, 1768, POC, X; James Kirby Martin, "The Return of the Paxton Boys and the Historical State of the Pennsylvania Frontier, 1764–1774," *Pennsylvania History* 38 (April 1971), 126.

15. Edmund Physick to Thomas Penn, February 4, 1769, Penn-Physick Correspondence, III, HSP; Martin, "Return of the Paxton Boys," 126–27.

16. Edmund Physick to Thomas Penn, April 19, 1769, Penn-Physick Correspondence, III, HSP.

17. *Minutes, Provincial Council,* 9:572–73.

18. Harvey, *History of Wilkes-Barre,* 475–76.

19. *Minutes, Provincial Council,* 9:583–85.

20. Ibid., 585–86.

21. *Pennsylvania Chronicle,* June 16, 1769.

22. *Minutes, Provincial Council,* 9:602.

23. Hazard, *Original Documents,* 4:350–51.

24. Thomas Penn to James Tilghman, July 3, 1769, PLB, X.

25. Thomas Penn to Henry Wilmot, December 10, 1769, PLB, X.

26. John Penn to Thomas Penn, January 1, 1770, PPC.

27. John Penn to Thomas Penn, March 10, 1770, PAML, II.

28. John Penn to Thomas Penn, May 22, 1770, PPC, V. The account appears to be based on a deposition by Nathan Ogden, Penn Papers, Wyoming Controversy, V.

29. John Penn to Thomas Penn, November 25, 1770, POC, X.

30. John Penn to Thomas Penn, March 6, 1771, POC, X.

31. Hazard, *Original Documents,* 4:386–88.

32. John Penn to Pennsylvania Assembly, February 4, 1771, Dreer Collection, HSP.

33. Hoban, *Votes of Assembly,* 7:6667–71.

34. Deposition of Joseph Morris, Penn Papers, Wyoming Controversy, V.

35. Richard Hockley to Thomas Penn, February 29, 1772, POC, XI.

36. Richard Penn Jr. to Thomas Penn, April 3, 1772, POC, XI.

37. John Penn to Edmund Physick, May 10, 1772, Penn-Bailey Collection, HSP.

38. *Minutes, Provincial Council,* 10:125–33.

39. "An Examination of the Connecticut Claim to the Lands in Pennsylvania," in *Early American Imprints,* no. 13629.

40. William Johnson to Thomas Penn, September 22, 1773, POC, XI.

41. John Penn to Thomas Penn, March 6, 1771, POC, X.

Chapter 10

1. Thomas Penn to John Penn, February 5, 1771, PLB, X.

2. Thomas Penn to Henry Wilmot, November 18, 1769, PLB, X.

3. Richard Penn Jr. to John Penn, "after January 1771," Penn-Bailey Collection, HSP.

4. Ibid.

5. Richard Penn Jr. to John Penn, November 10, 1771, Penn-Bailey Collection, HSP.

6. Richard Penn Jr. to John Penn, "after January 1771," Penn-Bailey Collection, HSP.

7. *Pennsylvania Chronicle,* October 17, 1768.

8. Richard Penn Jr. to John Penn, "after 28 January 1771," Penn-Bailey Collection, HSP.

9. Richard Hockley to Thomas Penn, July 5, 1771, PAML, II.

10. John Penn to Benjamin Chew, April 27, 1772, Society Collection, HSP.

11. Thomas Penn to John Penn, August 13, 1771, PLB, X; Thomas Penn to Richard Hockley, August 22, 1771, PLB, X.

12. John Penn to Thomas Penn, August 12, 1771, POC, X.

13. *Pennsylvania Chronicle,* October 21, 1771; *Pennsylvania Journal,* November 17, 1771; *Pennsylvania Packet and General Advertiser,* November 4, 1771.

14. Richard Penn Jr. to Thomas Penn, "December 1771," POC, X.

15. Richard Penn Jr. to John Penn, November 10, 1771, Penn-Bailey Collection, HSP.

16. Ibid.

17. John Penn to Thomas Penn, January 1, 1772, POC, XI.

18. Thomas Penn to Richard Penn Jr., December 29, 1771, and February 4, 1772, PLB, X.

19. John Penn to Lynford Lardner, May 12, 1772, Society Collection, HSP.

20. Richard Penn Jr. to John Penn, July 25, 1772, Penn-Bailey Collection, HSP.

21. Ibid.

22. Thomas Penn to James Tilghman, September 1, 1770, PLB, X.

23. Thomas Penn to Richard Penn Jr., February 4, 1772, PLB, X.

24. Thomas Penn to Richard Penn Jr., June 3, 1772, PLB, X.

25. John Penn to Lynford Lardner, May 17, 1772, Society Collection, HSP.

26. John Penn to Benjamin Chew, April 27, 1772, Society Collection, HSP.

27. John Penn to Benjamin Chew, June 1, 1773, Penn Papers, Box 9, HSP.

28. *Pennsylvania Chronicle,* August 30, 1773, and September 6, 1773; *Pennsylvania Journal,* September 1, 1773; *Pennsylvania Packet and General Advertiser,* August 30, 1773.

29. *Pennsylvania Packet and General Advertiser,* September 20, 1773.

30. John Penn to Thomas Penn, September 8, 1773, POC, IX.

31. John Penn to Lady Juliana Penn, October 28, 1773, POC, IX.

32. Richard Hockley to Thomas Penn, October 28, 1773, POC, XI.

33. *Pennsylvania Chronicle,* October 4, 1773.

34. James Tilghman to Thomas Penn, October 28, 1773, POC, XI.

Chapter 11

1. Hoban, *Votes of Assembly,* 8:6969–76, 6984.

2. Frederick D. Stone, "How the Landing of Tea Was Opposed in Philadelphia," *Pennsylvania Magazine of History and Biography* 15, no. 4 (1891), 386.

3. Doerflinger, *Vigorous Spirit of Enterprise,* 193–94; Lucas, *Portents of Rebellion,* 43; Gary B. Nash, *The Urban Crucible: Social Change, Political Consciousness, and the Origins of the American Revolution* (Cambridge, Mass.: Harvard University Press, 1979), 316–17.

4. Pigou and Booth to James and Drinker, October 13, 1773, Henry S. Drinker Papers, HSP.

5. "Inhabitants of Pennsylvania . . . ," in *Early American Imprints,* no. 12940.

6. *Pennsylvania Gazette,* October 20, 1773.

7. Stone, "How the Landing of Tea Was Opposed," 386–87.

8. Pigou and Booth to James and Drinker, October 27, 1773, Drinker Papers, HSP.

9. *Pennsylvania Gazette,* December 29, 1773.

10. Thomas Wharton to "Dear Brother," November 30, 1773, Letter Book of Thomas Wharton, HSP.

11. James and Drinker to Pigou and Booth, October 26, 1773, Drinker Papers, HSP.

12. Stone, "How the Landing of Tea Was Opposed," 389.

13. *Pennsylvania Gazette,* December 29, 1773.

14. *Pennsylvania Gazette,* December 1, 1773.

15. "Mucius to the Freemen of America," in *Early American Imprints,* no. 12873.

16. *Pennsylvania Journal,* December 1, 1773.

17. Thomas Wharton to "Dear Brother," November 30, 1773, Letter Book of Thomas Wharton, HSP.

18. "To the Tradesmen Mechanics Committee of the Province of Pennsylvania," in *Early American Imprints,* no. 13041.

19. "A Sermon on Tea," in *Early American Imprints,* no. 13606.

20. "From the Committee for Tarring and Feathering, To the Delaware Pilots," in *Early American Imprints,* no. 12941.

21. Stone, "How the Landing of Tea Was Opposed," 390–91.

22. Ibid.

23. *Pennsylvania Gazette,* December 24, 1773.

24. Thomas Wharton to Thomas Walpole, December 21, 1773, Letter Book of Thomas Wharton, HSP.

25. *Pennsylvania Gazette,* December 29, 1773.

26. Ibid.

27. Thomas Wharton to "Dear Friend," December 27, 1773. Letter Book of Thomas Wharton, HSP.

28. *Pennsylvania Gazette,* December 29, 1773.

29. Ibid.

30. Ibid.

31. Thomas Penn's secretary "P.U." to John Penn, February 8, 1774, PLB.

Chapter 12

1. Hazard, *Original Documents,* 4:480.

2. John Penn to Lady Juliana Penn, May 3, 1774, PPC, V; John Penn to Thomas Penn, May 15, 1774, POC, XI; John Penn to Henry Wilmot, May 1, 1774, POC, XI.

3. James Tilghman to Thomas Penn, March 31, 1774, POC, XI.
4. Thomas Penn to James Tilghman, March 2, 1774, PLB, X.
5. James Tilghman to Henry Wilmot, June 22, 1774, POC, XI.
6. Ryerson, *The Revolution Is Now Begun,* 40–42.
7. Ibid.
8. John Penn to Lady Juliana Penn, May 31, 1774, POC, XI.
9. In *Early American Imprints,* no. 13664.
10. In *Early American Imprints,* no. 13534.
11. Nash, *The Urban Crucible,* 377; Ryerson, *The Revolution Is Now Begun,* 50–52, 65, 86–88.
12. John Penn to Henry Wilmot, July 5, 1774, POC, XI.
13. Hoban, *Votes of Assembly,* 8:7087–91, 7097–7100.
14. Newcomb, *Franklin and Galloway,* 245–46.
15. John Penn to Lady Juliana Penn, June 24, 1774, PPC, V.
16. John Penn to Thomas Penn, August 2, 1774, POC, X.
17. *Pennsylvania Journal,* July 28, 1774.
18. John Penn to Lady Juliana Penn and William Baker, September 6, 1774, POC, XI.
19. Thomas Penn to James Tilghman, June 16, 1774, PLB, X.
20. Lady Juliana Penn to James Tilghman, September 4, 1774, PLB, X.
21. Lady Juliana Penn to James Tilghman, September 27, 1774, PLB, X.
22. Hazard, *Original Documents,* 4:539–40.
23. Ibid., 576–77.
24. John Penn to Lady Juliana Penn and William Baker, September 6, 1774, POC, XI.
25. John Penn to Henry Wilmot, November 1, 1774, POC, XI.
26. Caesar Rodney to Thomas Rodney, September 24, 1774, Gratz Collection, Stamp Act Congress, Case 2, Box 1, HSP.
27. James Tilghman to Henry Wilmot, October 2, 1774, PAML, II.
28. Newcomb, *Franklin and Galloway,* 258.
29. Ryerson, *The Revolution Is Now Begun,* 94, 98.
30. Thomas Penn to Edmund Physick, September 4, 1774, PLB, X.
31. Lady Juliana Penn to Edmund Physick, October 30, 1774, PLB, X.
32. Lady Juliana Penn to James Tilghman, November 28, 1774, PLB, X.
33. John Penn to Lady Juliana Penn, November 1, 1774, POC, XI.
34. Hoban, *Votes of Assembly,* 8:7185.
35. Ibid., 7192.
36. Ibid., 7221–25.
37. *Minutes, Provincial Council,* 10:213, 228–32.
38. Lady Juliana Penn to James Tilghman, February 1, 1775, PLB, X.
39. James Tilghman to Henry Wilmot, October 29, 1774, PAML, II.
40. John Penn to Lady Juliana Penn, February 28, 1775, POC, XI.

Chapter 13

1. John Penn to Henry Wilmot, May 1, 1774, POC, XI.
2. James Tilghman to Henry Wilmot, May 2, 1774, POC, XI.
3. Edmund Physick to Thomas Penn, September 29, 1774, Penn-Physick Correspondence, III, HSP.
4. Lady Juliana Penn to Richard Peters, October 30, 1774, PLB, X.

5. Ibid.

6. Lady Juliana Penn to James Tilghman, November 28, 1774, PLB, X.

7. Lady Juliana Penn to John Penn, January 10, 1775, PLB, X.

8. John Penn to Lady Juliana Penn, January 4, 1774, POC, XI. (Although this letter is dated 1774, I feel certain it was written in January 1775 because it refers to the death of Richard Hockley, which occurred in September 1774.)

9. "The Diary of James Allen, Esq., of Philadelphia, Counsellor at Law, 1770–1778," *Pennsylvania Magazine of History and Biography* 9, no. 2 (1885), 181.

10. John Penn to Lady Juliana Penn, April 5, 1774, POC, XI; John Penn to Thomas Penn, April 5, 1774, PPC, V.

11. Thomas Penn to Richard Hockley, June 16, 1774, PLB, X.

12. Edmund Physick to Thomas Penn, "1774," Penn-Physick Correspondence, V, HSP.

13. John Penn to Edmund Physick, June 10, 1774, Penn-Bailey Collection, HSP.

14. John Penn to Lady Juliana Penn, June 24, 1774, PPC, V.

15. Edmund Physick to Thomas Penn, September 29, 1774, Penn-Physick Correspondence, III, HSP.

16. John Penn to Thomas Penn, October 3, 1774, POC, XI.

17. Lady Juliana Penn to James Tilghman, November 28, 1774, PLB, X.

18. John Penn to Lady Juliana Penn, April 3, 1775, PPC, V.

19. Lady Juliana Penn to John Penn, October 5, 1774, PLB, X.

20. Lady Juliana Penn to John Penn, October 31, 1774, PLB, X.

21. Lady Juliana Penn to Edmund Physick, October 5, 1774, PLB, X.

22. Edmund Physick to Lady Juliana Penn, December 6, 1774, Penn-Physick Correspondence, III, HSP.

23. Lady Juliana Penn to Edmund Physick, January 10, 1775, PLB, X.

24. Lady Juliana Penn to John Penn, March 22, 1775, PLB, X.

25. Lady Juliana Penn to Richard Peters, April 5, 1775, PLB, X.

26. *Pennsylvania Gazette,* May 17, 1775.

27. William Baker to Lady Juliana Penn, September 30, 1774, Penn Papers in Boxes, HSP.

28. Lady Juliana Penn to Richard Peters, April 5, 1775, PLB, X.

29. Lady Juliana Penn to John Penn, May 29, 1775, PLB, X.

30. Lady Juliana Penn to the Rev. William Smith, August 31, 1775, Dreer Collection, HSP.

31. William Baker and Lady Juliana Penn to Richard Penn Jr., April 5, 1775, PLB, X.

32. Richard Penn to Lady Juliana Penn, May 10, 1775, PPC, V.

33. Lady Juliana Penn to Richard Penn, July 5, 1775, PLB, X.

34. William Baker and Lady Juliana Penn to John Penn, April 5, 1775, PLB, X.

35. William Baker and Lady Juliana Penn to John Penn, April 5, 1775, and April 15, 1775, PLB, X.

36. Edmund Physick to Lady Juliana Penn, September 4, 1775, Penn-Physick Correspondence, III, HSP.

Chapter 14

1. William Baker and Lady Juliana Penn to James Tilghman, April 5, 1775, PLB, X.

2. William Baker and Lady Juliana Penn to Edmund Physick, April 5, 1775, PLB, X.

3. William Baker and Lady Juliana Penn to James Tilghman, April 5, 1775, PLB, X.

4. Edmund Physick to William Baker and Lady Juliana Penn, June 30, 1775, and August 31, 1775, Penn-Physick Correspondence, III, HSP.

5. Lady Juliana Penn to Edmund Physick, June 17, 1775, PLB, X.

6. Lady Juliana Penn to Edmund Physick, June 20, 1775, PLB, X.

7. John Penn to Lady Juliana Penn, April 29, 1775, PPC, V.

8. William Baker to James Tilghman, July 15, 1775, PLB, X.

9. John Penn to Lady Juliana Penn, April 29, 1775, PPC, V.

10. Arthur J. Alexander, "Pennsylvania's Revolutionary Militia," *Pennsylvania Magazine of History and Biography* 69 (January 1945), 20–23; Nash, *The Urban Crucible*, 378–80.

11. "Diary of James Allen," 186.

12. Anne M. Ousterhout, *A State Divided: Opposition in Pennsylvania to the American Revolution* (Westport, Conn.: Greenwood Press, 1987), 107–8; Ryerson, *The Revolution Is Now Begun*, 117, 124.

13. Lady Juliana Penn to John Penn, May 29, 1775, PLB, X.

14. *Pennsylvania Journal*, August 9, 1775.

15. John Penn to Lady Juliana Penn, October 1, 1775, POC, XI.

16. John Penn to William Baker, October 1, 1775, POC, XI.

17. John Penn to Lady Juliana Penn, October 1, 1775, POC, XI.

18. "To the Tories," in *Early American Imprints,* no. 14739.

19. *Pennsylvania Gazette,* May 15, 1776; *Pennsylvania Journal,* May 8, 1776, and May 15, 1776.

20. David Hawke, *In the Midst of a Revolution* (Philadelphia: University of Pennsylvania Press, 1961), 116–18.

21. "Diary of James Allen," 187.

22. *Pennsylvania Gazette,* May 22, 1776.

23. J. Paul Selsam, *The Pennsylvania Constitution of 1776: A Study in Revolutionary Democracy* (Philadelphia: University of Pennsylvania Press, 1936), 122–24.

24. James E. Gibson, "The Pennsylvania Provincial Conference of 1776," *Pennsylvania Magazine of History and Biography* 58, no. 4 (1934), 331; Selsam, *Pennsylvania Constitution*, 136–38.

25. William Baker to Edmund Physick, June 10, 1776, PLB, X.

26. Edmund Physick to Lady Juliana Penn, June 11, 1776, Penn-Physick Correspondence, III, HSP; John Penn to Lady Juliana Penn, June 11, 1776, Gratz Collection, Governors of Pennsylvania, Case 2, Box 33a, HSP.

27. John Penn to Lady Juliana Penn, June 11, 1776, Gratz Collection, Governors of Pennsylvania, Case 2, Box 33a, HSP.

28. *Pennsylvania Gazette,* July 10, 1776.

29. Ousterhout, *A State Divided,* 147–48; Selsam, *Pennsylvania Constitution,* 152–62.

30. "Diary of James Allen," 188.

31. Edmund Physick to Lady Juliana Penn, September 17, 1776, Penn-Physick Correspondence, III, HSP.

32. Lady Juliana Penn to Edmund Physick, November 1, 1776, Penn-Physick Correspondence, I, HSP.

33. John Allen to Lady Juliana Penn, April 2, 1777, Dreer Collection in Boxes, HSP. The house Allen refers to is no doubt Lansdowne, John Penn's country estate. Allen's letter implies that Penn retired after the Declaration of Independence and was still there in April 1777. It is likely that he also remained there until his exile in August or early September 1777.

Chapter 15

1. Shepherd, *History of Proprietary Government,* 161–63.

2. Thomas Penn to William Allen, April 16, 1768, PLB, IX.

3. James Tilghman to Thomas Penn, October 10, 1771, POC, X.

4. Henry Wilmot to Thomas Penn, December 12, 1771, POC, XI.

5. Hoban, *Votes of Assembly,* 8:6914, 6918–19.

6. Ibid., 6936.

7. Ibid., 6956–57.

8. James Tilghman to Thomas Penn, January 30, 1773, March 1, 1773, and May 15, 1773, POC, XI.

9. James Tilghman to Thomas Penn, March 31, 1774, POC, XI.

10. *Minutes, Provincial Council,* 10:140–41.

11. Ousterhout, *A State Divided,* 251.

12. Hazard, *Original Documents,* 4:484.

13. *Minutes, Provincial Council,* 10:165.

14. Ibid., 168.

15. Ibid., 165.

16. Ibid., 169.

17. *Pennsylvania Gazette,* July 13, 1774.

18. Hoban, *Votes of Assembly,* 7:7085.

19. Kelley, *Pennsylvania: The Colonial Years,* 693–94.

20. *Pennsylvania Journal,* May 25, 1774.

21. *Pennsylvania Journal,* June 8, 1774.

22. *Pennsylvania Gazette,* July 6, 1774.

23. John Penn to Lady Juliana Penn, June 24, 1774, PPC, V.

24. *Pennsylvania Journal,* July 13, 1774; *Pennsylvania Gazette,* July 13, 1774.

25. *Pennsylvania Gazette,* July 13, 1774.

26. *Pennsylvania Journal,* November 16, 1774.

27. Hazard, *Original Documents,* 4:603–12.

28. John Penn to Henry Wilmot, January 30, 1775, POC, XI.

29. *Minutes, Provincial Council,* 10:149–50.

30. Ibid., 156–61.

31. Reed, *Papers of the Governors,* 3:506–7.

32. Ibid., 481.

33. *Minutes, Provincial Council,* 10:184–91; John Penn to Lady Juliana Penn, June 24, 1774, PPC, V.

34. John Penn to Henry Wilmot, November 6, 1774, POC, XI.

35. John Penn to Lady Juliana Penn, June 24, 1774, PPC, V.

36. Hoban, *Votes of Assembly,* 8:7085–87.

37. Ibid., 7171–2.

38. Ibid., 7095.

39. John Penn to Henry Wilmot, November 1, 1774, POC, XI; John Penn to Lady Juliana Penn, November 1, 1774, POC, XI.

40. Hoban, *Votes of Assembly,* 7:7085.

41. Reed, *Papers of the Governors,* 3:488–90.

42. John Penn to Lady Juliana Penn, April 29, 1775, PPC, V.

43. Ousterhout, *A State Divided,* 252–54.

44. John Penn to Lady Juliana Penn, April 5, 1774, POC, XI.

45. Ibid.

46. Hoban, *Votes of Assembly,* 8:7260.

47. Hazard, *Original Documents,* 4:661–62.

48. Harvey, *History of Wilkes-Barre,* 842–45.

49. Hoban, *Votes of Assembly,* 8:7364.

50. Ibid., 7315.

51. Ibid., 7330–32.

52. John Penn to William Plunket and the Justices of the Peace of Northumberland County, November 25, 1775, Dreer Collection, HSP.

53. Harvey, *History of Wilkes-Barre,* 860–62.

54. Ibid., 863.

55. Ousterhout, *A State Divided,* 236–39.

56. William Baker and Lady Juliana Penn to John Penn, April 5, 1775, PLB, X.

57. William Baker to John Penn, May 11, 1775, PLB, X.

58. John Penn to Thomas Penn, August 2, 1774, POC, XI.

59. Lady Juliana Penn to James Tilghman, September 27, 1774, PLB, X.

60. Hazard, *Original Documents,* 4:577.

61. Lady Juliana Penn to James Tilghman, September 4, 1774, PLB, X.

62. Henry Wilmot to William Baker, July 6, 1775, POC, XI.

63. Henry Wilmot to William Baker, November 12, 1775, POC, XI.

64. Henry Wilmot to William Baker, January 16, 1776, POC, XII.

65. Tully, *William Penn's Legacy,* 7.

66. Thomas Penn to the Line Commissioners, April 13, 1764, PLB, VIII.

67. Thomas Penn to Richard Hockley, July 23, 1768, PLB, IX.

68. James Hamilton to Thomas Penn, August 30, 1769, POC, X.

69. *Minutes, Provincial Council,* 10:220–22.

70. John Penn to Henry Wilmot, November 6, 1774, POC, XI.

71. William Baker to James Tilghman, July 15, 1775, PLB, X.

Chapter 16

1. "Diary of James Allen," 193.

2. Selsam, *Pennsylvania Constitution,* 226–27.

3. "Diary of James Allen," 189.

4. Wayne L. Bockelman and Owen S. Ireland, "The Internal Revolution in Pennsylvania: An Ethnic-Religious Interpretation," *Pennsylvania History* 41 (April 1974), 144–48.

5. Elisha P. Douglass, *Rebels and Democrats* (Chapel Hill: University of North Carolina Press, 1955), 274–75.

6. Robert L. Brunhouse, *The Counter Revolution in Pennsylvania, 1776–1790* (Harrisburg, Pa.: Pennsylvania Historical and Museum Commission, 1942), 18–20; Douglass, *Rebels and Democrats,* 278–80.

7. "Diary of James Allen," 189.

8. Ibid., 191.

9. Hazard, *Original Documents,* 5:73–75.

10. "Diary of James Allen," 189.

11. Reed, *Papers of the Governors,* 3:545–46.

12. Brunhouse, *The Counter Revolution,* 21–22.

13. Samuel B. Harding, "Party Struggles over the First Constitution of Pennsylvania," *American Historical Association Annual Report, 1894–1895,* 380.

14. "An Extract of a Letter from an Officer of Distinction in the American Army," in *Early American Imprints,* no. 14751.

15. "The Progress of British and Hessian Troops Through New Jersey," in *Early American Imprints,* no. 15037.

16. "In Assembly, December 24, 1776," in *Early American Imprints,* no. 14988.

17. John Allen to Lady Juliana Penn, April 2, 1777, Dreer Collection in Boxes, HSP.

18. John Penn to Edmund Physick, April 16, 1777, Penn Papers from Friends, HSP.

19. "Diary of James Allen," 193.

20. Ibid., 195–96.

21. Ibid., 296.

22. John Penn to Edmund Physick, April 16, 1777, Penn Papers from Friends, HSP.

23. John Penn to Edmund Physick, August 25, 1777, Penn-Bailey Collection, HSP.

24. Ousterhout, *A State Divided,* 161, 165–68.

25. "Diary of James Allen," 293.

26. John Penn to Edmund Physick, August 25, 1777, Society Miscellaneous Collection, HSP.

27. *Minutes of the Supreme Executive Council of Pennsylvania,* vol. 11, Pennsylvania Archives, Colonial Records (Harrisburg, Pa.: Theo Fenn and Company, 1852), 264–65.

28. *Pennsylvania Gazette,* August 13, 1777.

29. James Hamilton to President of the Executive Council, September 11, 1777, Society Miscellaneous Collection, HSP.

30. "Diary of James Allen," 195.

31. Frederick Weiner, "The Military Occupation of Philadelphia in 1777–1778," *American Philosophical Society Proceedings* 111 (October 1967), 310–11.

32. Anne Penn to Lady Juliana Penn, December 14, 1777, Society Miscellaneous Collection, HSP.

33. Darlene Emmert Fisher, "Social Life in Philadelphia During the British Occupation," *Pennsylvania History* 37 (July 1970), 244–45, 249–52.

34. Ibid., 238–39, 241, 243, 246.

35. Willard O. Mishoff, "Business in Philadelphia During the British Occupation," *Pennsylvania Magazine of History and Biography* 61 (April 1937), 167, 173, 181.

36. John Penn, "After May 1778," Dreer Collection in Boxes, HSP.

37. "Diary of James Allen," 434–35, 440.

38. Lady Juliana Penn to Edmund Physick, July 27, 1778, Penn-Physick Correspondence, I, HSP.

39. Hazard, *Original Documents,* 6:367, 389–90.

40. William Baker to Edmund Physick, April 9, 1778, Penn-Physick Correspondence, I, HSP.

41. William Baker to James Hamilton, April 9, 1778, James Hamilton Papers, HSP.

42. Edmund Physick to Lady Juliana Penn, May 28, 1778, Penn-Physick Correspondence, III, HSP.

43. Edmund Physick to Lady Juliana Penn, December 12, 1777, Penn-Physick Correspondence, III, HSP.

44. Lady Juliana Penn to Edmund Physick, March 4, 1778, Penn-Physick Correspondence, I, HSP.

45. John Penn to Lady Juliana Penn, July 20, 1778, Gratz Collection, Governors of Pennsylvania, Case 2, Box 33a, HSP.

46. Bockelman and Ireland, "Internal Revolution," 155.

47. Doerflinger, "Philadelphia Merchants," 225.

48. O. S. Ireland, "The Crux of Politics: Religion and Party in Pennsylvania, 1778–1789," *William and Mary Quarterly,* 3rd ser., 42 (October 1985), 455.

49. Steven Rosswurm, *Arms, Country, and Class: The Philadelphia Militia and the Lower Sort During the American Revolution, 1775–1783* (New Brunswick, N.J.: Rutgers University Press, 1987), 203.

50. John K. Alexander, "The Fort Wilson Incident of 1779: A Case Study of the Revolutionary Crowd," *William and Mary Quarterly,* 3rd ser., 31 (October 1974), 602–6.

51. Ousterhout, *A State Divided,* 232, 240–42.

52. Onuf, *Origins of the Federal Republic,* 57.

Chapter 17

1. John Allen to Lady Juliana Penn, April 2, 1777, Dreer Collection in Boxes, HSP.
2. "Diary of James Allen," 286.
3. Ousterhout, *A State Divided,* 171–72.
4. "Diary of James Allen," 296.
5. James Tilghman to the Council of Safety, January 3, 1777, Society Miscellaneous Collection, HSP.
6. Brunhouse, *The Counter Revolution,* 50.
7. Bockelman and Ireland, "Internal Revolution," 144–48.
8. "Diary of James Allen," 440.
9. Bockelman and Ireland, "Internal Revolution," 155–56.
10. *Pennsylvania Gazette,* February 10, 1779.
11. *Journals of the House of Representatives of the Commonwealth of Pennsylvania, 28 November 1776 to 2 October 1781,* vol. 1 (Philadelphia, 1782), 339.
12. Ibid., 365.
13. Ibid.
14. Reed, *Papers of the Governors,* 3:734.
15. *Pennsylvania Gazette,* December 8, 1779.
16. Ibid.
17. Shepherd, *History of Proprietary Government in Pennsylvania,* 89–91.
18. Ibid., 87–88.
19. *Journals, Pa. House of Representatives,* 402.
20. John Bayard to John Penn, March 4, 1779, Penn-Bailey Collection, HSP.
21. Drafted Letter by John Penn, 1779?, Society Collection, HSP.
22. *Journals, Pa. House of Representatives,* 402–4.
23. Hazard, *Original Documents,* 8:113.
24. Edmund Physick to John Bayard, February 24, 1780, Penn-Physick Correspondence, III, HSP.
25. Drafted Letter by John Penn, 1779?, Society Collection, HSP.

Chapter 18

1. John Penn to Dr. Parke, August 1780, Etting Papers, Early Quakers, HSP.
2. Anne Penn to Dr. Parke, August 27, 1780, Etting Papers, Early Quakers, HSP.
3. John Penn to Dr. Parke, 1781 and March 1781, Etting Papers, Early Quakers, HSP.
4. *Pennsylvania Journal,* April 19, 1783.
5. Richard Penn Jr. to Benjamin Franklin, July 30, 1782, Gratz Collection, Governors of Pennsylvania, Case 2, Box 33, HSP.
6. William Baker to James Hamilton, September 25, 1781, PAML, II, HSP.
7. Edmund Physick to John Penn, April 2, 1782, Penn-Physick Correspondence, III, HSP.
8. John Penn to Benjamin Chew, November 22, 1782, Penn-Physick Correspondence, I, HSP.
9. Reed, *Papers of the Governors,* 3:973.
10. Onuf, *Origins of the Federal Republic,* 58–62.
11. Samuel West to Lady Juliana Penn, December 26, 1782, Society Miscellaneous Collection, HSP.
12. William Baker to James Hamilton, January 13, 1783, James Hamilton Papers, HSP.
13. Lady Juliana Penn to Edmund Physick, March 20, 1783, Penn-Physick Correspondence, I, HSP.

14. William Baker to James Hamilton, January 13, 1783, James Hamilton Papers, HSP.

15. Memorial of John Penn, John Penn and Richard Penn, March 1784, Wilson Manuscripts, X, HSP.

16. Hazard, *Original Documents,* 10:485–88.

17. Edmund Physick to Lady Juliana Penn, September 1, 1785, Penn-Physick Correspondence, III, HSP.

18. Brunhouse, *The Counter Revolution,* 119–20, 140–41, 164.

19. John Penn, John Penn, and Richard Penn to Thomas Mifflin, Speaker of the Assembly, March 16, 1787, Etting Papers, Early Quakers, HSP.

20. Benjamin Chew to John Penn, 1786, Cadwalader Papers, Box 19, HSP.

21. John Penn's Commonplace Book, HSP.

22. John Penn to Dr. Parke, August 2, 1789, Gratz Collection, Governors of Pennsylvania, Case 2, Box 33a, HSP.

23. Tench Francis to Richard Penn Jr., May 13, 1788, Cadwalader Papers, Box 25, HSP.

24. Edmund Physick to John Penn, May 13, 1788, and June 30, 1788, Penn-Physick Correspondence, III, HSP.

25. "Family of William Penn," 90.

26. John Penn to Edmund Physick, July 9, 1788, Penn-Physick Correspondence, I, HSP.

27. John Penn to Edmund Physick, September 2, 1788, Penn-Bailey Collection, HSP.

28. John Penn to Edmund Physick, August 4, 1789, Penn-Physick Correspondence, II, HSP.

29. To Thomas McKean, February 1795, McKean Papers, III, HSP.

30. Agreement between John and Richard Penn, March 14, 1787, Penn-Physick Correspondence, III, HSP.

31. "Family of William Penn," 91.

32. Richard Penn to Edmund Physick, September 5, 1797, Penn-Physick Correspondence, II, HSP.

33. Anne Penn to J. Mifflin, January 6, 1796, Shippen Papers, XXXIII, HSP.

34. Anne Penn to John Mifflin, September 10, 1795, Shippen Papers, XXXIII, HSP.

35. Anne Penn to John Mifflin, June 26, 1801, Shippen Papers, XXXIII, HSP.

Bibliography

Primary Sources

"The Diary of James Allen, Esq., of Philadelphia, Counsellor at Law." *Pennsylvania Magazine of History and Biography* 9, nos. 2, 3, and 4 (1885), 176–96, 278–96, 424–41.

Early American Imprints, 1639–1800. Edited by Clifford K. Shipton. Worcester, Mass.: American Antiquarian Society, 1967–74.

Hazard, Samuel, ed. *Original Documents of the Secretary of the Commonwealth.* 12 vols. Pennsylvania Archives, 1st series, vols. 4–6, 8, 10. Philadelphia, Pa.: Joseph Severns & Co., 1853–54.

Historical Society of Pennsylvania, Philadelphia, Pennsylvania. Various items from the following collections:

Cadwalader Papers
Dreer Collection
Dreer Collection in Boxes
Etting Papers, Early Quakers
Gratz Collection, Case 1, Box 1
Gratz Collection, Governors of Pennsylvania, Case 2, Boxes 33 and 33a
Gratz Collection, Stamp Act Congress, Case 1, Box 1
Henry S. Drinker Papers
James Hamilton Papers
James Steel's Letter Book
John Penn's Commonplace Book
Lancaster County Collection 1724–73
Letter Book of Thomas Wharton
P. E. Bishops Collection
Penn-Bailey Collection
Penn-Hamilton Correspondence
Penn Letter Books
Penn Manuscripts, Unbound

Penn Papers, Additional Miscellaneous Letters
Penn Papers, Box 9
Penn Papers from Friends
Penn Papers in Boxes
Penn Papers, Indian Walk
Penn Papers, Official Correspondence
Penn Papers, Penn Family, 1732–67
Penn Papers, Personal Correspondence
Penn Papers, Saunders-Coates Collection
Penn Papers, Saunders Collection
Penn Papers, Wyoming Controversy
Penn-Physick Correspondence
Pennsylvania Miscellaneous Collection, Penn and Baltimore
Pennsylvania Miscellaneous Papers
Shippen Papers
Society Collection
Society Miscellaneous Collection
Wilson Manuscripts

Hoban, Charles F., ed. *Votes of Assembly.* 8 vols. Pennsylvania Archives, 8th series, vols. 6–8, 1935.

Journals of the House of Representatives of the Commonwealth of Pennsylvania, November 28, 1776 to October 2, 1781. Vol. 1. Philadelphia, 1782.

Minutes of the Provincial and Supreme Executive Council of Pennsylvania. Vols. 9–11 of *Pennsylvania Archives, Colonial Records.* Harrisburg, Pa.: Theo Fenn & Co., 1852.

Pennsylvania Chronicle. 1767–74.

Pennsylvania Gazette. 1732, 1763–90.

Pennsylvania Journal. 1767–92.

Pennsylvania Packet and Weekley Advertiser. 1771–73.

Reed, George Edward, ed. *Papers of the Governors.* 12 vols. Pennsylvania Archives, 4th series, vol. 3. Harrisburg, Pa.: William Stanley Ray, 1900.

Secondary Sources

Alexander, Arthur J. "Pennsylvania's Revolutionary Militia." *Pennsylvania Magazine of History and Biography* 69 (January 1945), 15–25.

Alexander, John K. "The Fort Wilson Incident of 1779: A Case Study of the Revolutionary Crowd." *William and Mary Quarterly,* 3rd ser., 31 (October 1974), 589–612.

Bockelman, Wayne L., and Owen S. Ireland. "The Internal Revolution in Pennsylvania: An Ethnic-Religious Interpretation." *Pennsylvania History* 41 (April 1974), 125–59.

Brobeck, Stephen. "Revolutionary Change in Colonial Philadelphia: The Brief Life of the Proprietary Gentry." *William and Mary Quarterly,* 3rd ser., 33 (July 1976), 410–34.

Brunhouse, Robert L. *The Counter Revolution in Pennsylvania, 1776–1790.* Harrisburg, Pa.: Pennsylvania Historical and Museum Commission, 1942.

———. "Effects of the Townshend Acts in Pennsylvania." *Pennsylvania Magazine of History and Biography* 54, no. 4 (1930), 355–73.

Buxbaum, Melvin H. *Ben Franklin and the Zealous Presbyterians.* University Park: The Pennsylvania State University Press, 1974.

Cavaioli, Frank J. "A Profile of the Paxton Boys: Murderers of the Conestoga Indians." *Journal of the Lancaster County Historical Society* 87, no. 3 (1983), 74–96.

Crowley, James E. "The Paxton Disturbances and Ideas of Order in Pennsylvania Politics." *Pennsylvania History* 37 (October 1970), 317–39.

Currey, Cecil B. *The Road to Revolution: Benjamin Franklin in England, 1765–1775.* Garden City, N.Y.: Anchor Books, Doubleday, 1968.

Daudelin, Don. "Numbers and Tactics at Bushy Run." *Western Pennsylvania Historical Magazine* 68 (April 1985), 153–79.

Doerflinger, Thomas M. "Philadelphia Merchants and the Logic of Moderation, 1760–1775." *William and Mary Quarterly,* 3rd ser., 40 (April 1983), 197–226.

———. *A Vigorous Spirit of Enterprise: Merchants and Economic Development in Revolutionary Philadelphia.* Chapel Hill: University of North Carolina Press, 1986.

Douglass, Elisha P. *Rebels and Democrats.* Chapel Hill: University of North Carolina Press, 1955.

"The Family of William Penn: A Collated Record." *Pennsylvania Genealogical Magazine* 25, no. 2 (1967), 69–96.

Fisher, Darlene Emmert. "Social Life in Philadelphia During the British Occupation." *Pennsylvania History* 37 (July 1970), 237–60.

Gibson, James E. "The Pennsylvania Provincial Conference of 1776." *Pennsylvania Magazine of History and Biography* 58, no. 4 (1934), 312–41.

Hanna, William S. *Benjamin Franklin and Pennsylvania Politics.* Stanford, Calif.: Stanford University Press, 1964.

Harding, Samuel B. "Party Struggles over the First Pennsylvania Constitution." *American Historical Association Annual Report, 1894–1895,* 371–402.

Harvey, Oscar Jewell. *A History of Wilkes-Barre.* Wilkes-Barre, Pa.: Raeder Press, 1909.

Hawke, David. *In the Midst of a Revolution.* Philadelphia: University of Pennsylvania Press, 1961.

Hindle, Brook. "The March of the Paxton Boys." *William and Mary Quarterly* 3, no. 4 (October 1946), 461–86.

Hutson, James H. "Benjamin Franklin and Pennsylvania Politics, 1751–1755: A Reappraisal." *Pennsylvania Magazine of History and Biography* 93 (July 1969), 303–71.

———. "The Campaign to Make Pennsylvania a Royal Province." *Pennsylvania Magazine of History and Biography,* 94 (October 1970), 427–63, and 95 (January 1971), 28–49.

———. "An Investigation of the Inarticulate: Philadelphia's White Oaks." *William and Mary Quarterly,* 3rd ser., 28 (January 1971), 3–25.

———. *Pennsylvania Politics, 1746–1770: The Movement for Royal Government and Its Consequences.* Princeton: Princeton University Press, 1972.

Illick, Joseph E. *Colonial Pennsylvania: A History.* New York: Charles Scribner's Sons, 1976.

Ireland, O. S. "The Crux of Politics: Religion and Party in Pennsylvania, 1778–1789." *William and Mary Quarterly,* 3rd ser., 42 (October 1985), 453–75.

Jenkins, Howard M. *The Family of William Penn, Founder of Pennsylvania: Ancestry and Descendants.* Philadelphia: Author, 1899.

Kelley, Joseph J. Jr. *Pennsylvania: The Colonial Years, 1681–1776.* Garden City, N.Y.: Doubleday, 1980.

Lincoln, Charles H. *The Revolutionary Movement in Pennsylvania, 1760–1776.* Philadelphia: University of Pennsylvania, 1901.

Lucas, Stephen E. *Portents of Rebellion: Rhetoric and Revolution in Philadelphia, 1765–1776.* Philadelphia: Temple University Press, 1976.

Marietta, Jack D. *The Reformation of American Quakerism, 1748–1783.* Philadelphia: University of Pennsylvania Press, 1984.

Martin, Kames Kirby. "The Return of the Paxton Boys and the Historical State of the Pennsylvania Frontier, 1764–1774." *Pennsylvania History* 38 (April 1971), 117–33.

Mishoff, Willard O. "Business in Philadelphia During the British Occupation." *Pennsylvania Magazine of History and Biography* 61 (April 1937), 165–81.

Morgan, Edmund S., and Helen M. Morgan. *The Stamp Act Crisis: Prologue to Revolution.* Chapel Hill: University of North Carolina Press, 1953.

Nash, Gary B. *The Urban Crucible: Social Change, Political Consciousness, and the Origins of the American Revolution.* Cambridge, Mass.: Harvard University Press, 1979.

Newcomb, Benjamin H. "Effects of the Stamp Act on Colonial Pennsylvania Politics." *William and Mary Quarterly,* 3rd ser., 23 (April 1966), 257–72.

———. *Franklin and Galloway: A Political Partnership.* New Haven: Yale University Press, 1972.

Onuf, Peter. *The Origins of the Federal Republic.* Philadelphia: University of Pennsylvania Press, 1983.

Ousterhout, Anne M. "Controlling the Opposition in Philadelphia During the American Revolution." *Pennsylvania Magazine of History and Biography* 105 (January 1981), 3–34.

———. *A State Divided: Opposition in Pennsylvania to the American Revolution.* Westport, Conn.: Greenwood Press, 1987.

Ries, Linda A. "The Rage of Opposing Government: The Stump Affair of 1768." *Cumberland County History* 1 (Summer 1984), 21–45.

Rosswurm, Steven. *Arms, Country, and Class: The Philadelphia Militia and the Lower Sort During the American Revolution, 1775–1783.* New Brunswick, N.J.: Rutgers University Press, 1987.

Rowe, G. S. "The Frederick Stump Affair, 1768, and Its Challenge to Legal Historians of Early Pennsylvania." *Pennsylvania History* 49 (October 1982), 259–88.

Ryerson, Richard Alan. *The Revolution Is Now Begun: The Radical Committee of Philadelphia, 1765–1776.* Philadelphia: University of Pennsylvania Press, 1977.

Schlesinger, Arthur M. *The Colonial Merchants and the American Revolution.* New York: Atheneum, 1968.

Selsam, J. Paul. *The Pennsylvania Constitution of 1776: A Study in Revolutionary Democracy.* Philadelphia: University of Pennsylvania Press, 1936.

Shepherd, William R. *The History of Proprietary Government in Pennsylvania.* New York: Columbia University Press, 1896.

Sloan, David. "A Time of Sifting and Winnowing: The Paxton Riots and Quaker Non-Violence in Pennsylvania." *Quaker History* 66 (Spring 1977), 3–22.

Stone, Frederick D. "How the Landing of Tea Was Opposed in Philadelphia." *Pennsylvania Magazine of History and Biography* 15, no. 4 (1891), 385–93.

Stone, Lawrence. *The Family, Sex, and Marriage in England, 1500–1800.* New York: Harper & Row, 1977.

Thayer, Theodore. *Pennsylvania Politics and the Growth of Democracy, 1740–1776.* Harrisburg, Pa.: Pennsylvania Historical and Museum Commission, 1953.

Tully, Alan. *William Penn's Legacy: Politics and Social Structure in Provincial Pennsylvania, 1726–1755.* Baltimore: Johns Hopkins University Press, 1977.

Van Doren, Carl. *Benjamin Franklin.* New York: Viking Press, 1938.

Wainwright, Nicholas B. *George Croghan: Wilderness Diplomat.* Chapel Hill: University of North Carolina Press, 1959.

———. "The Penn Collection." *Pennsylvania Magazine of History and Biography* 87 (October 1963), 393–419.

Weiner, Frederick. "The Military Occupation of Philadelphia in 1777–1778." *American Philosophical Society Proceedings* 111 (October 1967), 310–13.

Index